I0795896

IMAGES
of America

IDLEWILD

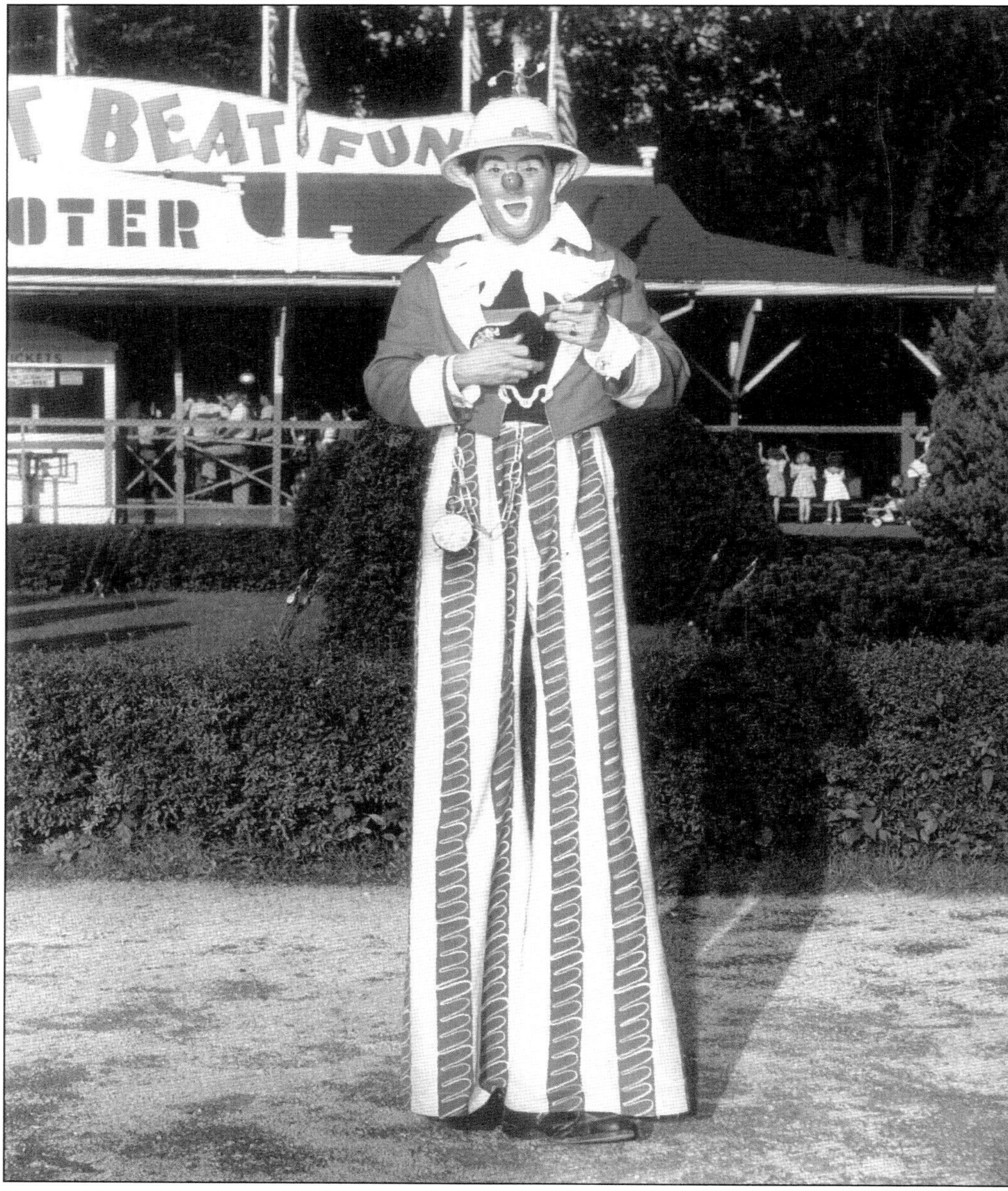

Happy Dayze was a popular fixture at Idlewild in the 1950s. The clown's portrayer, Arthur Jennings, delighted children of all ages with his musical and juggling talents. The performer was also an accomplished engineer who later joined forces with Idlewild management to design and create the beloved Story Book Forest.

IMAGES
of America

IDLEWILD

Jeffrey S. Croushore

ARCADIA
PUBLISHING

ISBN 978-0-7385-3564-7

Published by Arcadia Publishing
Charleston, South Carolina

Printed in the United States of America

Library of Congress Catalog Card Number: 2004100868

For all general information contact Arcadia Publishing at:
Telephone 843-853-2070
Fax 843-853-0044
E-mail sales@arcadiapublishing.com
For customer service and orders:
Toll-Free 1-888-313-2665

Visit us on the Internet at www.arcadiapublishing.com

To Zachary, Jacob, Kaci, and Rachel

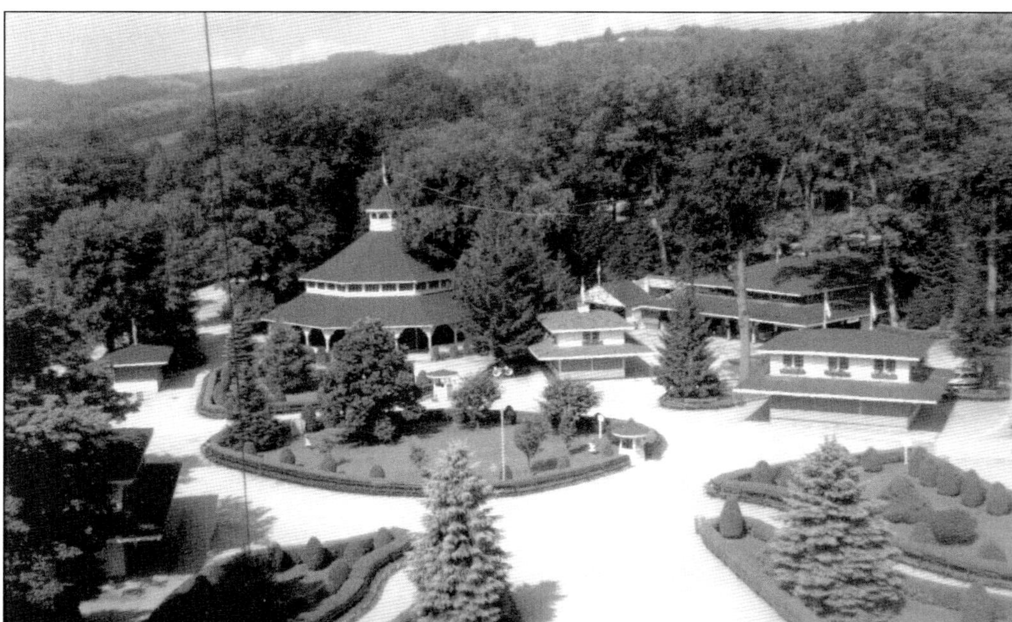

This aerial view, focusing on Idlewild's central mall, illustrates why the park has been referred to as a mountain playground. The rolling hills and heavy forests of the Laurel Highlands surround Idlewild's classic cedar-sided, red-shingled buildings.

Contents

ACKNOWLEDGMENTS

While this project has truly been a labor of love for me, its completion is due to the efforts of many individuals who I would like to sincerely thank. I would not have been involved in this writing if it was not for Brandon Leonatti—general manager of Idlewild and SoakZone—who recommended me for the project. Your confidence in me is greatly appreciated. I also owe a lot to Brandon's predecessor, Jerome Gibas, for getting me involved with the park archives beginning in 2000, and to Mary Lou Rosemeyer from Kennywood Entertainment Partners for adhering to Brandon's recommendations and allowing me this opportunity. Kathy Sichula, you have my extreme gratitude for your constant encouragement and belief in me. Your thoughts and suggestions were always helpful. I am thrilled that we both love what we do.

It was a privilege to meet R. Z. Macdonald, who shared his photographs and memories with me; the book is definitely better because of it, and Idlewild is definitely better because of his family. Thanks go to the Ligonier Valley Library and to Cheryl Wegener, my proofreader for portions of the book. Thanks also go to Christy Goswick, Carol Croushore, Shirley Conley, and Lori Ellis for their contributions to these pages. While most of the photographs featured within are from the Idlewild archives, those from other sources have been credited.

Finally, I would like to thank my family, friends, and the Lord above: your love and support has meant the world to me. I am forever grateful.

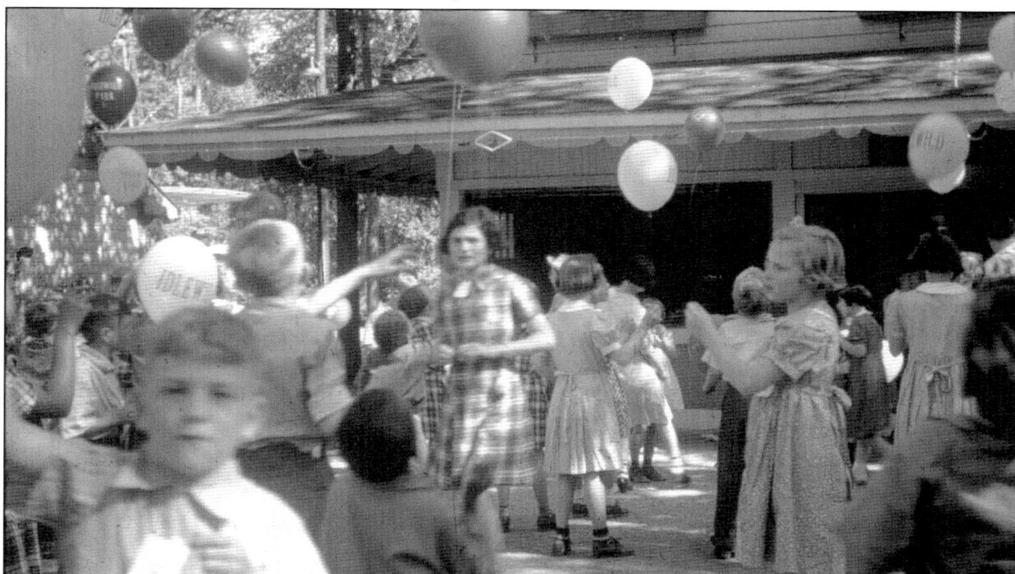

Children from an area children's home enjoy their visit to the park in this image from the 1950s. The souvenir balloons helped brighten their day.

Introduction

On April 15, 1853, the Commonwealth of Pennsylvania granted a charter to a small group of investors who desired to build a railroad between the towns of Latrobe and Ligonier in the Laurel Mountains of Pennsylvania. For years, the corporation known as the Latrobe and Ligonier Rail Road Company accomplished little in the way of actually constructing a rail line. After renewing the charter in 1866, 1869, and again in 1871, the company changed its name to the Ligonier Valley Rail Road and finally acquired a 10.3-mile stretch of land to construct a narrow-gauge railroad. In 1875, the partially constructed railway was sold at a sheriff's sale to cover an unpaid construction bill. The purchaser at the sale was Judge Thomas Mellon, who was one of the original creditors of the carrier. Mellon, whose term as a common pleas court judge in nearby Allegheny County expired in 1869, had quickly become known as an ambitious and shrewd businessman. He founded T. Mellon and Sons Bank in downtown Pittsburgh and was heavily invested in coal, steel, oil, glassmaking, and railroad ventures. Mellon's wealth led him to become a prominent force in the nation's industrial revolution, financially backing such corporate giants as Gulf Oil, Alcoa, Westinghouse Electric, and PPG Industries. Mellon also launched the career of steel magnate Henry Clay Frick by loaning him money to build his first coke ovens. It was Thomas Mellon who oversaw the completion of the short-line Ligonier Valley Rail Road, nicknamed "the Millionaire's Line," in December 1877.

The railroad was originally intended to carry timber and coal from mines near Ligonier, and later Fort Palmer, to Latrobe where it connected with the main line of the Pennsylvania Railroad. However, Mellon was not content with that. His drive to increase profits led him to seek ways to use the line to move passengers as well as freight. He decided to offer a pleasure ground along the route where people could enjoy picnics and recreation. This practice had become popular with rail lines across the country, giving rise to resort destinations that were known as railroad parks. Mellon found the ideal location in a 350-acre wooded estate owned by William M. and Mary C. Darlington. The property, located three miles west of Ligonier, was located in a scenic valley and graced with the natural beauty of the Loyalhanna Creek.

In response to Thomas Mellon's request, Darlington issued the following grant.

> Pittsburgh, PA, May 1, 1878
> Thos. Mellon Esq.
>
> Dear Sir:
>
> In compliance with your request, I will and do hereby agree to grant to the Ligonier Valley Rail Road Company the right and privilege to occupy for picnic purposes or pleasure grounds that portion of land in Ligonier Township, Westmoreland County as follows – the strip or piece of ground lying between the railway and the creek and extending from the old cornfield to Byards run – also two or three acres on the opposite side of the creek adjoining near the same. Without compensation in the shape of rent for three years from the first of April

1878 provided no timber or other trees are to be cut or injured – the underbrush you may clear out if you wish to do so.

Yours respectfully,
Wm. M. Darlington

Shortly thereafter, a train depot was built, and the property known as Idlewild became a favorite destination for many city dwellers wishing to escape to a mountain playground. So began the legacy of Idlewild, one of the nation's oldest and most beautiful amusement parks.

One

A Mountain Playground 1878–1930

Idlewild in its early days offered simple pleasures to its guests such as hiking trails, bicycle courses, ball fields, tennis courts, swings, shaded walks, and fine picnic pavilions. Three lakes were dug: Lake Woodland in the 1880s, Lake St. Clair in 1891, and the largest, Lake Bouquet in 1896. Fishing and boating quickly became popular attractions. A bridge led to a large island, known as Flower Island, in the middle of Lake Bouquet. Here, thousands of sweet smelling flowers, grasses, and shrubs were planted offering the perfect natural studio to the early photographer of the times. Another bridge spanned the Loyalhanna Creek, leading to the Woodlands—an area that remained more rustic and pastoral.

Along with the train depot, the early buildings of the park included the Auditorium. Located atop the hillside overlooking the train depot, it was often used as a dance hall. The dining hall, which could seat nearly 1,000 people, offered running water and a kitchen. The boathouse served as a dock for the vapor launch and swan boats that cruised Lake Bouquet. In 1896, the carousel pavilion was constructed to house the park's new T. M. Harton Company steam-powered carousel, which replaced an earlier merry-go-round from 1891. These structures still stand today as evidence of their quality construction and management's commitment to maintenance and preservation.

While the early success of Idlewild can indeed be credited in part to its natural beauty, fine facilities, and easy access via the Ligonier Valley Rail Road, one factor that cannot be ignored is its marketing success with churches, schools, communities, family reunions, and major corporations. Thomas Mellon heavily advertised the park in Pittsburgh and throughout western Pennsylvania, offering discount rates on his rail line for groups of 200 or more. Therefore, Idlewild played host to large group outings as well as small family excursions. Records show that as many as 12,000 guests would disembark from the trains for a single picnic. Some of the most popular events included the Sunday school picnic, the Lutheran church picnic, the Ligonier Valley reunion, and the Westinghouse Air Brake Company and H. J. Heinz Company picnics. Group outings were a flourishing concept and would continue to be one of the most important contributing factors to the success of Idlewild during the next century.

The Ligonier Valley Rail Road remained a part of the Mellon family after the death of Judge Thomas Mellon in 1908. His sons, Andrew W. and Richard B. Mellon, who together had managed the railroad for several years, gained controlling interest of Idlewild. Later in life, Andrew became the treasury secretary of the United States under presidents Harding, Coolidge, and Hoover. Richard continued his association with the railroad and Idlewild while watching his son Richard K. Mellon go on to become president of the Mellon Bank empire.

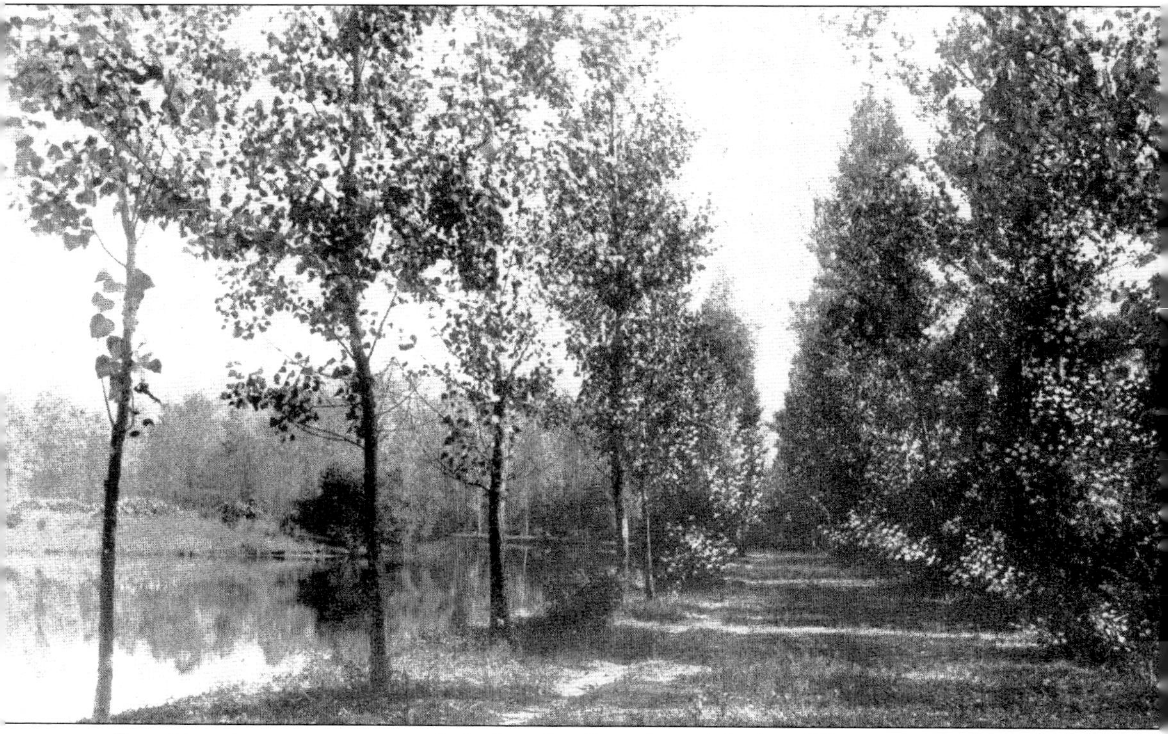

Fort Ligonier was constructed during the French and Indian War as a supply post for the final assault against the French-occupied Fort Duquesne, which was 40 miles westward. In November 1758, after multiple skirmishes, the British forces, led by Gen. John Forbes, were successful in taking control of Fort Duquesne. The fort, burned by retreating French forces, was rebuilt and renamed Fort Pitt, which later became Pittsburgh. While serving at Fort Ligonier during the campaign, George Washington received word of a conflict between French forces and a British party commanded by Lieutenant Colonel Mercer. Washington led a group of volunteers three miles from the post to aid Mercer's men. In the darkness, Mercer's forces mistook the volunteers as the enemy. Several volleys were exchanged, killing 13 soldiers and one lieutenant. Realizing the mistake, Washington rushed between the opposing commands, knocking up rifles to prevent further unnecessary bloodshed. He later recalled that he was never in more imminent danger than those moments between the firing lines. While the exact location of the occurrence has not been ascertained, it is widely believed to have taken place at what later became the Woodlands area of Idlewild.

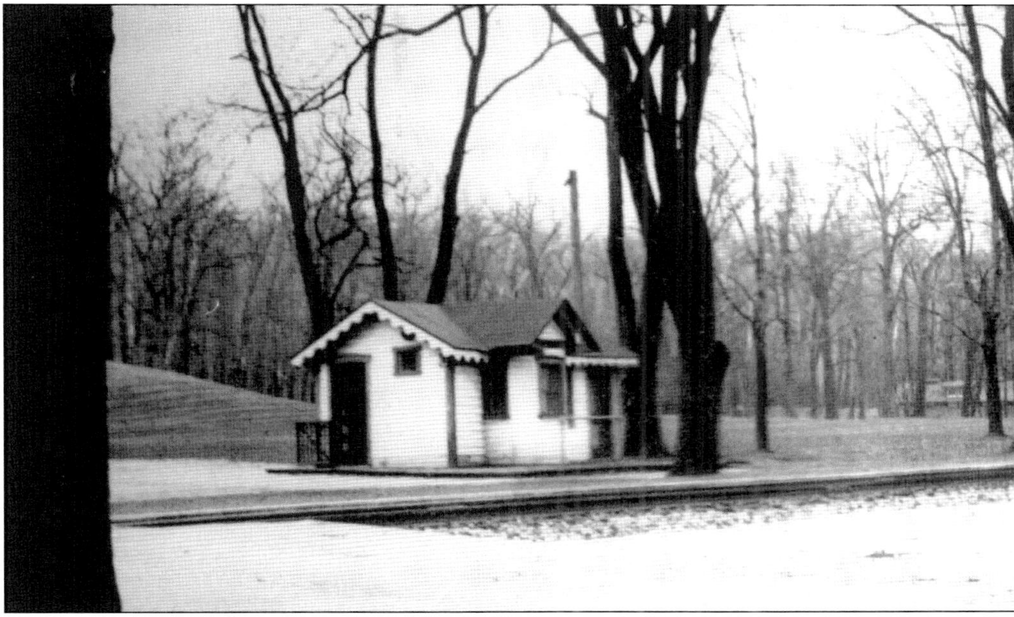

The original Idlewild depot was built in 1878. Measuring 9 feet by 16 feet, the structure was described by Robert Ripley as the smallest full-service depot in the United States. A passenger waiting room occupied one-half of the interior space, while the remainder was used for the ticket agent, the telegraph operator, and a freight and express office.

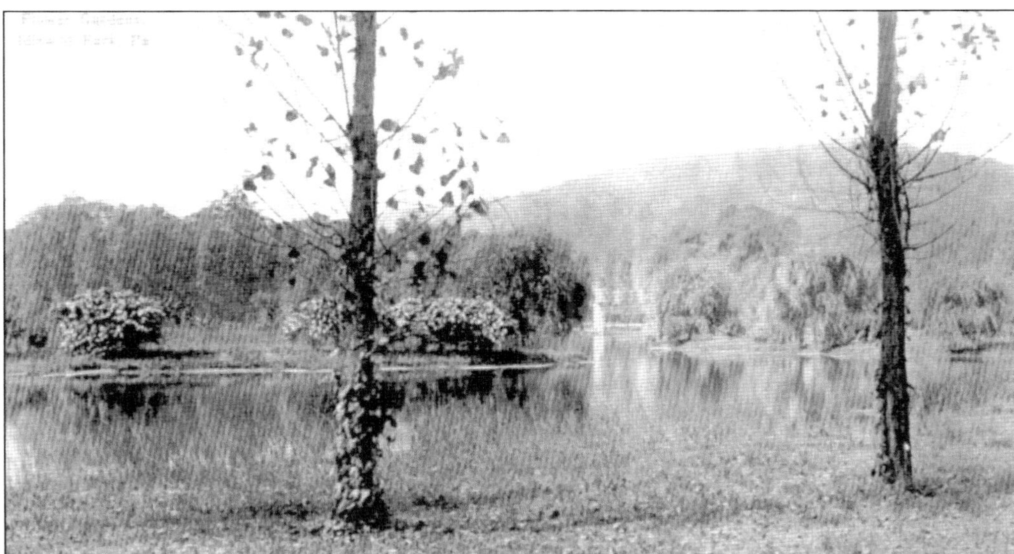

In addition to being a picnic ground Idlewild served as a campground. The Pennsylvania Militia camped along the Loyalhanna Creek in July 1886, and many religious camp meetings also took place at the resort. Many of the latter would last for several weeks at a time. One of the amenities the campers enjoyed was Lake Bouquet, a portion of which is seen here in this postcard from the early 1900s. In the distance is Darlington Station, a stop on the Ligonier Valley Rail Road located just one-half mile from the depot at Idlewild.

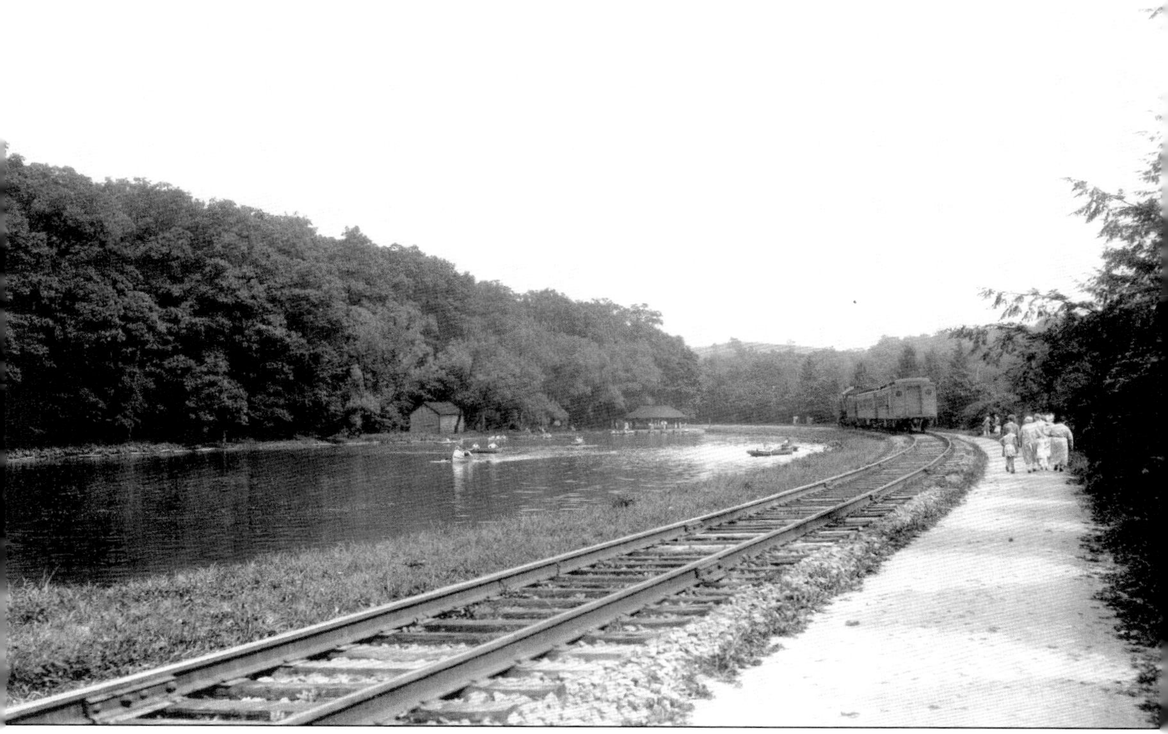

From Darlington Station the Ligonier Valley Rail Road skirted past Lake St. Clair and on to the Idlewild depot (not pictured). The lake covers nearly four acres and was named in honor of Arthur St. Clair, a member of the British Army who came to America in 1857 to serve in the French and Indian War. After serving as civilian commander of Fort Ligonier (beginning in 1764), he went on to become a court justice of Westmoreland County, major general in the Revolutionary War, president of the Continental Congress, and governor of the Northwest Territory.

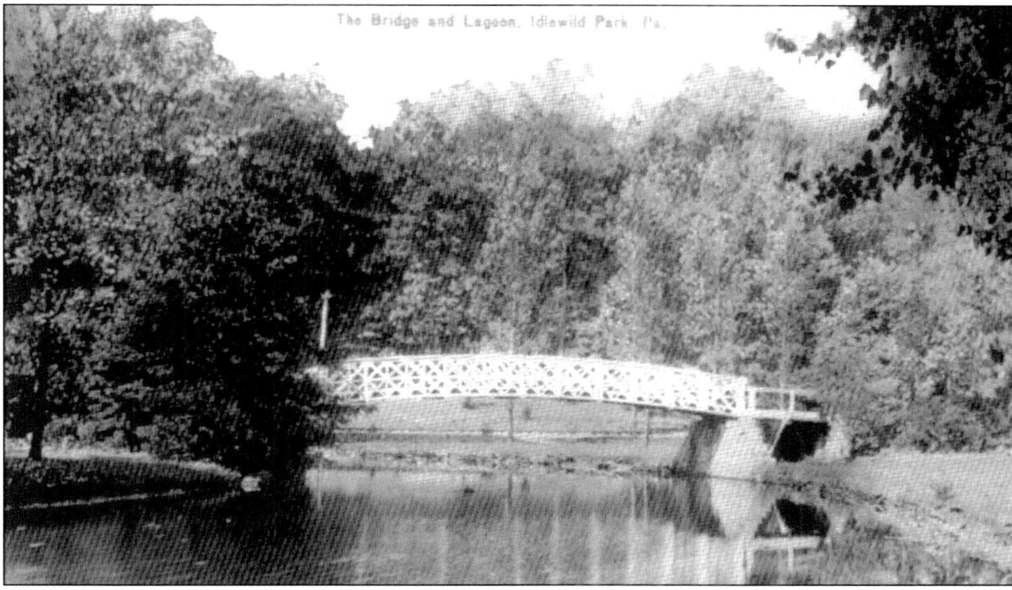

Lake Bouquet was named for Col. Henry Bouquet, another celebrated hero of the French and Indian War. Four times the size of Lake St. Clair, it also featured many canals and tributaries. This bridge, spanning the eastern edge of Lake Bouquet, led to Flower Island. In the background, visible underneath the bridge, are the tracks of the Ligonier Valley Rail Road.

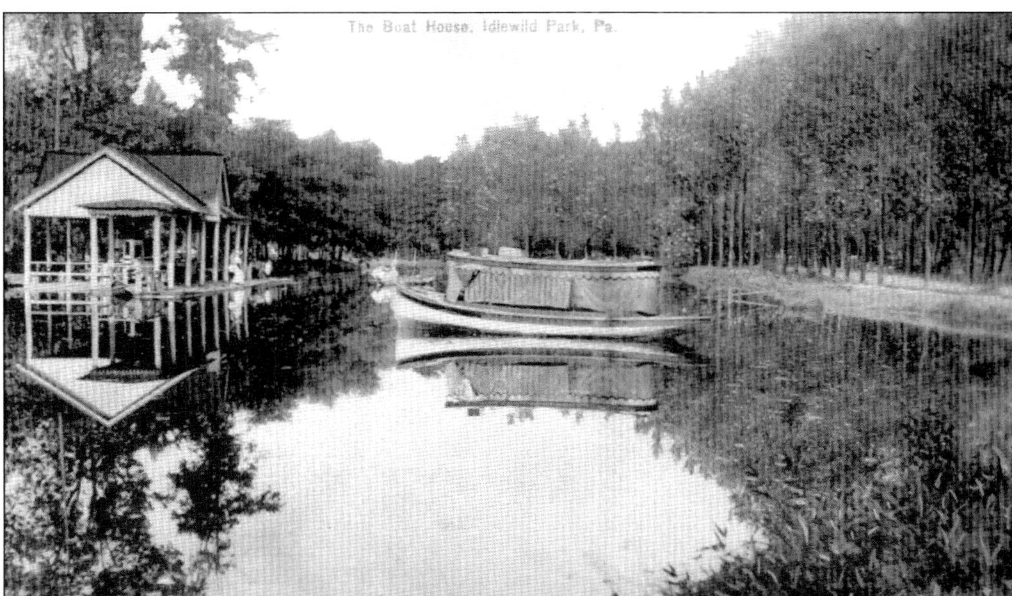

The boathouse served as the boarding location for the park's vapor launch (a heavy boat fueled by naphtha) and swan boats. Decades later the Idlewild showboat also docked here. Though the appearance of the structure changed throughout the years, it remains at the park serving as a pavilion for guests dining on the island.

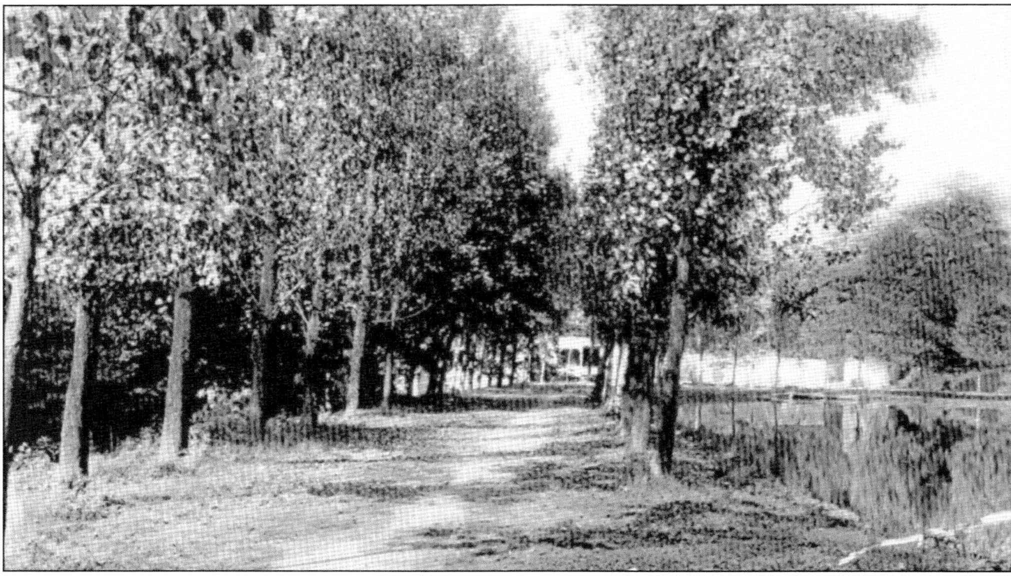

The shady walks surrounding Lake Bouquet offered a romantic setting for young couples visiting the park. Dubbed "Lover's Lane," the scenic pathways are captured in this postcard from the early 1900s.

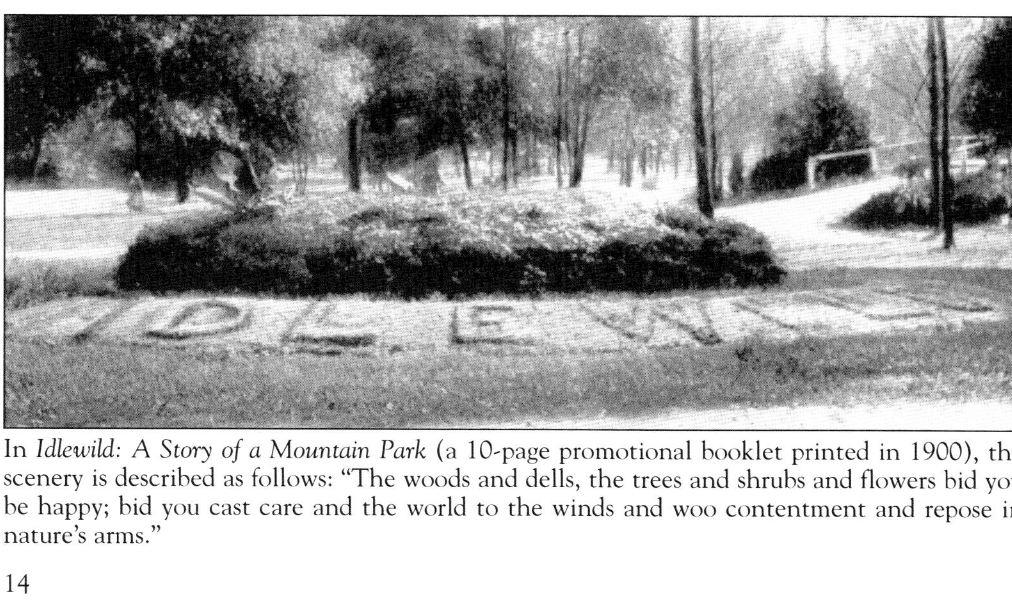

In *Idlewild: A Story of a Mountain Park* (a 10-page promotional booklet printed in 1900), the scenery is described as follows: "The woods and dells, the trees and shrubs and flowers bid you be happy; bid you cast care and the world to the winds and woo contentment and repose in nature's arms."

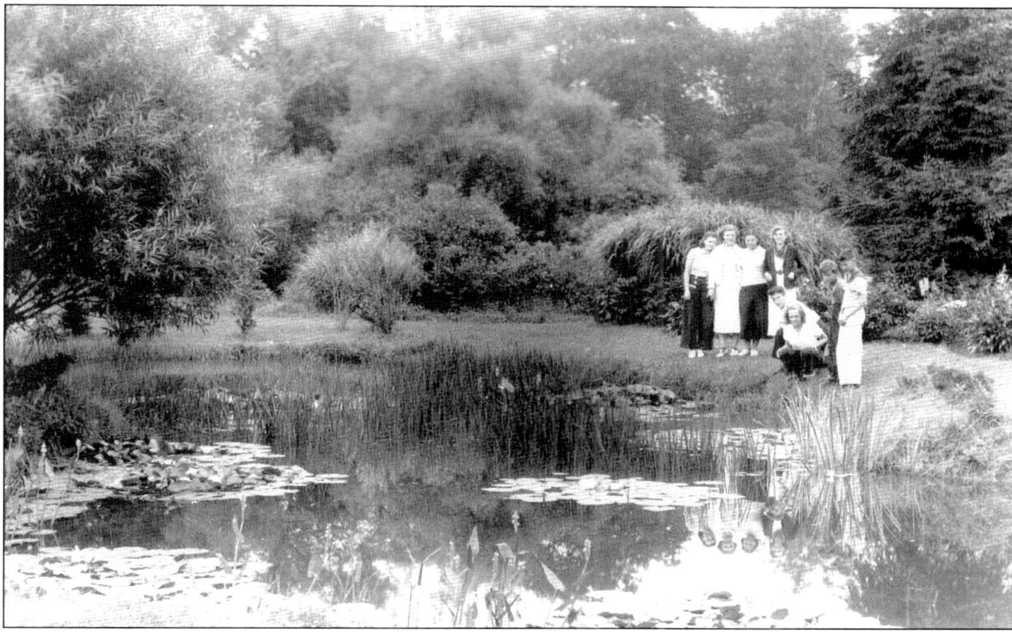

These two postcards depict the beauty of Flower Island. Children of all ages enjoyed the abundant trees, grasses, shrubs, flowers, and lily pads. *Idlewild: A Story of a Mountain Park* notes, "The landscape gardener has done his work well and on every hand is found beautiful specimens of his skill. Flowers and shrubs abound."

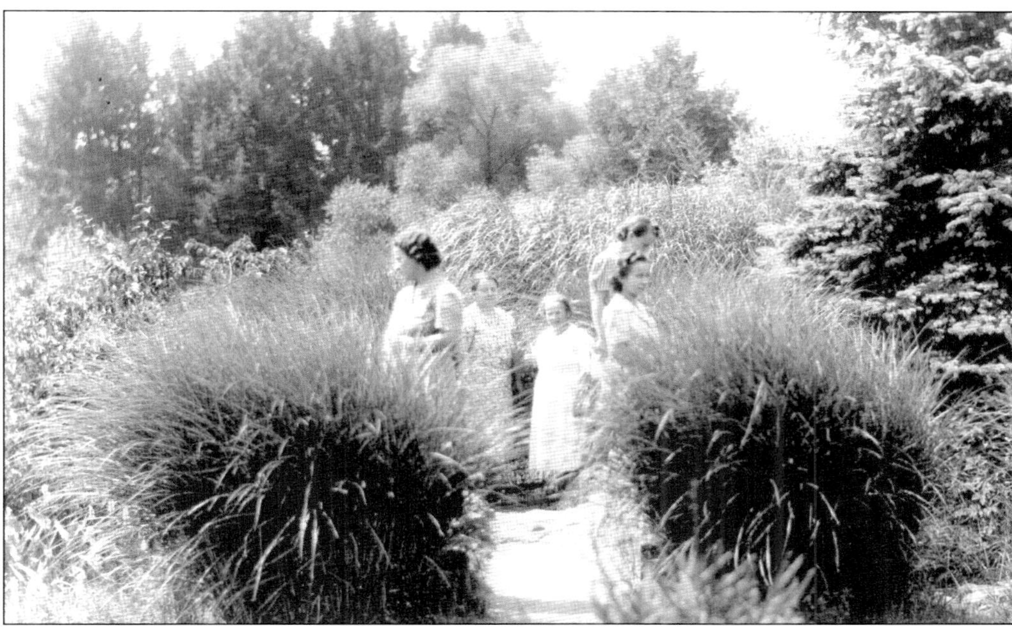

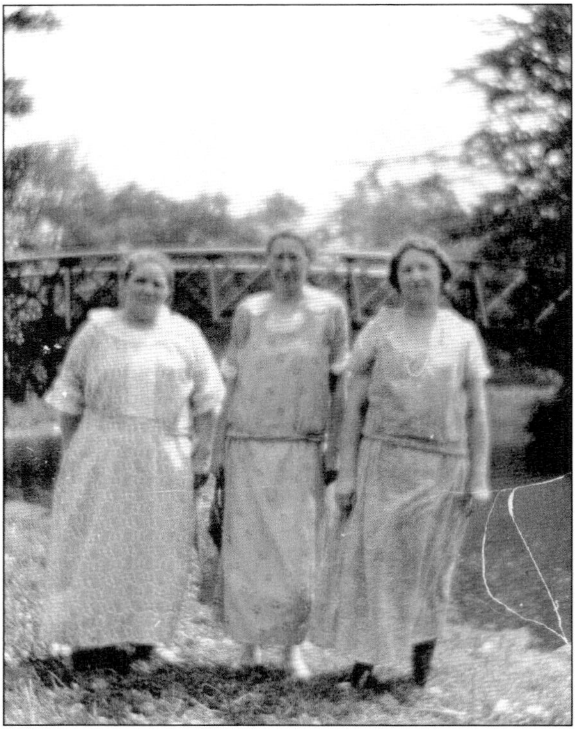

These photographs show an outing to the park in 1924. The lovely ladies standing in front of the Flower Island bridge in the above image are, from left to right, Anna Kennewey, May Hormathy, and Gertrude Stuver. The image below shows the visitors amid the picturesque flora of the island. Pictured are, from left to right, as follows: (sitting) unidentified, Chester Stuver, and unidentified; (kneeling) unidentified, and Ida May Hormathy; (standing) Anna Kennewey, May Hormathy, and Gertrude Stuver. (Photographs donated to the Idlewild Archives courtesy Shirley Conley.)

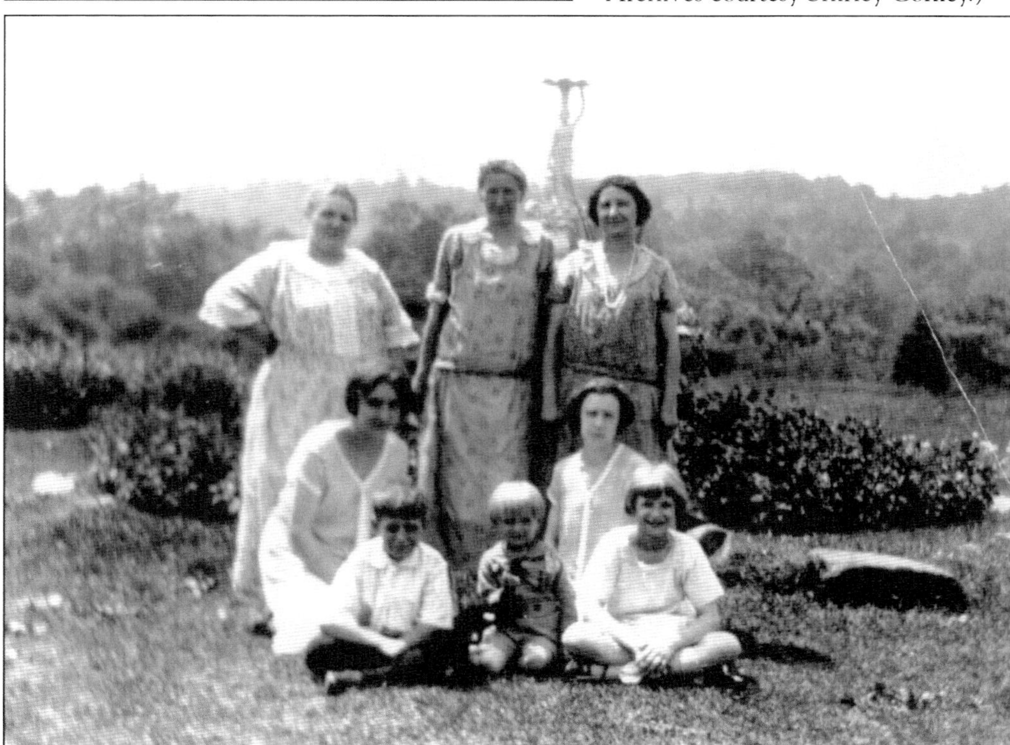

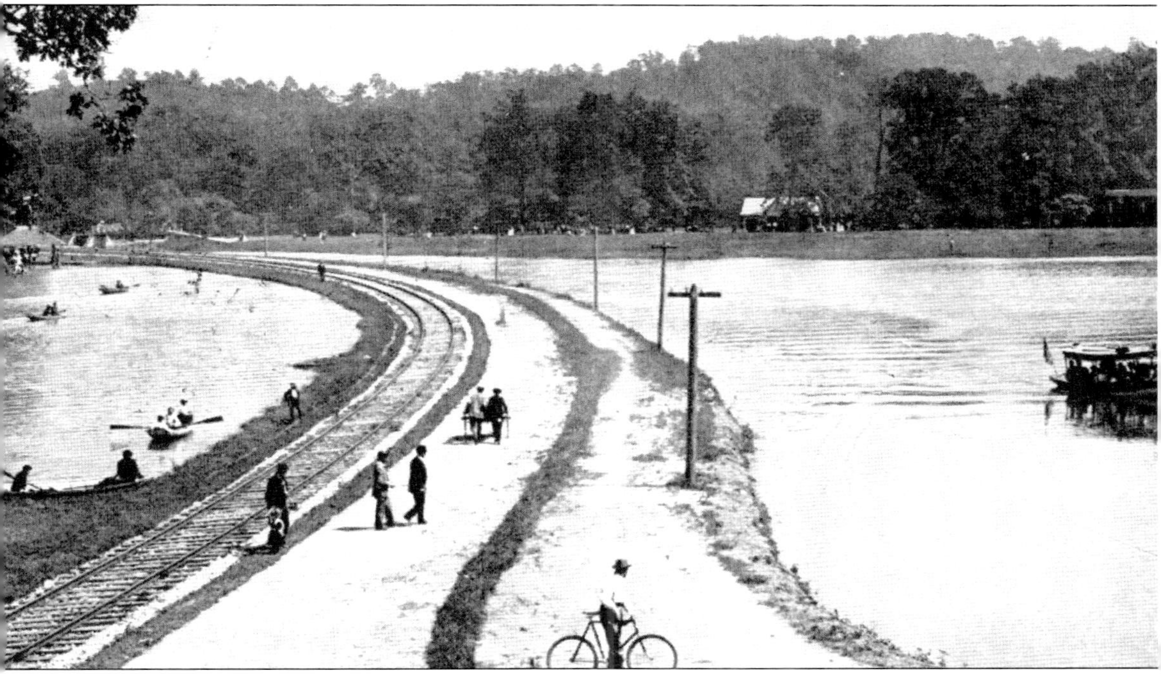

Many picnickers enjoyed the rowboats in Lake St. Clair, whereas others opted to tour Lake Bouquet on the motor launch. While he appears to be taking a break to watch the boaters, the gentleman in the foreground is enjoying the bicycle course that circled the larger lake.

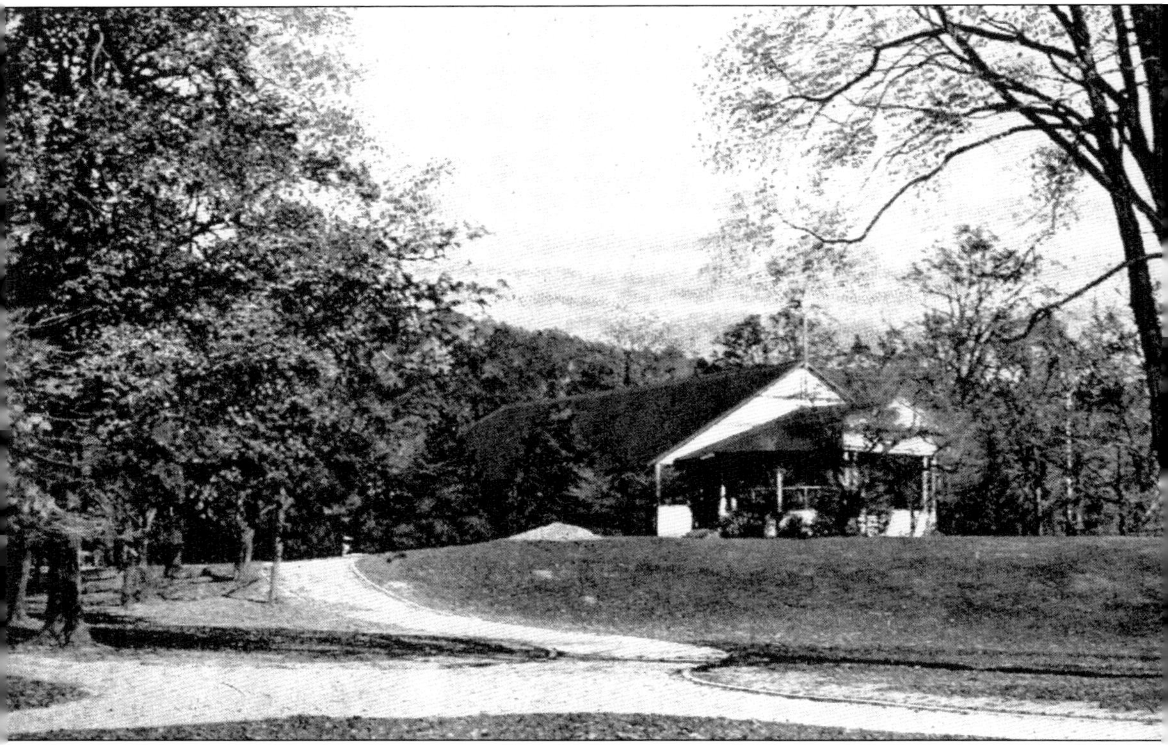

Up until the early 1890s, the park was limited to the strip of land between the railroad tracks and the Loyalhanna Creek (measuring 400 feet wide and one-half mile long) and a few acres on the south side of the creek. In 1891, the operators of the park were allowed to expand to the northern side of the tracks. This expansion doubled the size of Idlewild and featured many new additions. In this postcard, the park's dance hall, known as the Auditorium, stands atop the hillside in the center of the new Idlewild. The dance floor accommodated 200 people and was surrounded by three rows of seating on either side. A raised music stand was centrally located with a large room underneath for coats and wraps.

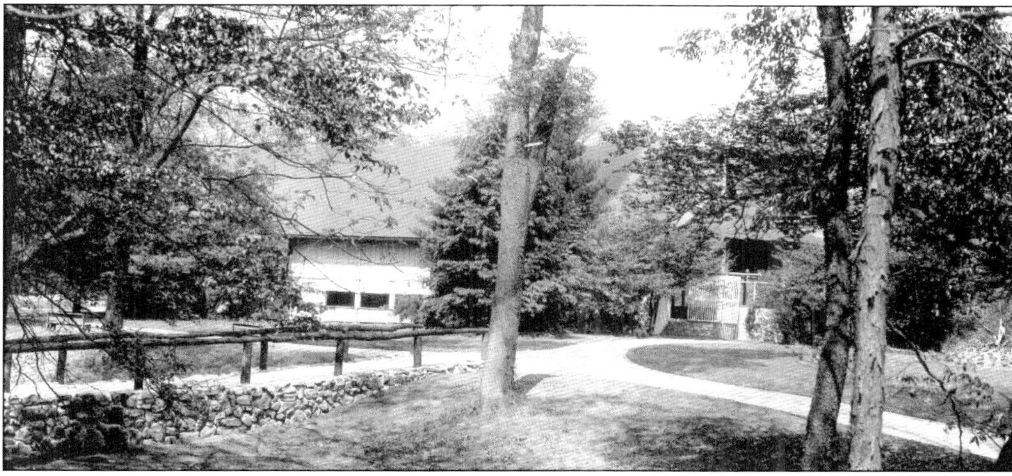

A side view of the Auditorium is featured in the above image, whereas the image below depicts what one might have seen by looking out the southern side of the grand building. From its perch on the hillside, the Auditorium offered exquisite views of the lush central lawn, the train station at left, and the Idlewild bandstand at right.

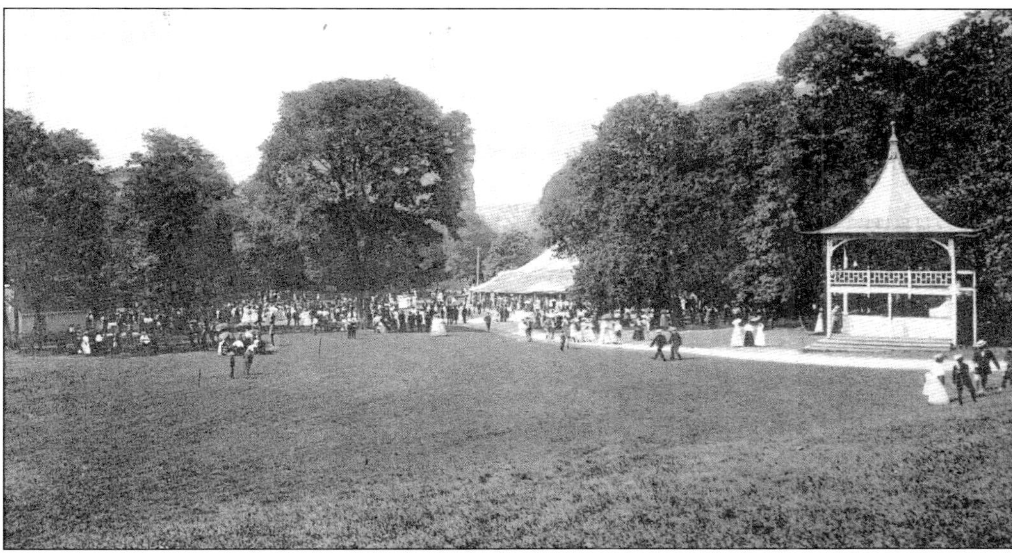

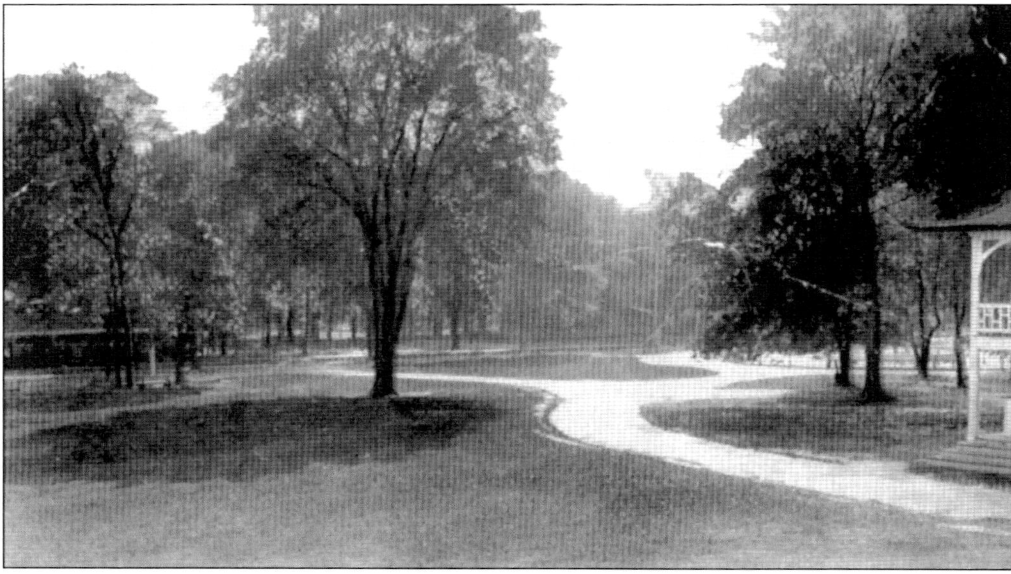

Idlewild's grassy lawns and winding promenades proved popular among its visitors. The postcard above shows the central area of the park that would become home to the Hillside Theater nearly a century later. The postcard below shows the reverse angle from the one above. It depicts a fine view of the bandstand and the Auditorium. Today, the Auditorium serves as a picnic pavilion and is used for large corporate outings or community picnics.

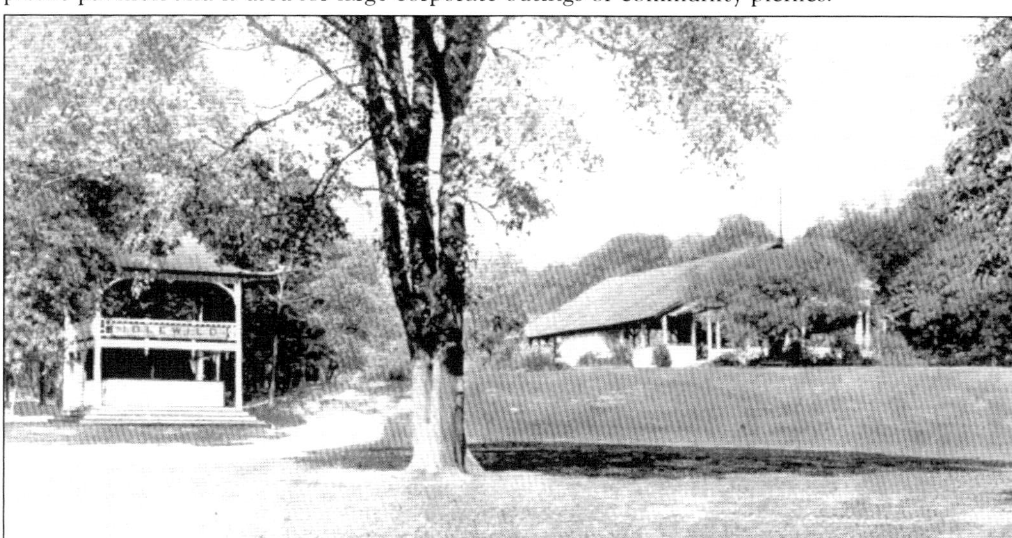

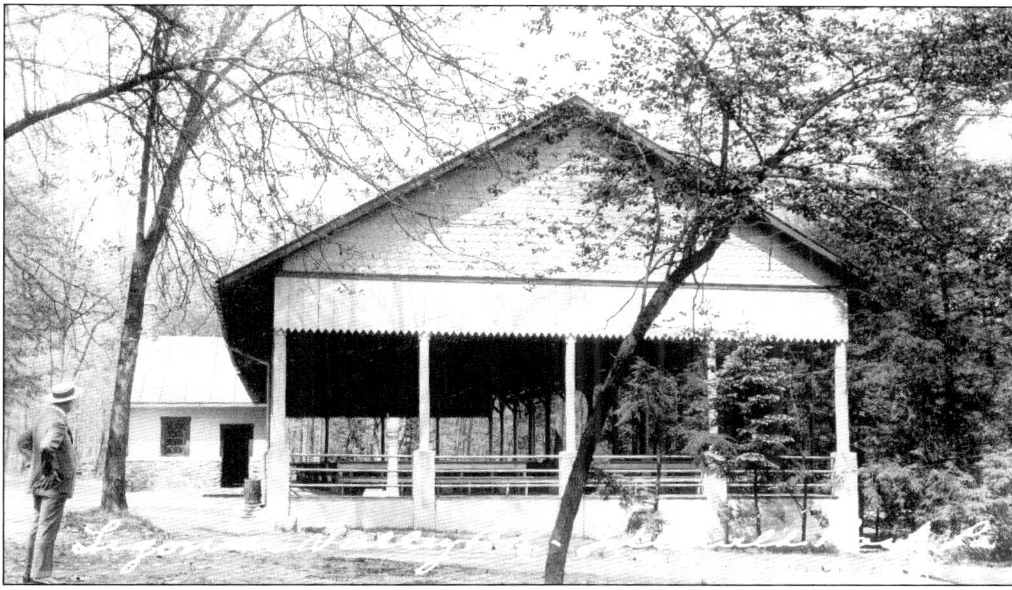

Through a grove of trees west of the Auditorium stands another immense pavilion, which was used as the dining hall. With 7,000 feet of floor space, the structure could accommodate 1,000 diners at a time. It also featured a kitchen with iron sinks, running water, gas ranges, cupboards, and tables. An artesian well stood outside. Today, this building is called Picnic Pavilion E-1 and is located behind the Idlewild administration building. These images show the dining hall from the west (above) and from the east (below).

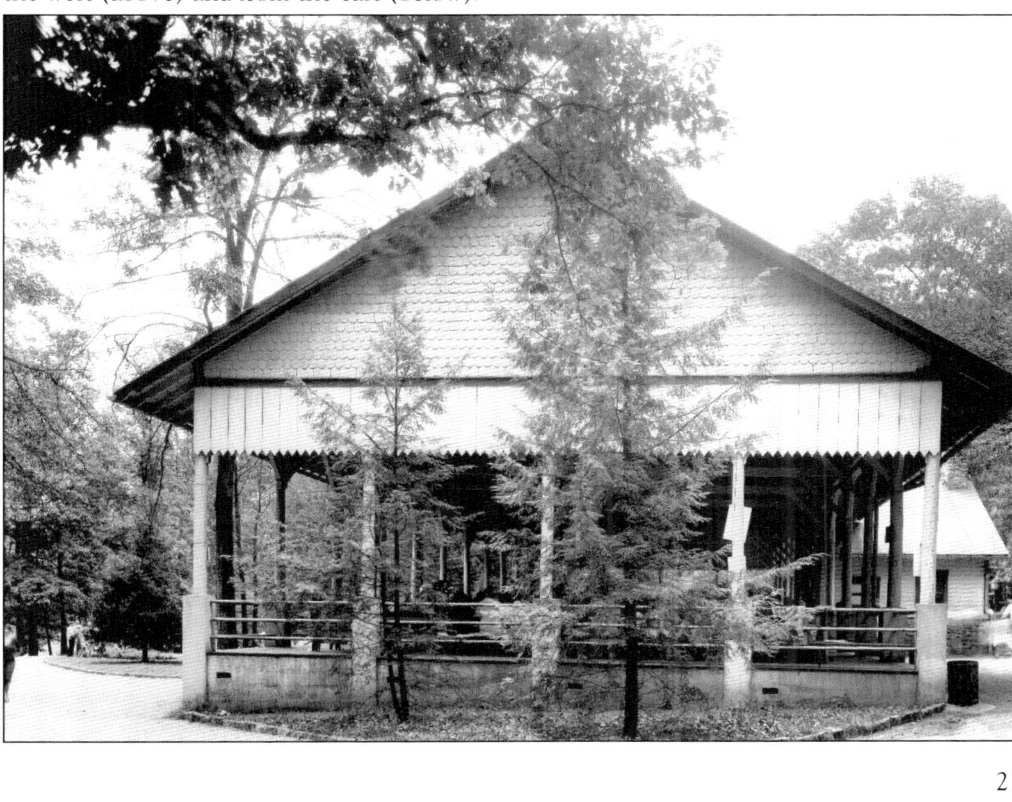

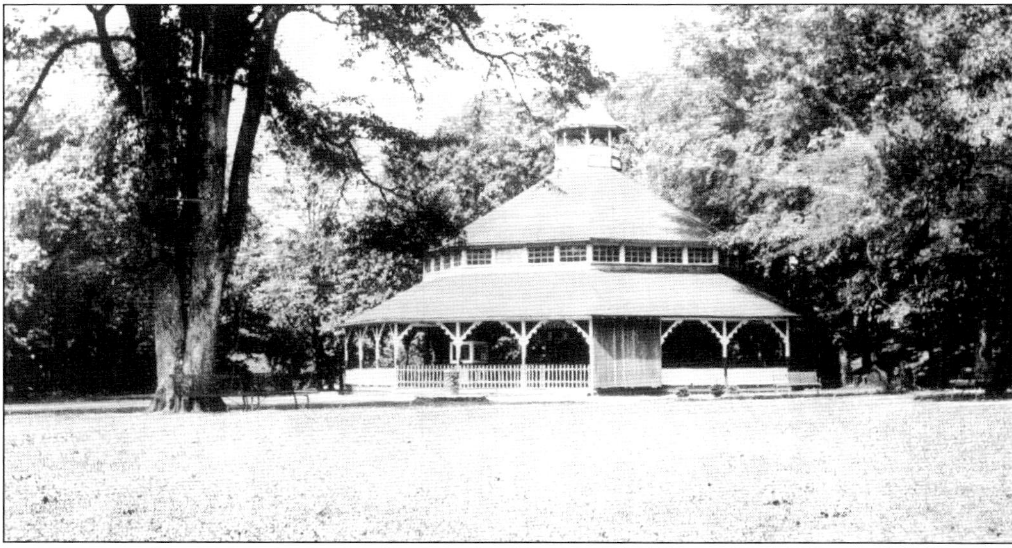

A carousel has been present at Idlewild since 1891. That year, George Senft, superintendent of the Ligonier Valley Rail Road, signed a lease with M. B. Parsons of Ligonier, whereby Parsons would operate a "steam riding gallery" capable of accommodating 56 people. The lease called for Parsons to assure safety of the riders, maintain order and cleanliness, and present employees of "strictly sober habits, courteous and gentlemanly in their purpose." The carousel pavilion was constructed in 1896 to house Idlewild's second carousel, manufactured by the T. M. Harton Company.

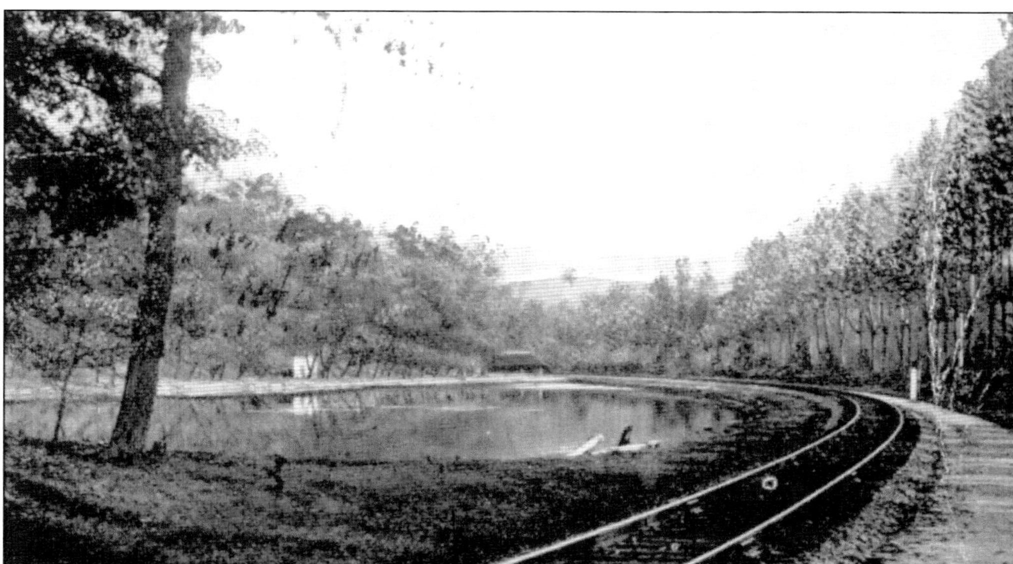

The reverse of this card (its front view shows the tracks and Lake St. Clair) is postmarked July 25, 1923. Addressed to Mr. John P. Kuhn from his nephew Alfred, the message speaks of Idlewild's abundance of wildlife: "Every time we go for milk we see 3 quails and a rabbit. The woods are polluted with them. I have seen 4 deers [*sic*], 3 bucks and a doe."

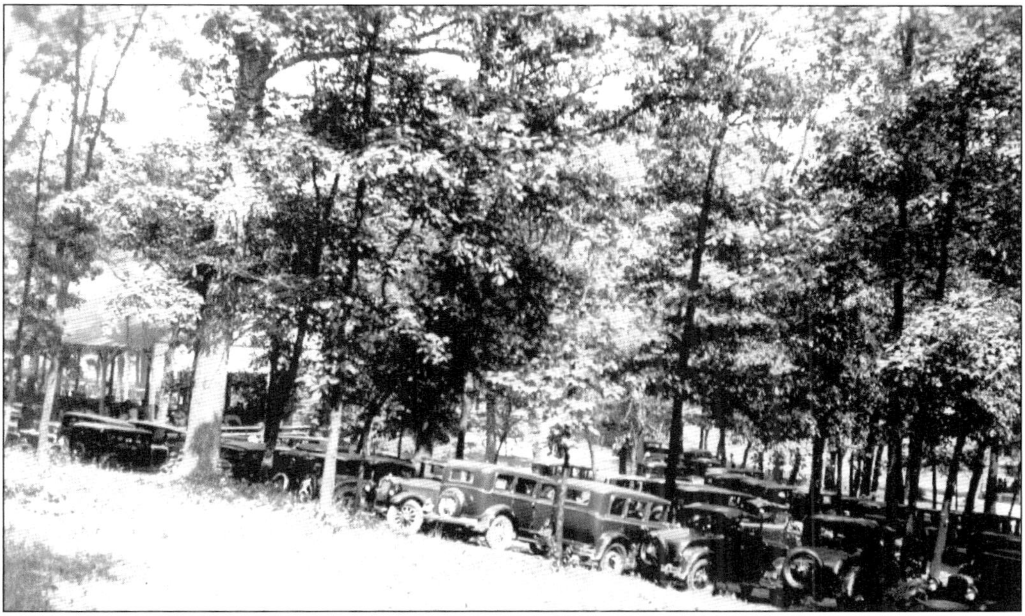

With technological advances in transportation and the improvements of roads and highways in the area, the effect of the Ligonier Valley Rail Road on the success of Idlewild began to lessen. By the time these undated photographs were taken, many travelers were choosing to reach the park by driving on the Lincoln Highway. As witnessed by these images, once the visitors arrived, they were assured a shady spot to park their vehicle.

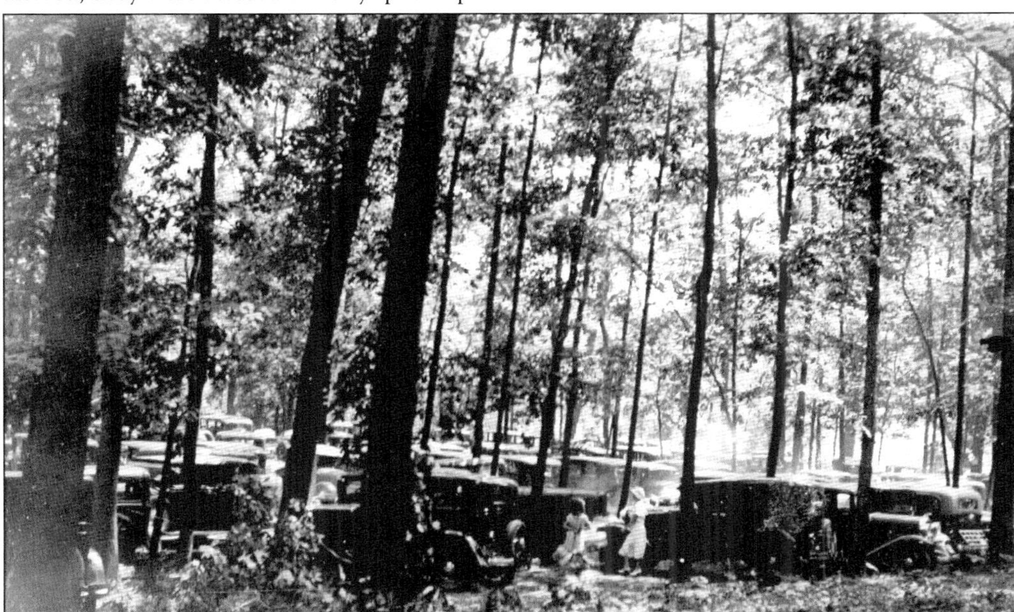

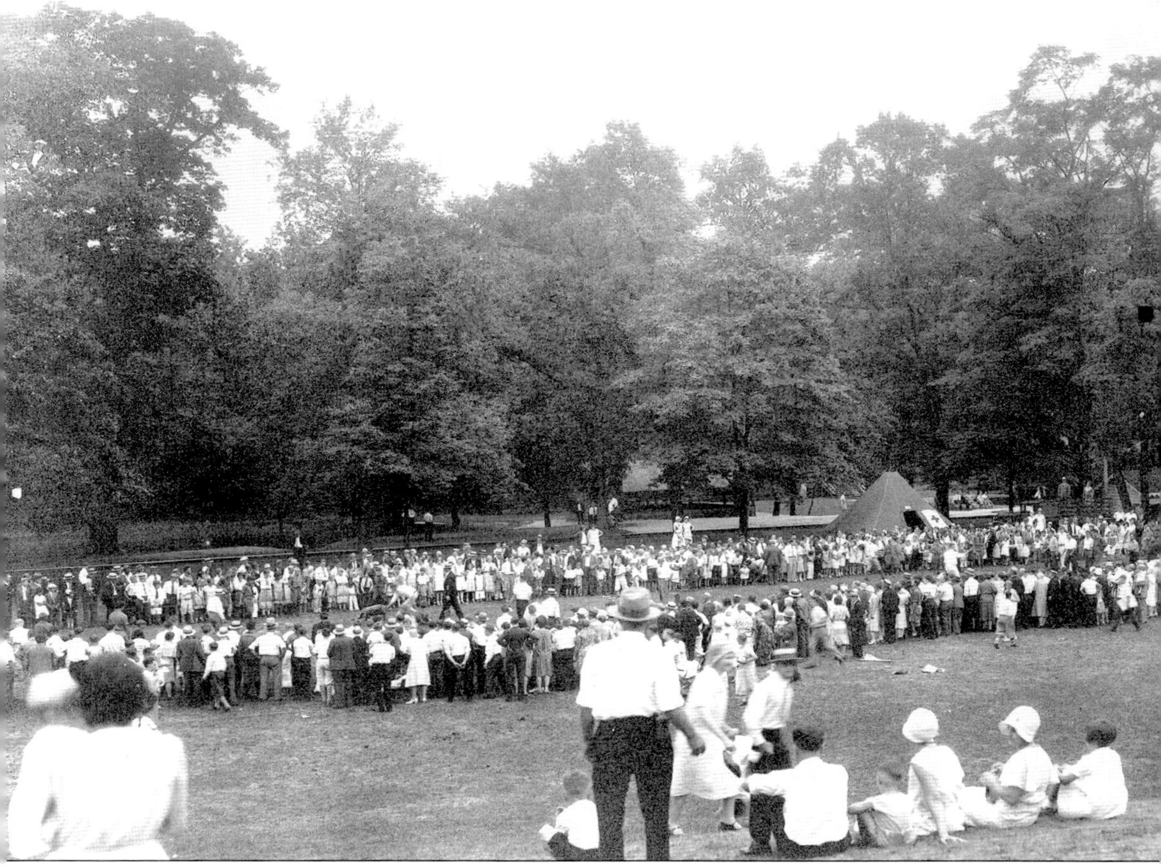

Many groups held games and races on the large central lawn at Idlewild. The presence of a pig in this photograph is evidence that a greased pig contest is about to begin. The contestants stand between the lines of onlookers ready to chase down the catch. The dress of the picnickers certainly seems formal by today's standards but was customary for the time.

Two

The Park Beautiful 1931–1952

In 1931, Idlewild was sold to the Idlewild Management Company, a partnership between Richard B. Mellon and Clinton (C. C.) Macdonald. Macdonald, who had more than 30 years of previous amusement park experience, became general manager and was assisted by his wife, Grace, and their two sons. Throughout the next few decades, the Macdonald family transformed Idlewild from a recreational picnic resort into a full scale, family-oriented amusement facility. Their first season brought electricity to the park allowing for later operating hours and new electric-powered amusement rides. A new carousel built by the Philadelphia Toboggan Company replaced the old steam merry-go-round underneath the carousel pavilion. In addition, many new refreshment stands were built.

The ensuing years saw many more changes. In 1932, the giant swimming pool located on the former Flower Island debuted. A circle swing, a Ferris wheel, a Whip, a miniature railroad, and a dark ride called the Rumpus were soon added. Macdonald also booked several traveling performance shows as free attractions; circuses, rodeos, high wire acts, and grand firework displays frequently delighted the crowds. The highlight of the early Macdonald years was the construction of the Rollo Coaster, designed by Herbert Schmeck of the Philadelphia Toboggan Company. It was built using wood harvested from the property, utilizing a sawmill built on site specifically for the project. World War II caused severe rationing across the United States, and Idlewild was forced to close during the 1943 season. Reopened in 1946, the improvements continued with the addition of the Caterpillar, the Showboat, and some children's rides by the end of the decade.

One of the most important elements the Macdonald family brought to Idlewild was a commitment to build on its natural beauty. Ten-thousand shrubs were planted during their first season, and a landscaping project was undertaken that defined the park's midways for decades. Thousands of trees were planted throughout the 1930s, and Idlewild was billed as "the Park Beautiful." This commitment would continue to guide the family's management style as they assumed complete ownership of the park in 1950.

In 1952, with the closing of area coal mines and with a steady decrease in passenger traffic, the decision was made by the Mellon family to abandon the Ligonier Valley Rail Road. Although Idlewild's inception was a product of the railroad, its continued existence was not dependent on the Millionaire's Line. In 1913, the Lincoln Highway had been laid out as a transcontinental automobile route. Running from New York City to San Francisco, the route traveled directly passed Idlewild. By the 1930s, a Gulf Oil service station and several parking lots were added to accommodate the many automobile travelers. While Idlewild certainly owed its early success to the Ligonier Valley Rail Road, its closing on August 31, 1952, did little to diminish the amusement park's popularity.

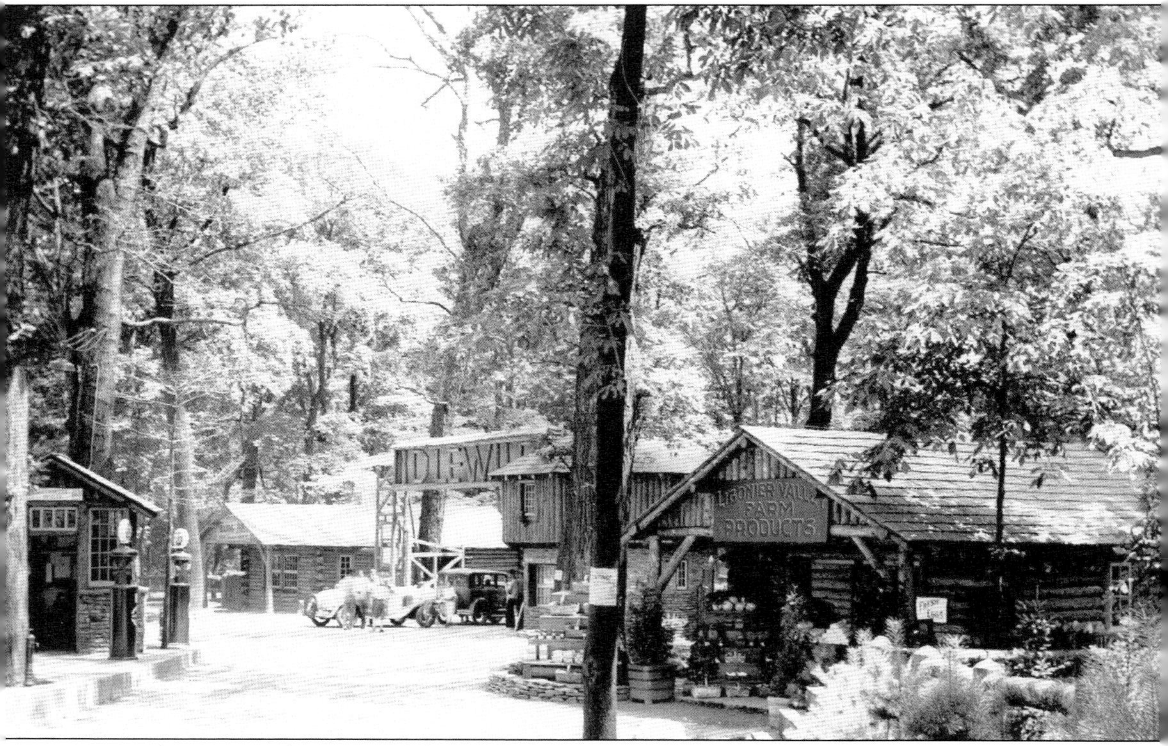

In the 1930s, the automobile entrance featured several businesses. Pictured here are, from left to right, a Gulf Oil station, the Trading Post gift shop, the Roundhouse, and the Ligonier Valley produce market. C. C. Macdonald had begun his love of log structures while operating Rock Springs Park in Chester, West Virginia. There, many buildings, including the home of the Macdonald family, were made from logs shipped from Canada. The inclusion of the Gulf Oil station was only logical since the Mellons had a financial interest in the company and Idlewild adjoined a transcontinental highway. A former parachutist who had previously performed at the park operated the station in its later years. The Roundhouse often served as rooming quarters for some of the park's seasonal help.

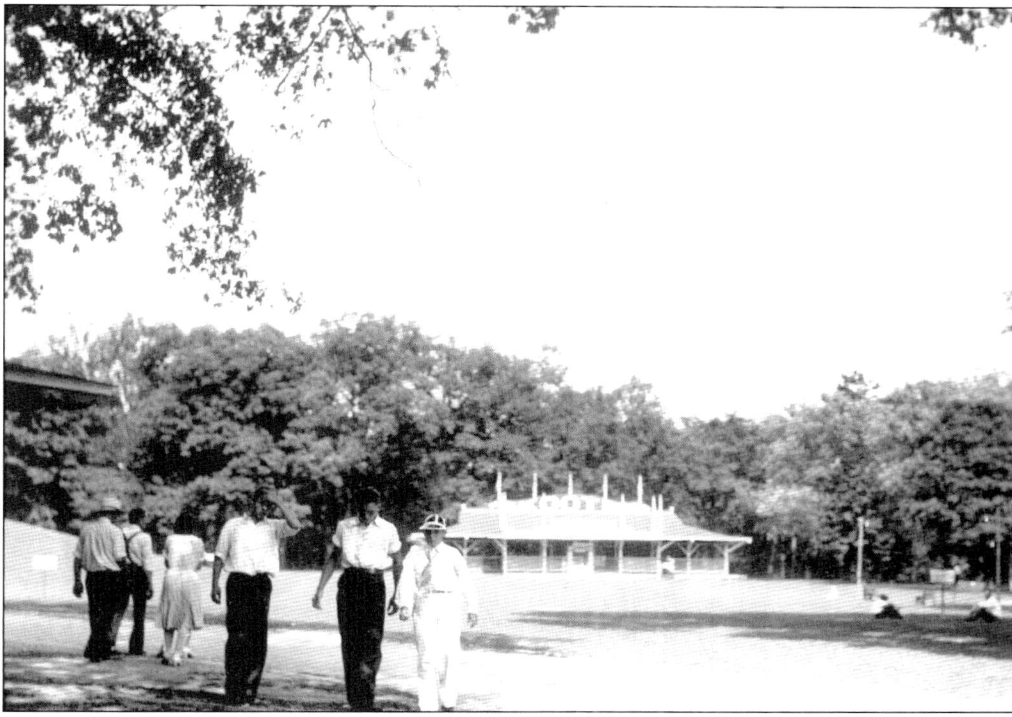

The main lawn became home to the Skooters in 1931. The 40-by-80-foot building was ornately decorated with spires and flags and included 20 electrically operated Lusse bumper cars.

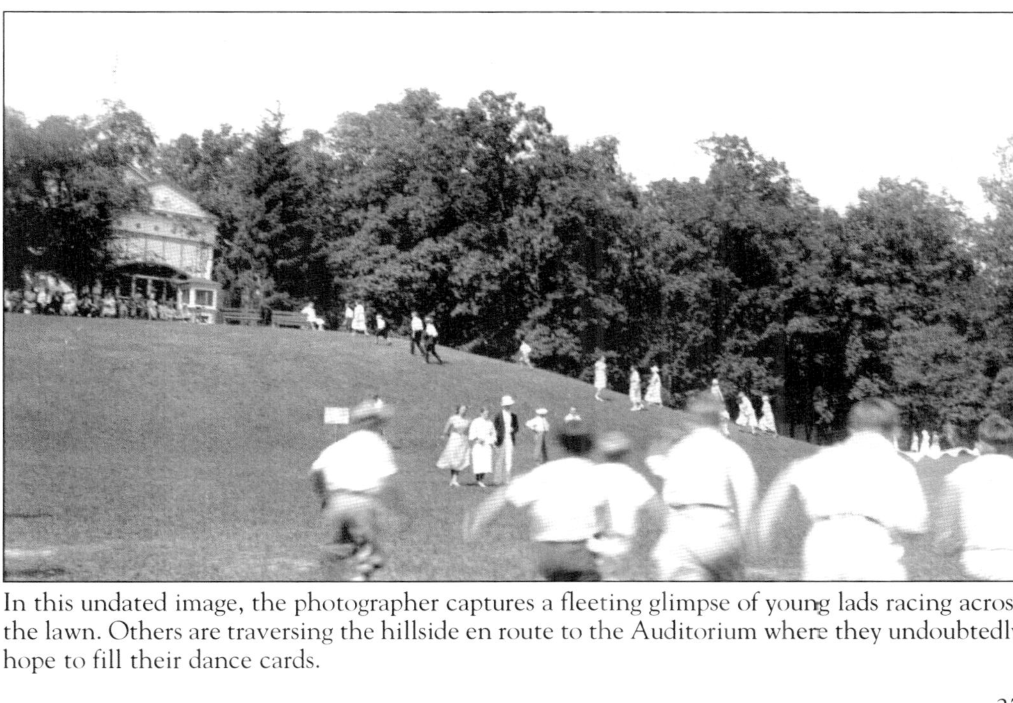

In this undated image, the photographer captures a fleeting glimpse of young lads racing across the lawn. Others are traversing the hillside en route to the Auditorium where they undoubtedly hope to fill their dance cards.

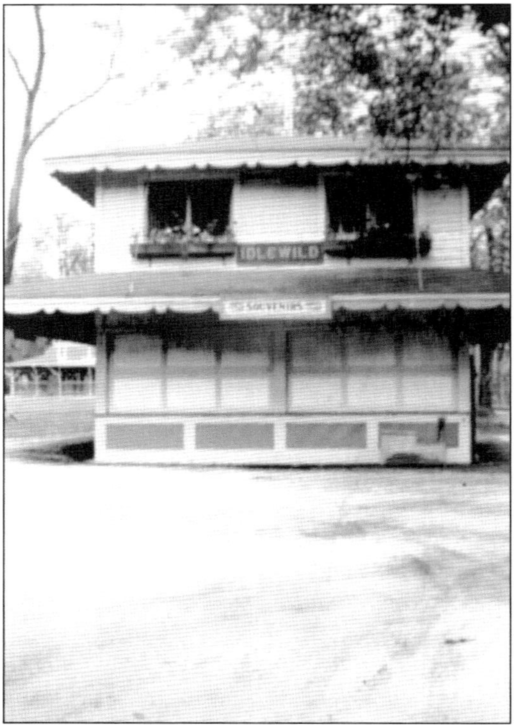

A new two-story depot was built in 1931. Offices for park management were on the second floor and a souvenir stand, refreshment stand, and waiting room on the first floor. Today, the building houses the Odds and Ends gift shop, a committee room, and storage rooms.

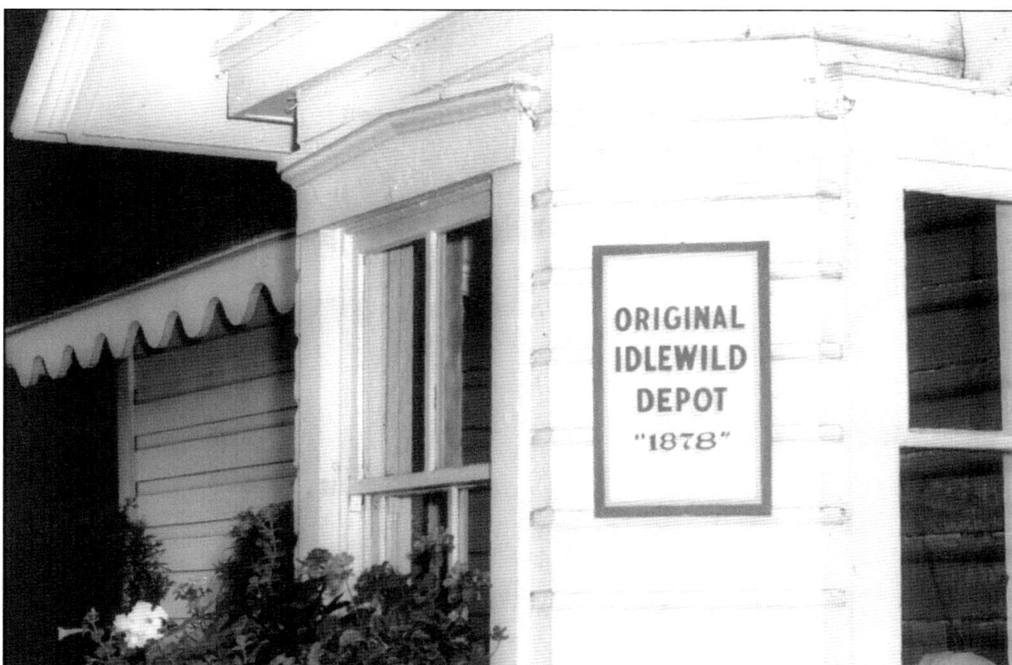

The tiny depot that served the park since 1878 was not torn down when the new two-story building was erected. Since the building was used for other purposes, a simple sign reminded visitors of the structure's significance to the history of Idlewild.

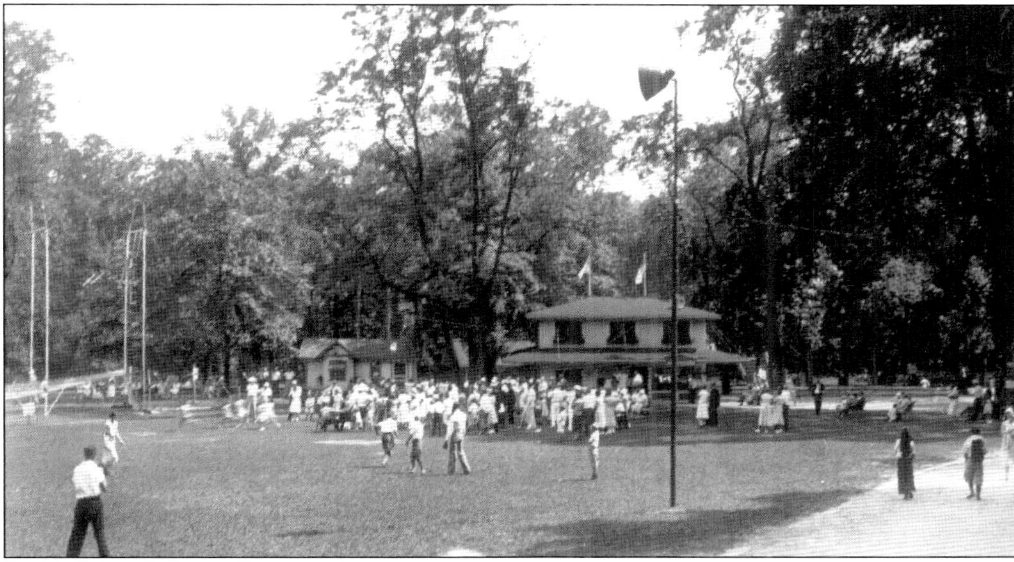

The old depot can be seen next to its successor in this photograph from 1932. The crowd is probably gathering to watch artists perform on the trapeze tower located to the left. The floodlight on top of the pole was one of many throughout the park added by the Macdonalds. The lights allowed for much later operating hours.

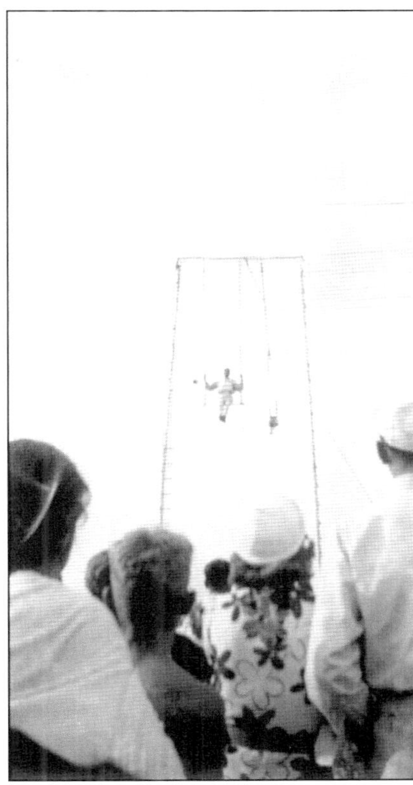

The Macdonald family brought many types of entertainment to the patrons of the park. The free acts, such as this trapeze artist, were customarily presented once in the afternoon and once in the evening. In 1933, a new outdoor stage was constructed with microphone connections so that guests could better see and hear the many circus acts, musical groups, and stunt performances.

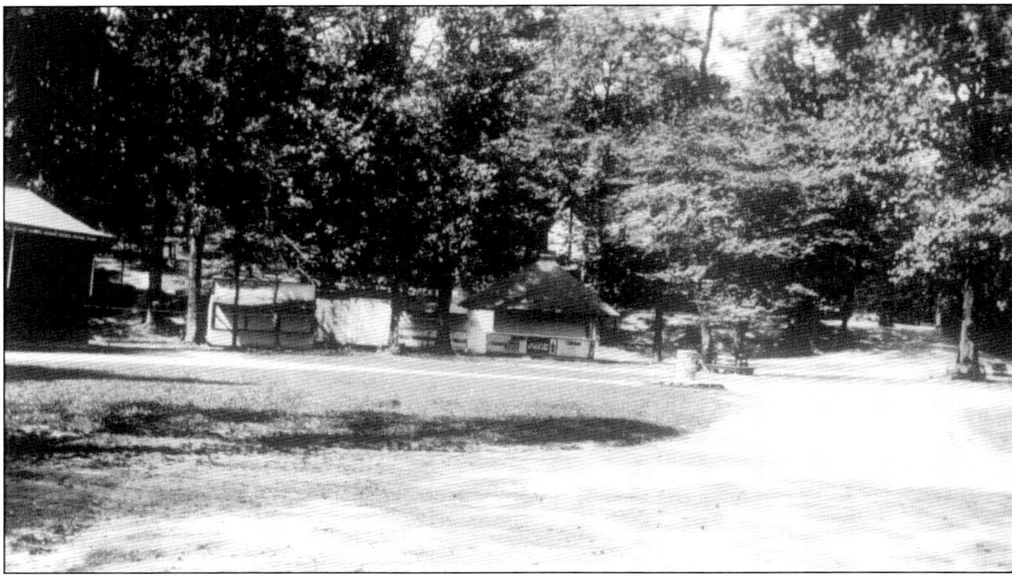

Small refreshment stands were scattered among the trees in the early 1930s. A few years later, C. C. Macdonald built new, larger lunch stands, snack counters, and restaurants—many of which still stand to this day. Beef from cattle raised on the Macdonald's Texas ranch was served up in many of the new eateries.

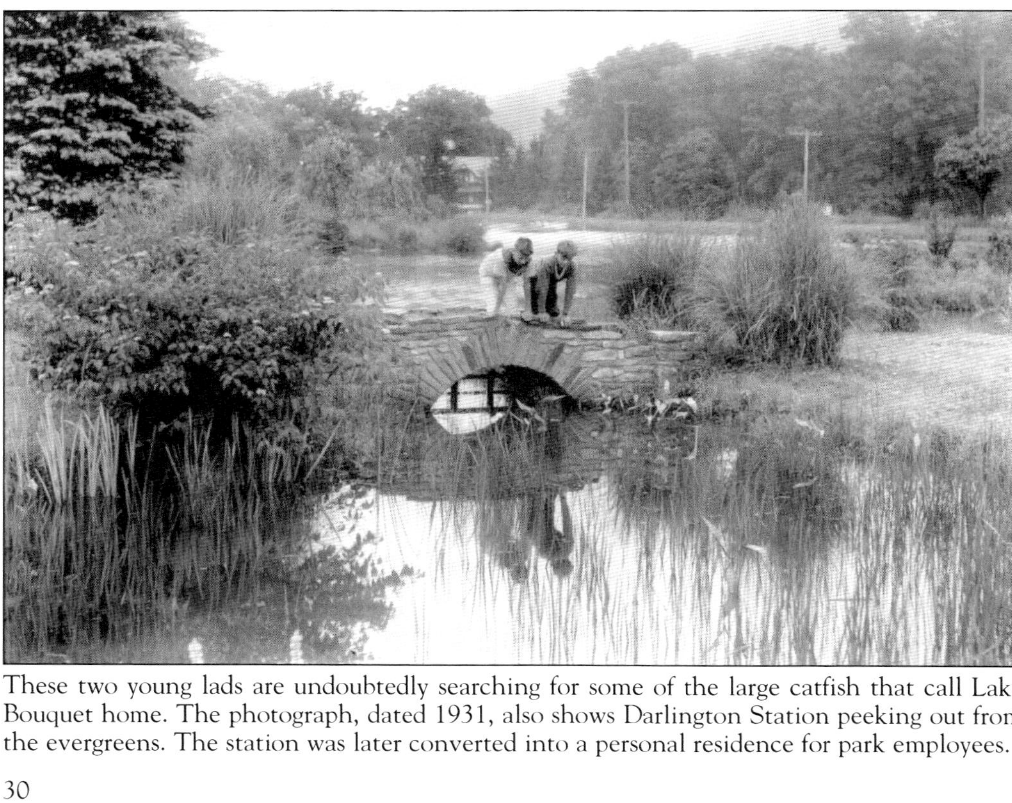

These two young lads are undoubtedly searching for some of the large catfish that call Lake Bouquet home. The photograph, dated 1931, also shows Darlington Station peeking out from the evergreens. The station was later converted into a personal residence for park employees.

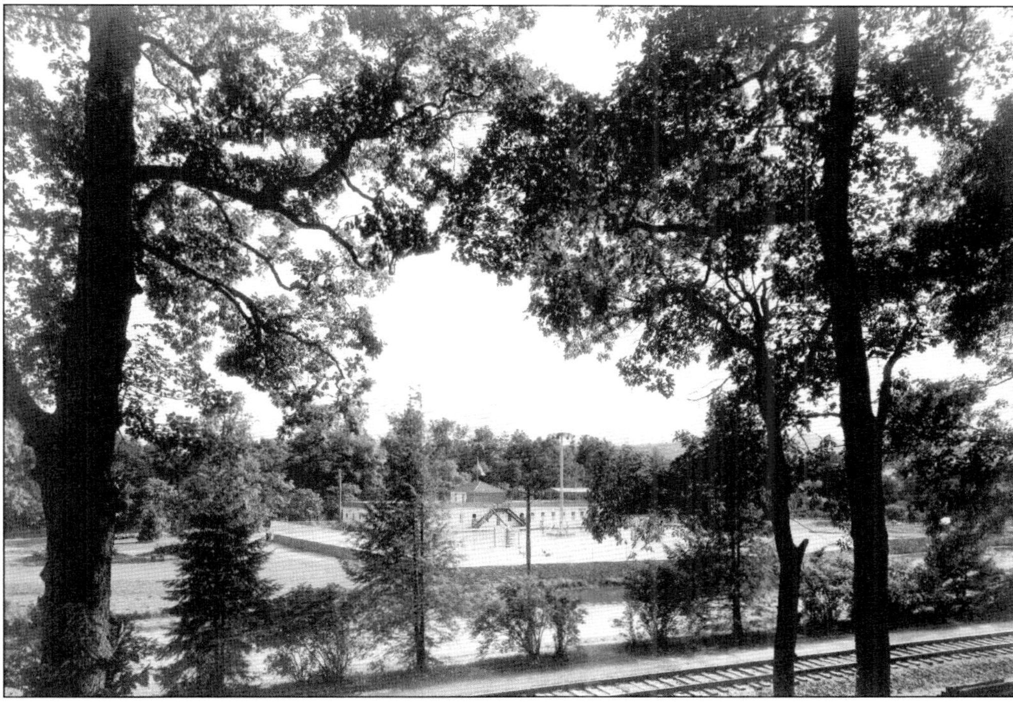

In 1932, a large modern swimming pool opened on the island in the middle of Lake Bouquet. Measuring 80 feet by 100 feet, it was equipped with the finest sand filtering system available at the time. The project also included a bathhouse and a sand beach. Two images of the new attraction are featured here. The image above offers a fine view of the railroad tracks.

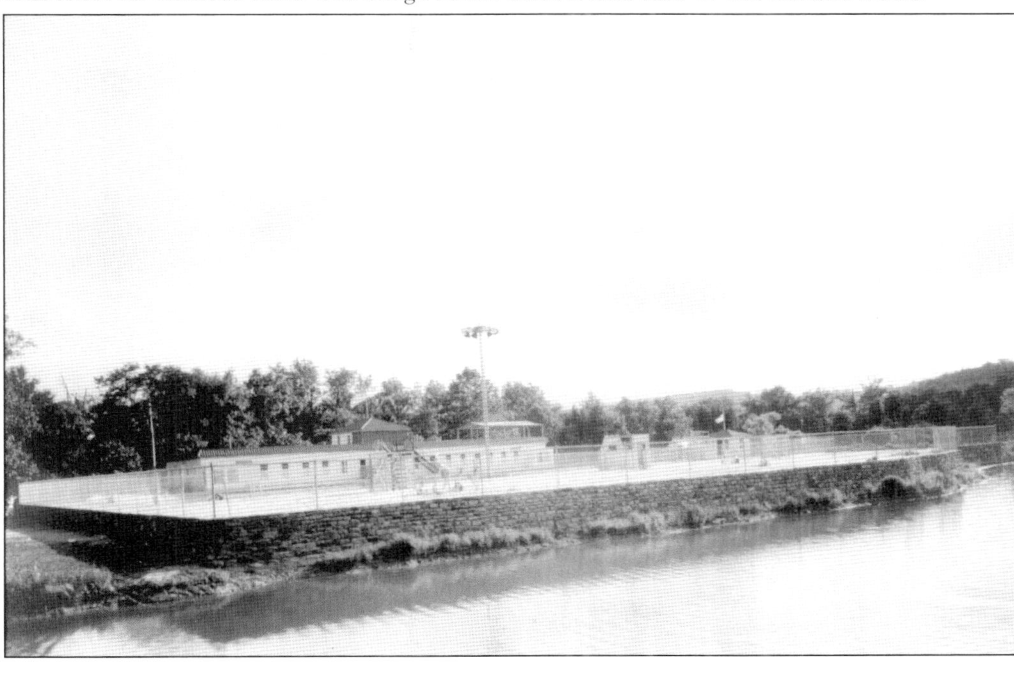

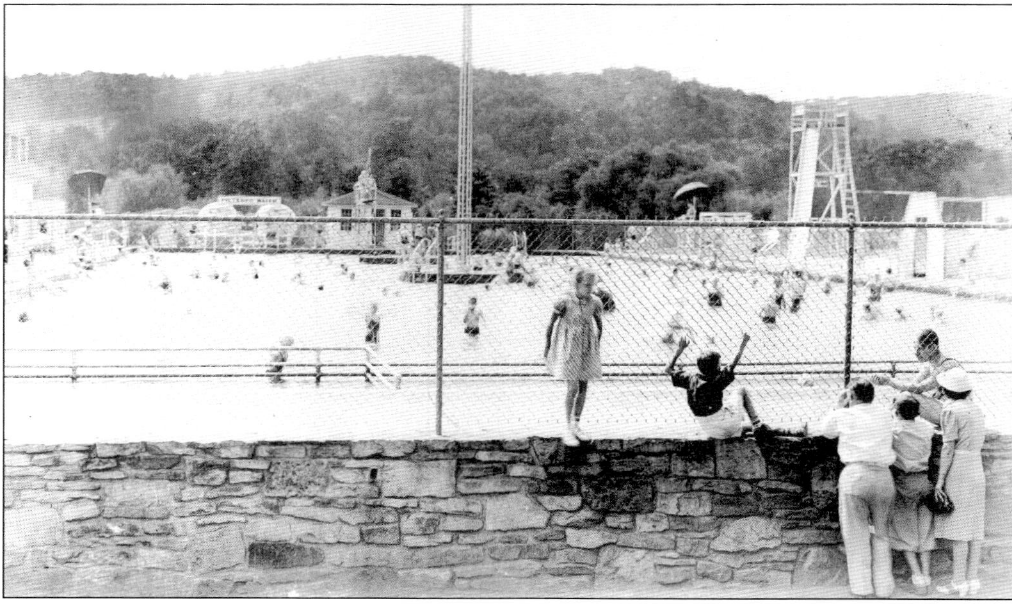

From its first season, the swimming pool proved very popular among many Idlewild guests. However, these photographs show that some people liked to stand outside the gate and just watch, or perhaps they forgot their bathing suit. Prominent in the image below is the floodlight tower that rose from the center of the pool. This allowed for swimming after dark.

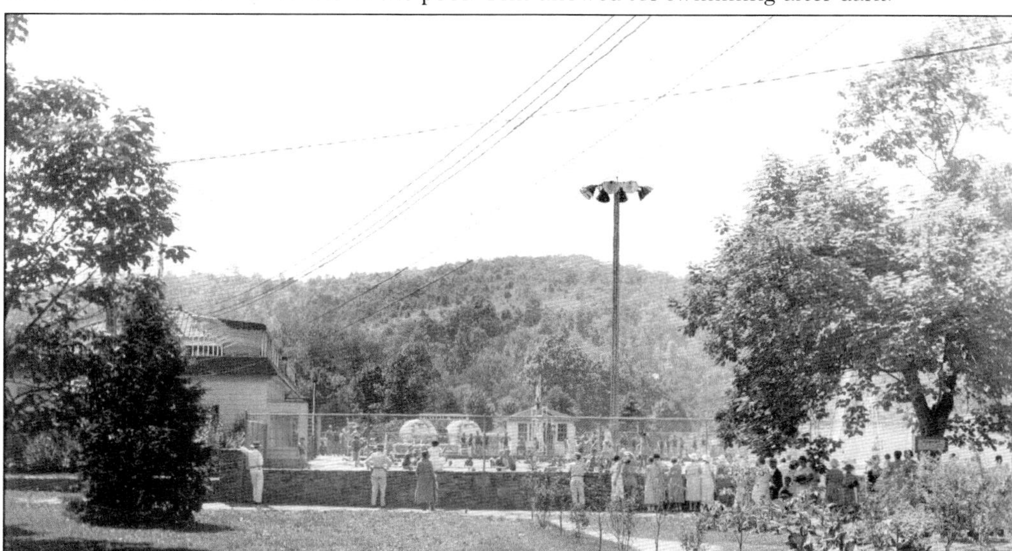

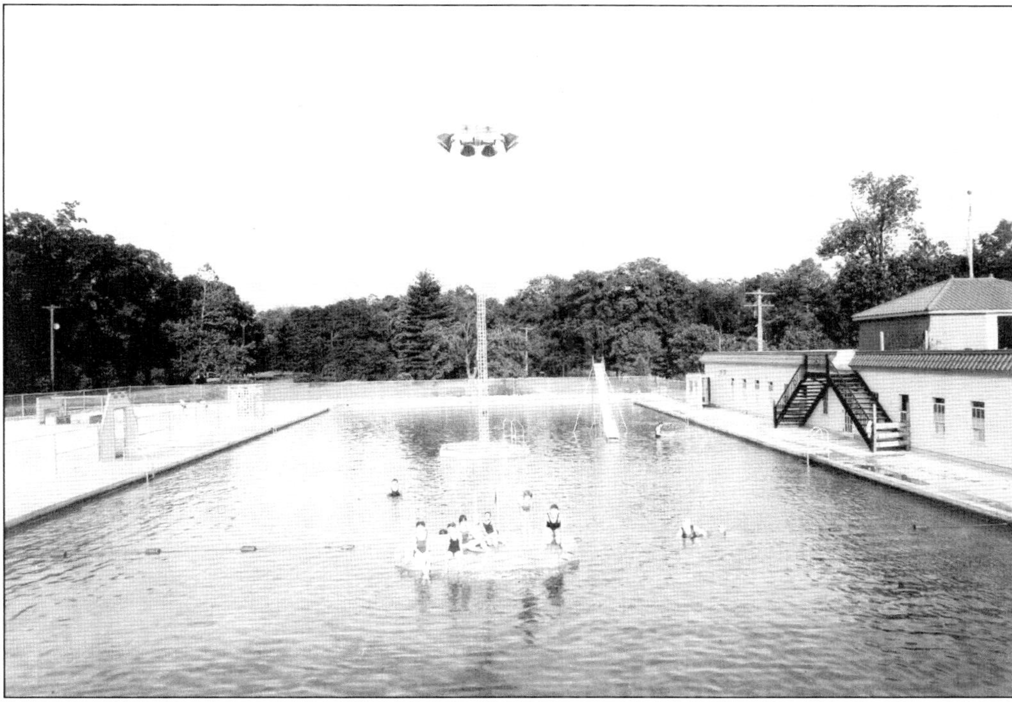

The bathhouse adjoining the swimming pool was equipped with changing rooms for both gentlemen and ladies. Showers were also included through which all bathers passed before entering the pool. Concrete islands stood in the center of the water and served as diving platforms.

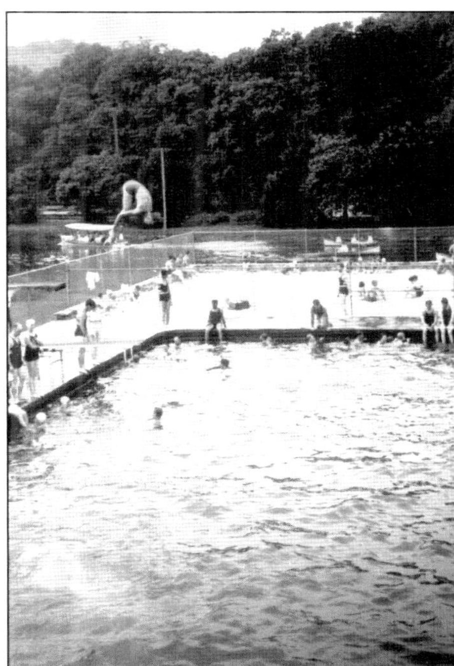

This image, dated July 21, 1935, shows the deep end of the swimming pool where three diving boards were present. Beyond the water is the sand beach that would later be removed. Clogged drains and filters led management to replace it with a lawn beach.

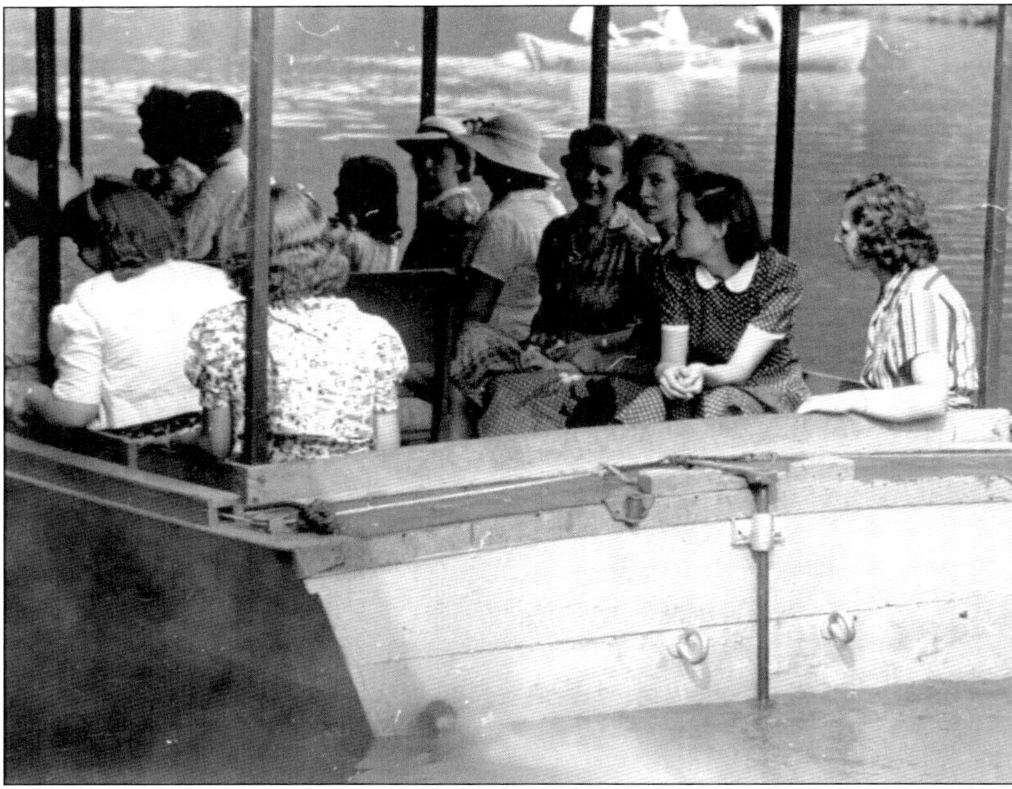

A new motor launch, capable of carrying 25 passengers, replaced the earlier vapor launches in 1930. It continued to dock at the boathouse just as its predecessor had done. The image below is dated June 30, 1935.

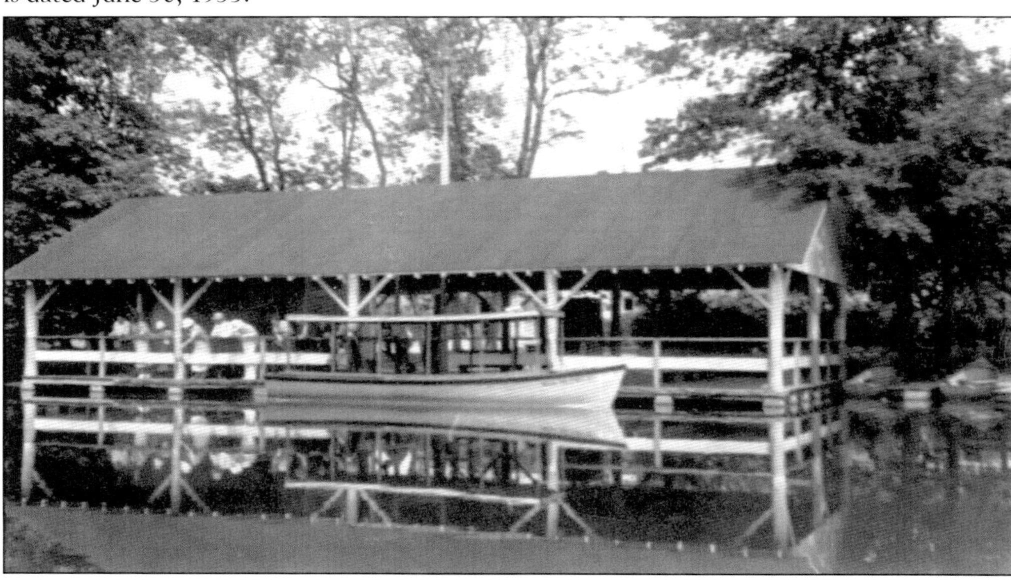

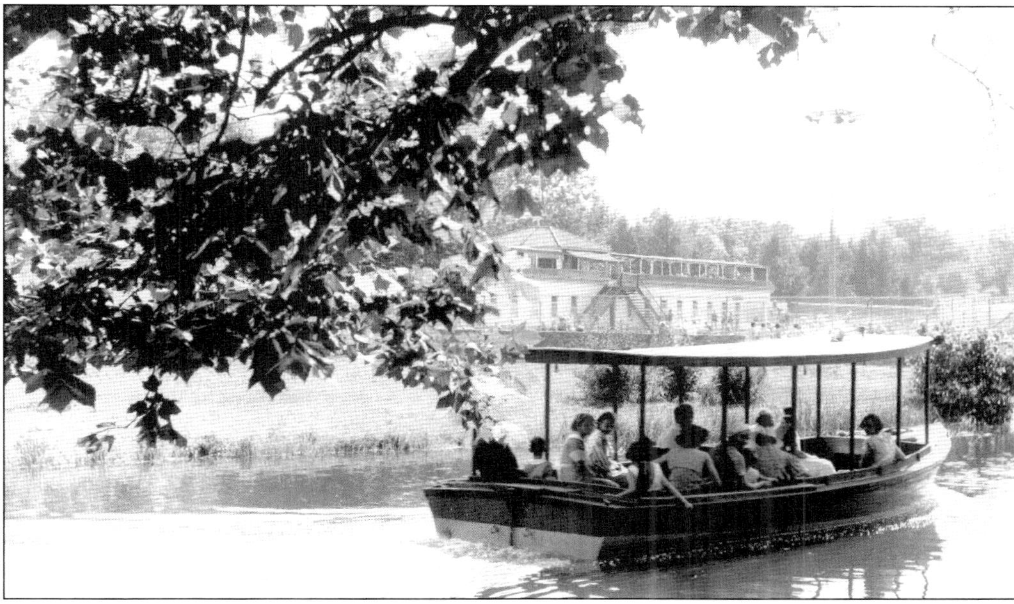

The motor launch offered great views of the swimming pool, as did the second floor of the bathhouse. There, sunbathers could grab a snack and watch the swimmers frolic in the water below.

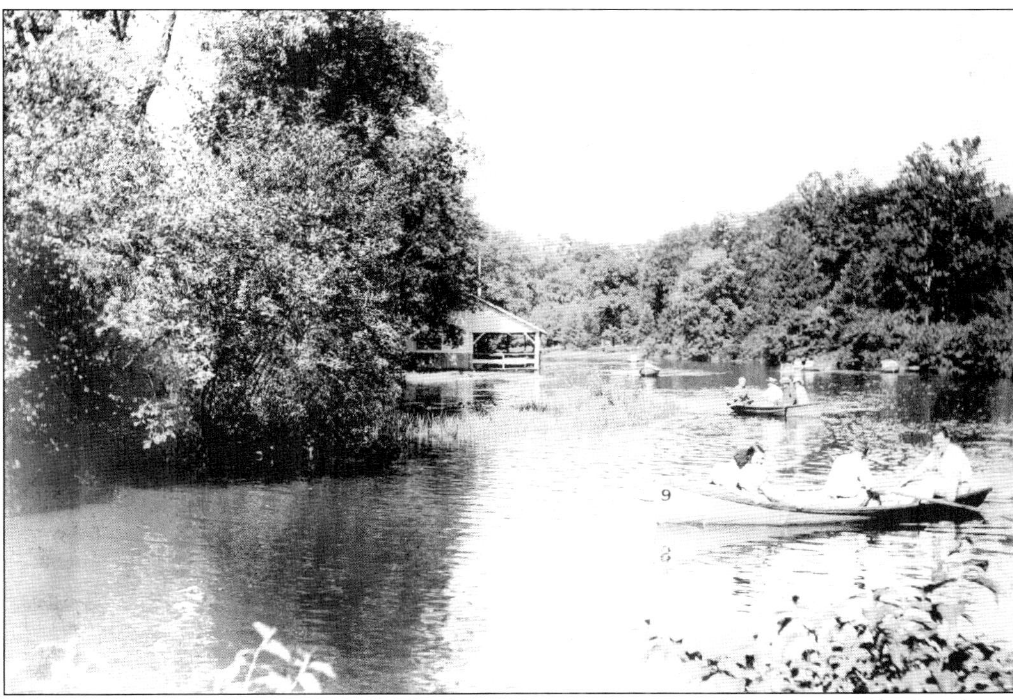

A warm sunny day in 1932 proved to be the perfect time to enjoy the rowboats. The boathouse is shown in the center of the photograph. Much of this portion of Lake Bouquet later became filled in when Idlewild expanded its water park facilities in 2000.

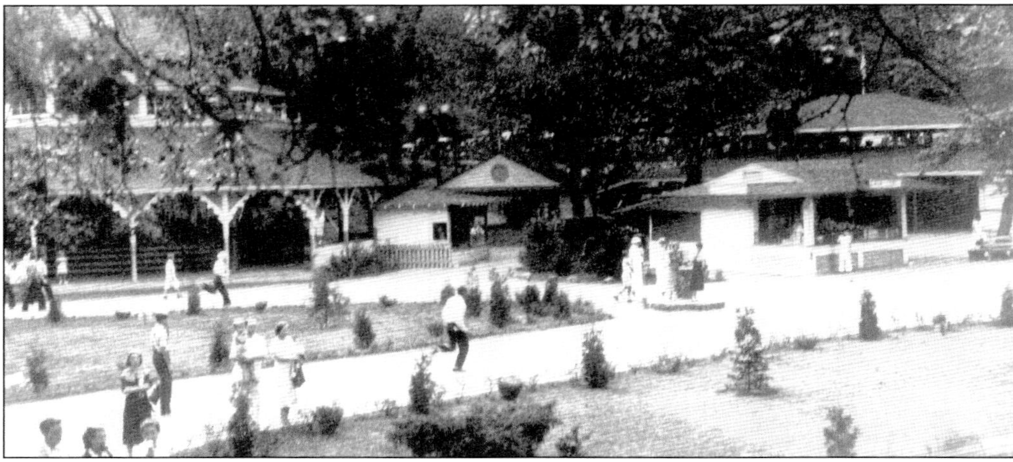

Seen here in its early stages, the landscaping efforts of the Macdonald family gave structure to the park's midways. The buildings in the background are, from left to right, the carousel pavilion, the shooting gallery, the popcorn stand, and the administration building.

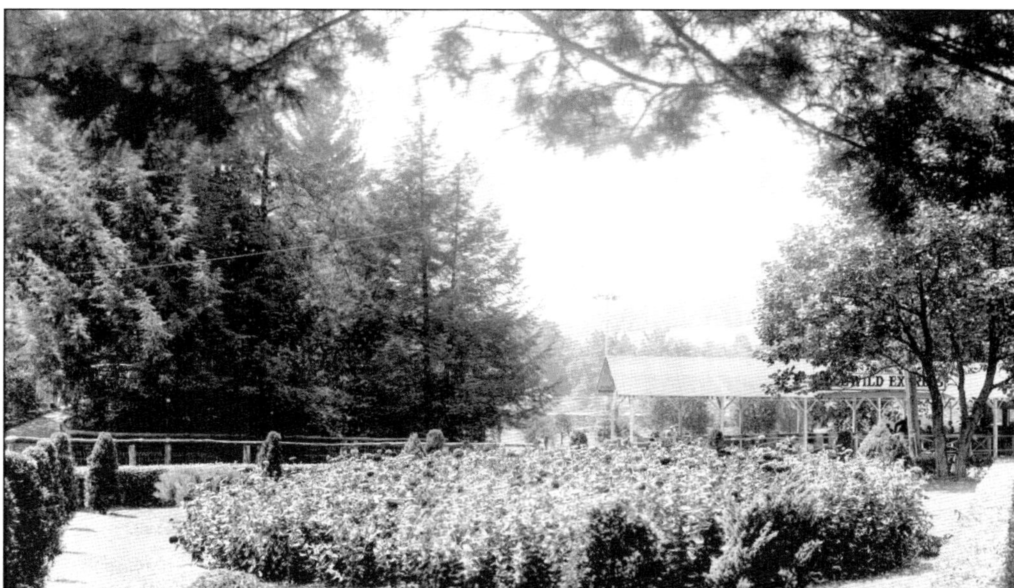

The station for the Idlewild Express miniature railroad can be seen beyond this attractive flower garden. The innovative ride had a two-foot gauge track that covered nearly one mile. Starting at the station, the track ran between Lakes Bouquet and St. Clair along the line of the Ligonier Valley Rail Road until it reached Darlington Station. From there, it turned sharply left and traveled through a patch of evergreen trees. It followed the north bank of the Loyalhanna Creek until it cut back to the station.

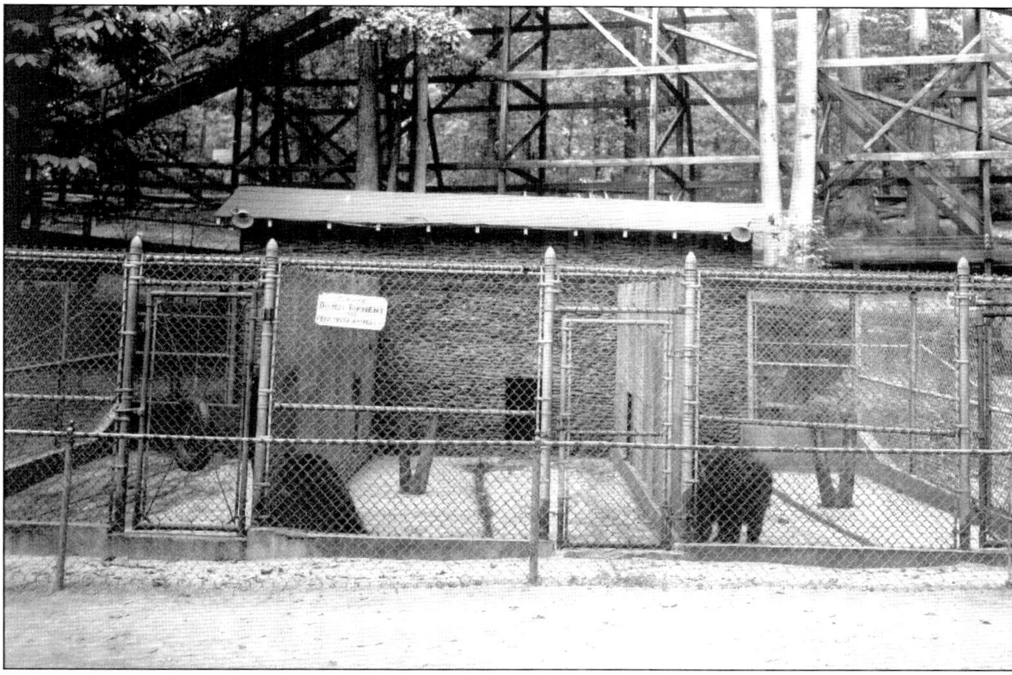

A popular attraction that debuted in 1931 was the den of Canadian black bears. It was a neighbor to the monkey cage pictured below. The monkeys were notorious for escaping their confine. In 1932, a reward of $3 per head was offered for the capture of seven monkeys that had gotten loose. Later, it was believed that an unauthorized person had freed the monkeys. While he stopped short of making any formal accusations against his father, R. Z. Macdonald noted in an interview with this author that C. C. Macdonald always seemed quite amused (and pleased) with the publicity the escaped monkeys generated for the park. A warren of raccoons completed the animal menagerie.

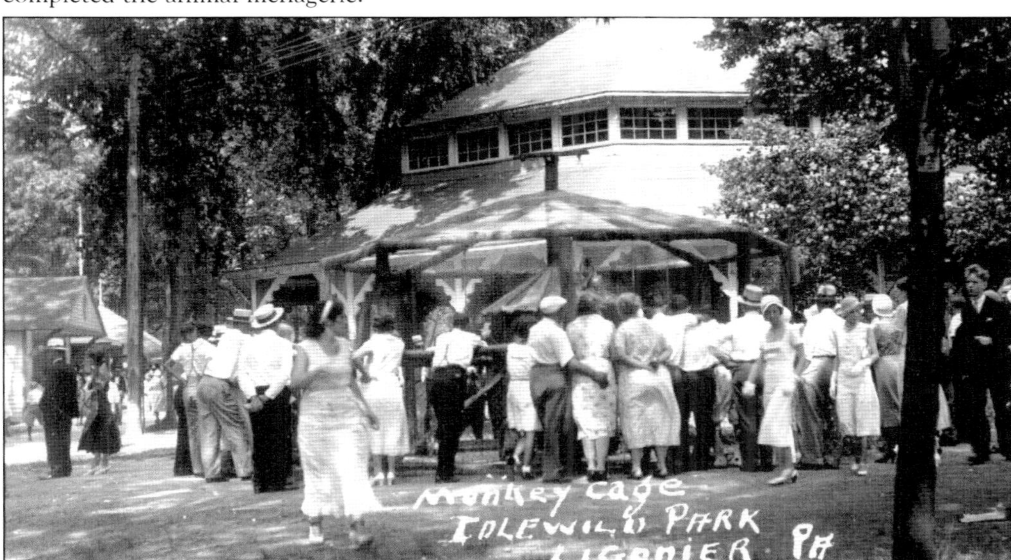

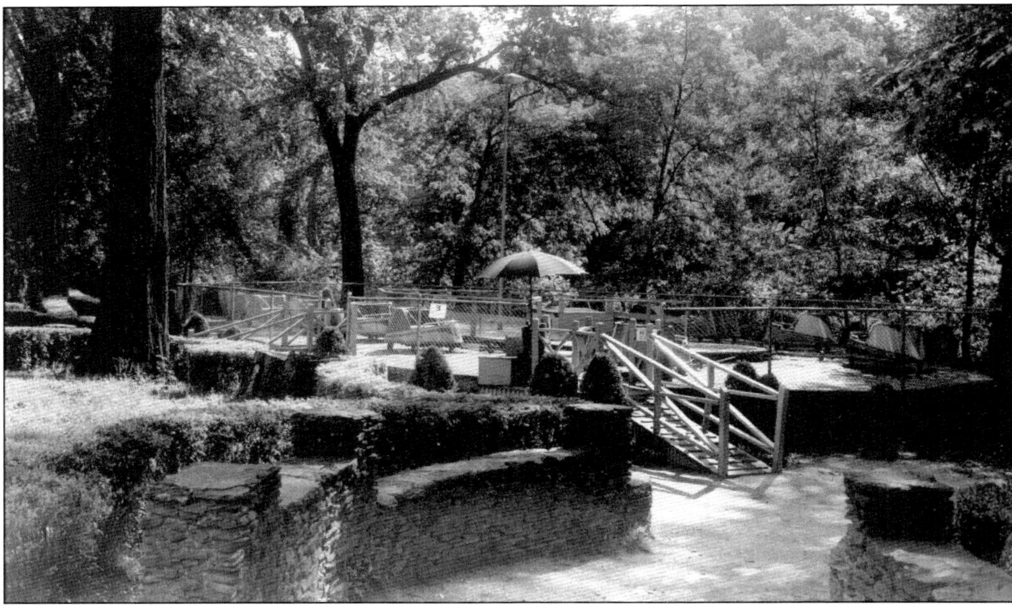

In 1939, the park's current Whip, manufactured by the W. F. Mangels Company, replaced a small portable version that had stood since 1934. The classic ride has remained popular through the years because it offers a thrill that even the youngest and oldest generations can enjoy. Its location next to the Loyalhanna Creek has led to the ride being flooded several times over the course of its existence. One of these floods led to the replacement of the original 12 cars.

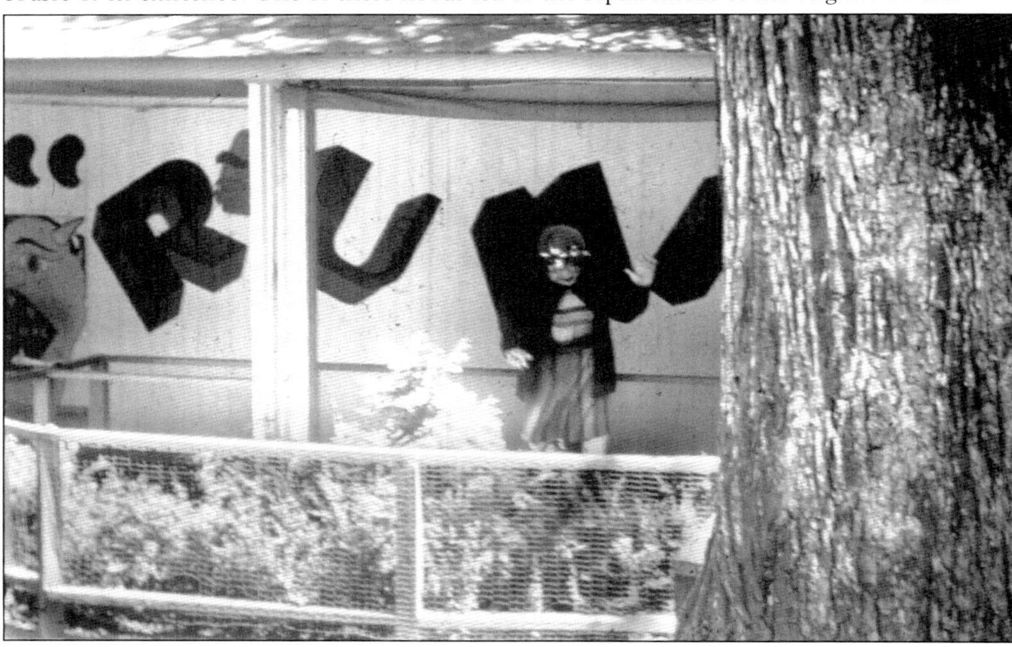

In the 1930s, a picnic pavilion was converted into the Rumpus, a dark ride manufactured by the Pretzel Amusement Company. The attraction featured a laughing Sal, a popular fixture of the time, at its entrance. The Rumpus and Sal were destroyed in a fire two days before the 1947 season began.

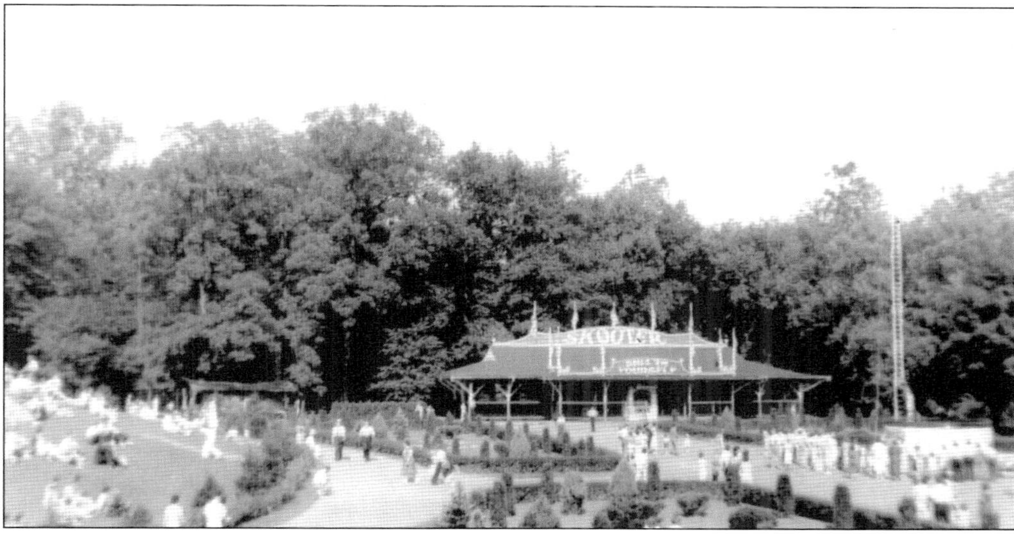

The Skooter building stands at the east end of the redesigned Idlewild mall in this image from the 1930s. C. C. Macdonald joined forces with local landscaper John Deeds to bring a host of new greenery to the former central lawn. Forty-thousand privet bushes made up the myriad hedges that lined the walkways, while several hundred evergreens were also planted.

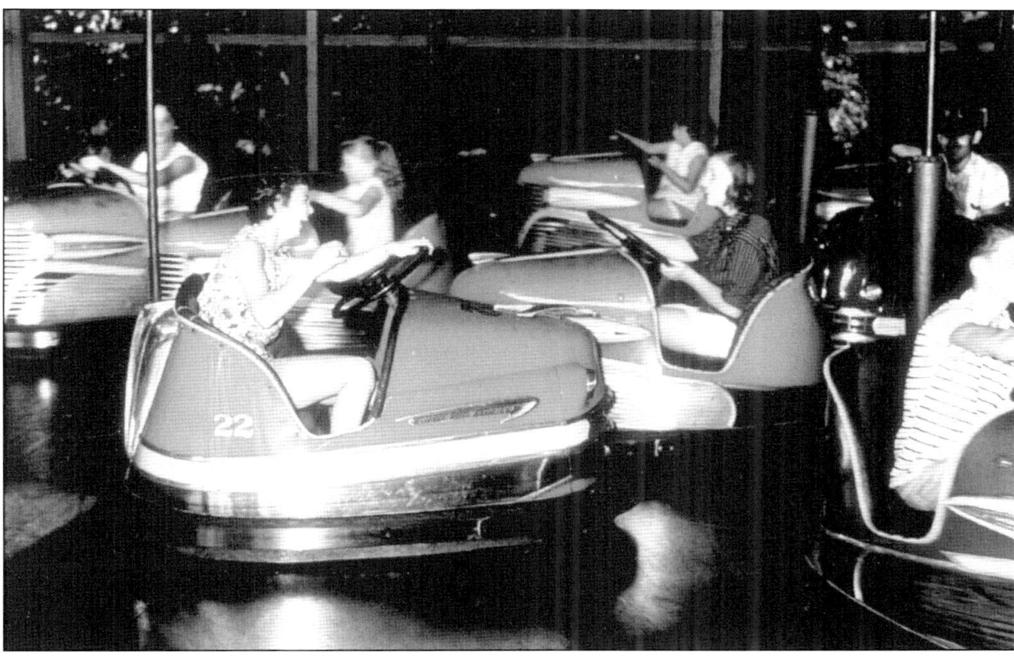

The original Lusse Skooter cars provided fun for park guests dating back to 1931. During World War II, adding new rides or obtaining parts for existing rides became a struggle for many parks. Idlewild sold their Skooter cars to one of these suffering parks. When the war ended, shiny new replacement cars took their place.

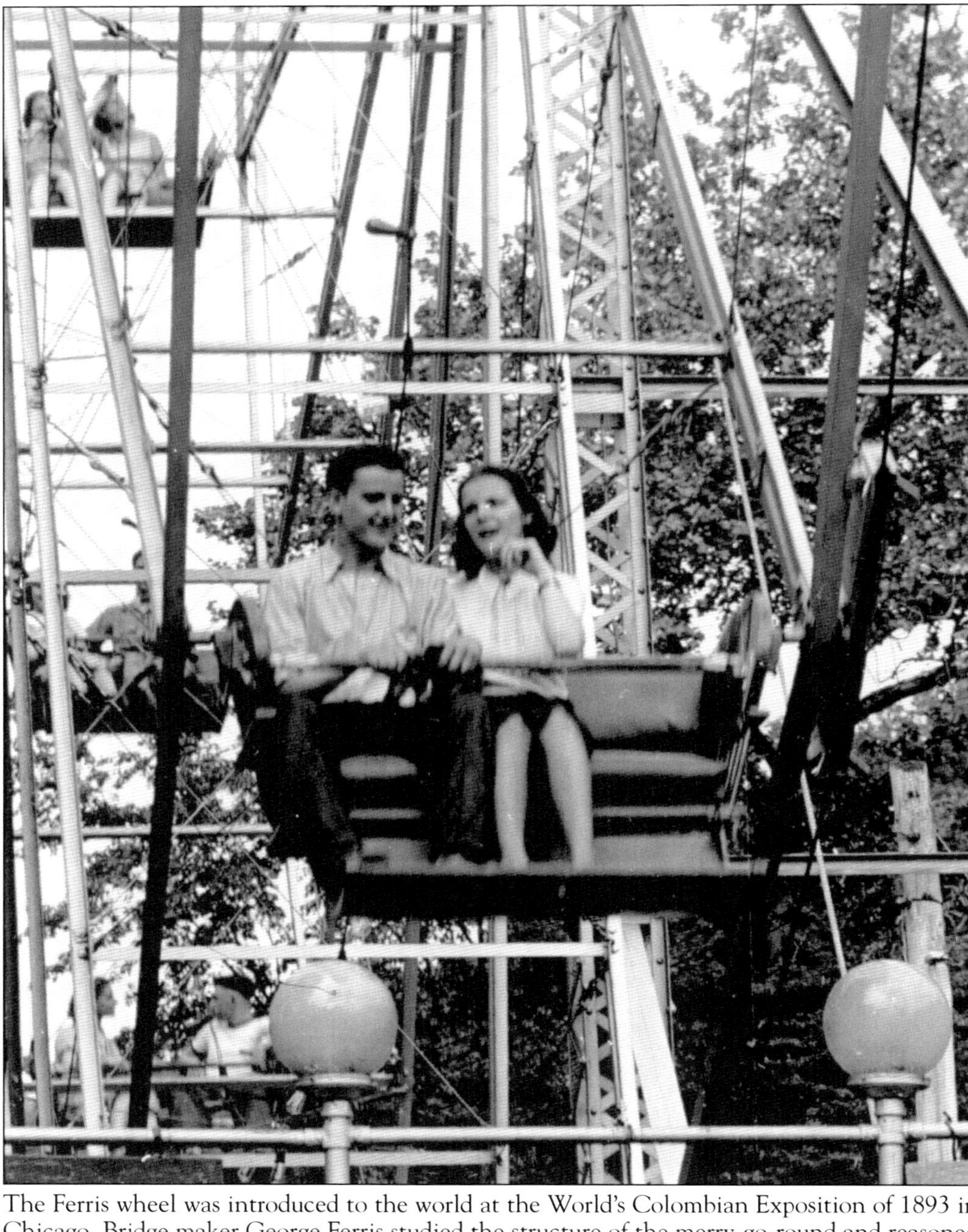

The Ferris wheel was introduced to the world at the World's Colombian Exposition of 1893 in Chicago. Bridge maker George Ferris studied the structure of the merry-go-round and reasoned that people would enjoy a vertical wheel just as much as a horizontal wheel. His creation contained 36 wooden cars that held 60 passengers each. Considerably smaller than the one at the exposition, Idlewild's first Ferris wheel stood from 1934 until 1941 near the bridge crossing the Loyalhanna. As one can see from this photograph, the smaller seat capacity made it a popular ride for young couples.

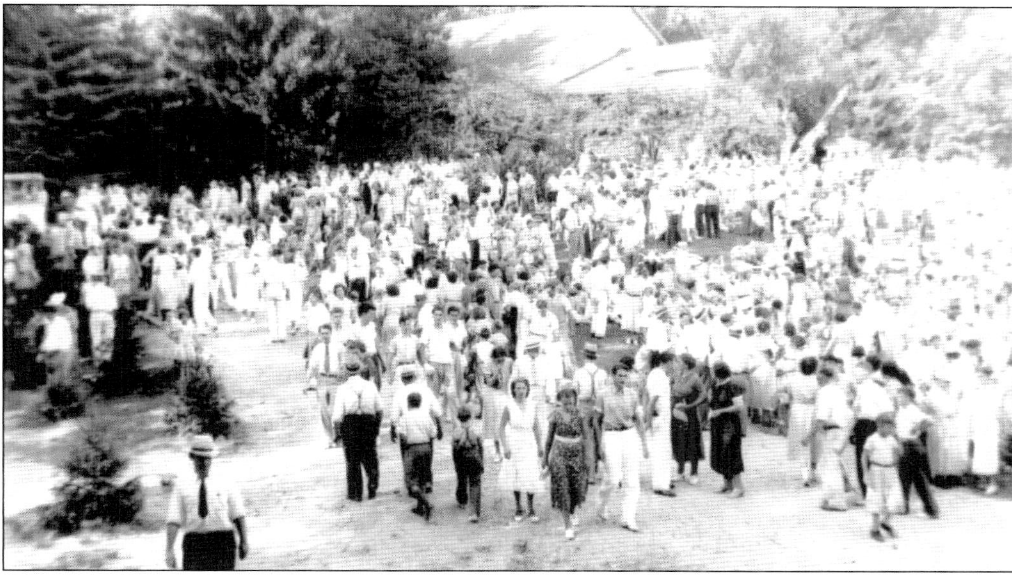

Huge crowds pack the hillside in these two images from the 1930s. While it is unknown what particular events they are enjoying, aerial acts were commonly held at this location. Prize drawings for company and community picnics also took place here. The drawings often attracted thousands of hopefuls waiting to hear if their ticket would be chosen.

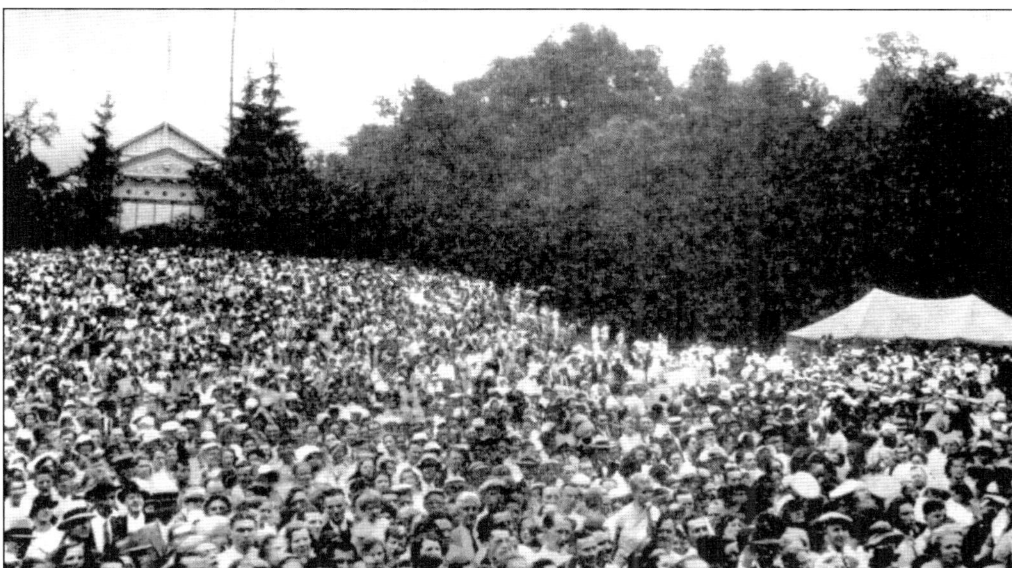

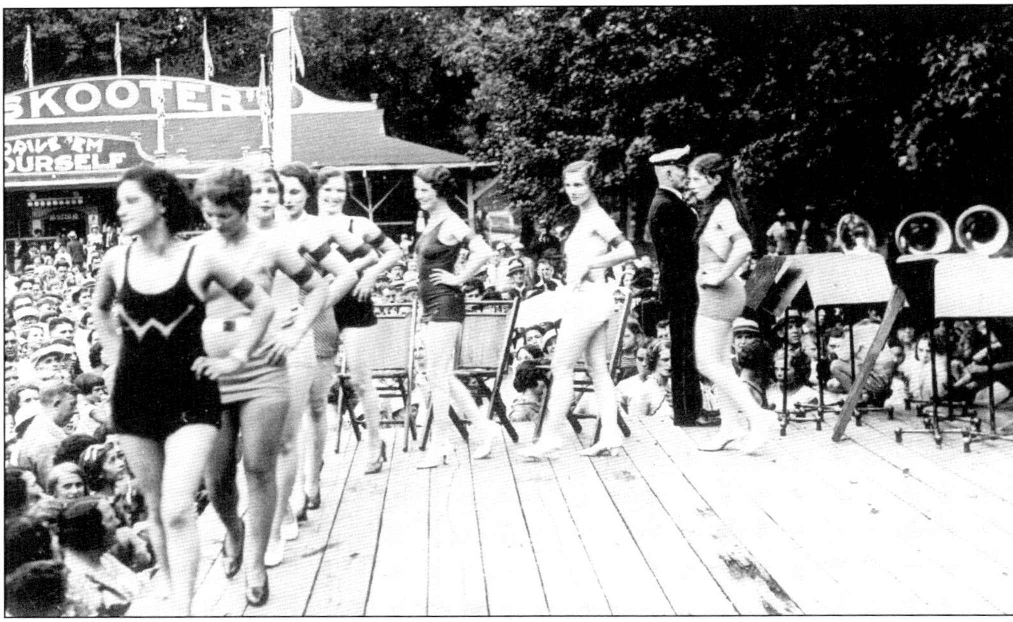

Beauty pageants, sponsored by business or community organizations, occasionally were held on the main stage. Pictured in these two photographs are scenes from the Miss Westinghouse pageant held in the 1930s. The contestants parade across the stage in the above image. The image below shows the lovely champion.

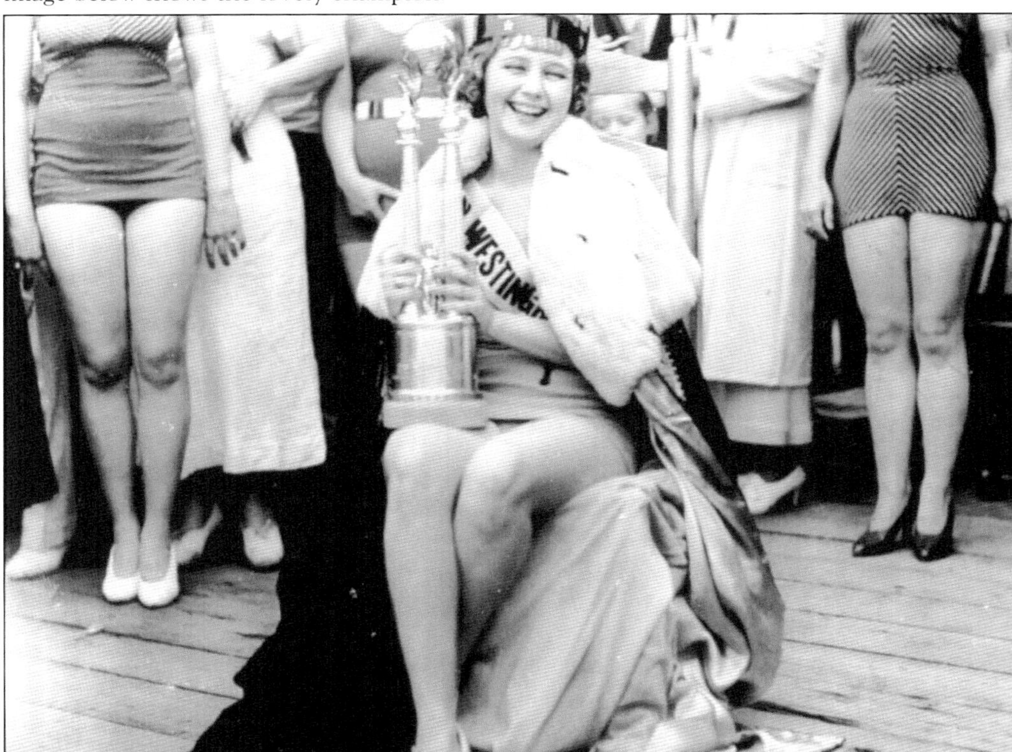

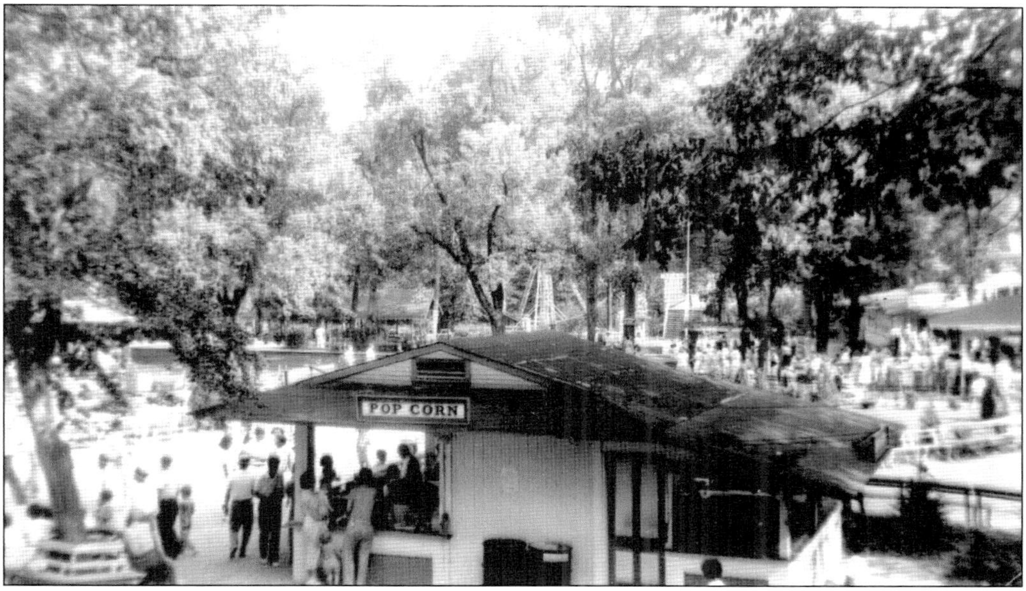

The park's popcorn stand was the favorite of manager C. C. Macdonald. *The Ligonier Valley Rail Road and Its Communities*, by James Madison Meyers, notes that only a "white corn with no outside silver," was sold here. Through the trees just above the roof of the popcorn stand are the steps to the Shadowlands, the renamed Woodlands area. To the left of the steps is the Ferris wheel, and the ill-fated Rumpus stands at right.

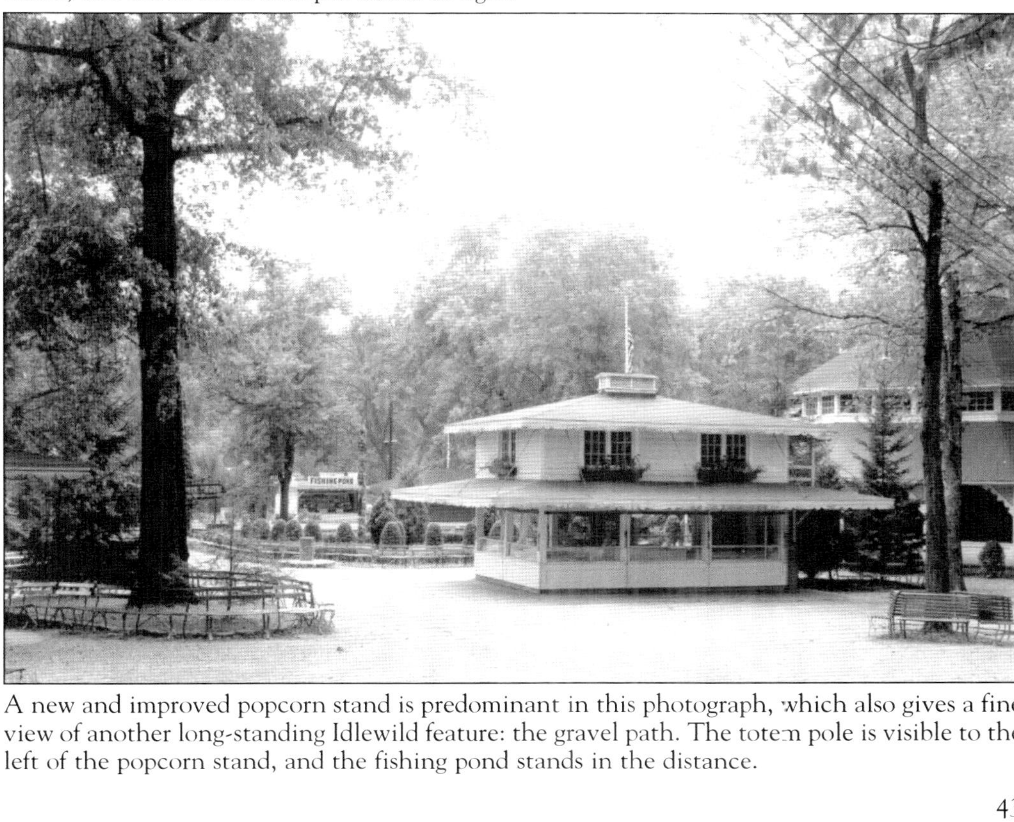

A new and improved popcorn stand is predominant in this photograph, which also gives a fine view of another long-standing Idlewild feature: the gravel path. The totem pole is visible to the left of the popcorn stand, and the fishing pond stands in the distance.

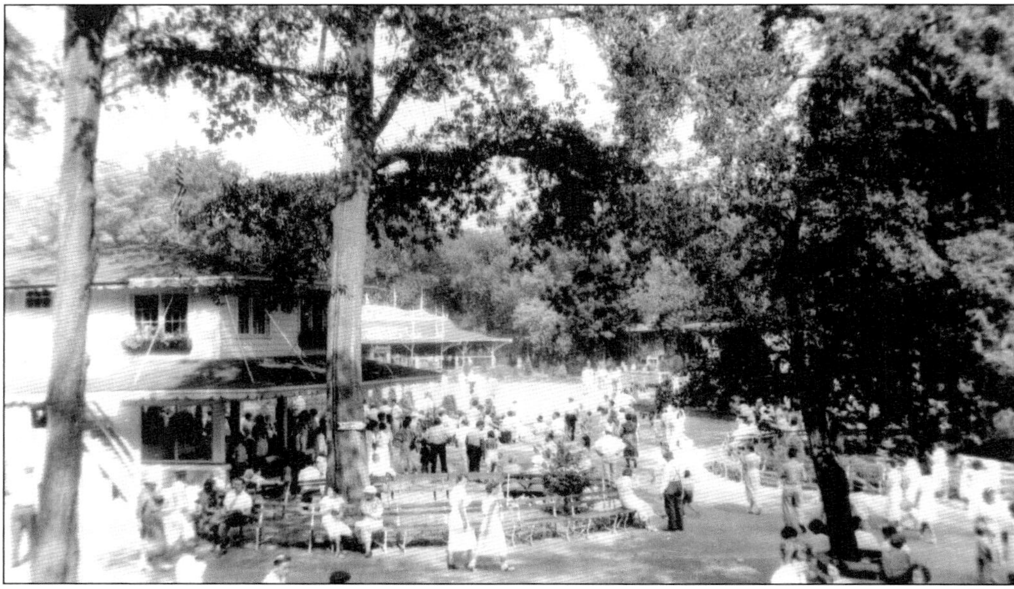

The lunch stand, shown here on the left, served such favorites as hamburgers, hot dogs, and French fries. In later years, it sold steak hoagies. Eventually, the building was replaced by a new eatery called the Sandwich Factory. Idlewild's infamous green benches had already found their place skirting the park's midways by the time this undated photograph was taken.

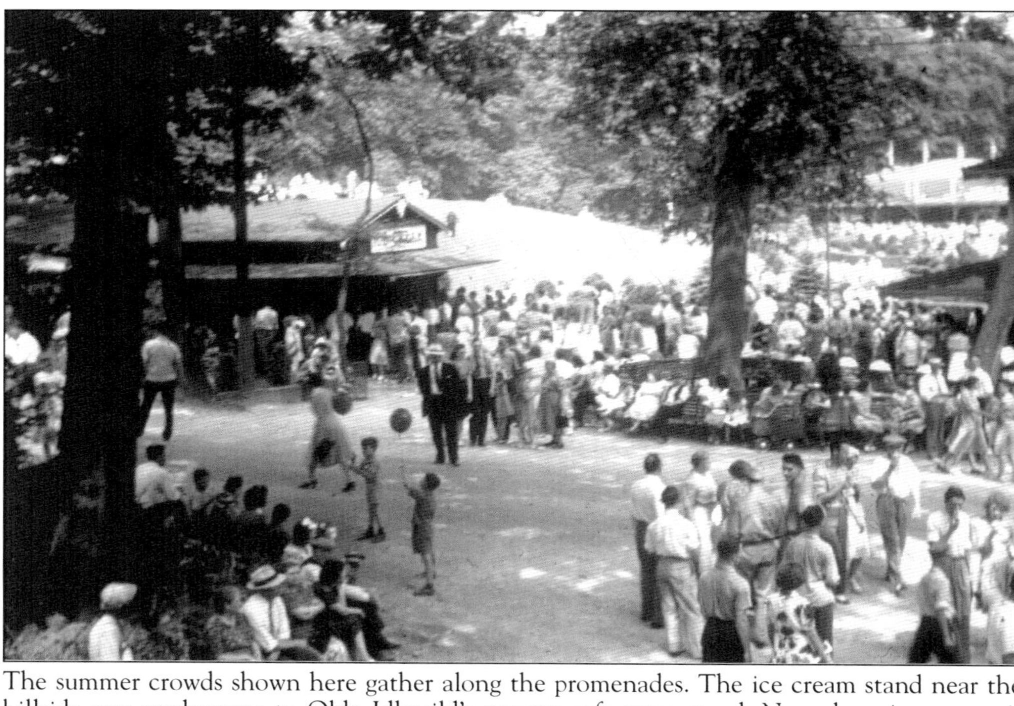

The summer crowds shown here gather along the promenades. The ice cream stand near the hillside was predecessor to Olde Idlewild's current soft serve stand. Nowadays, ice cream is offered in multiple locations to alleviate some of the long lines on hot summer days.

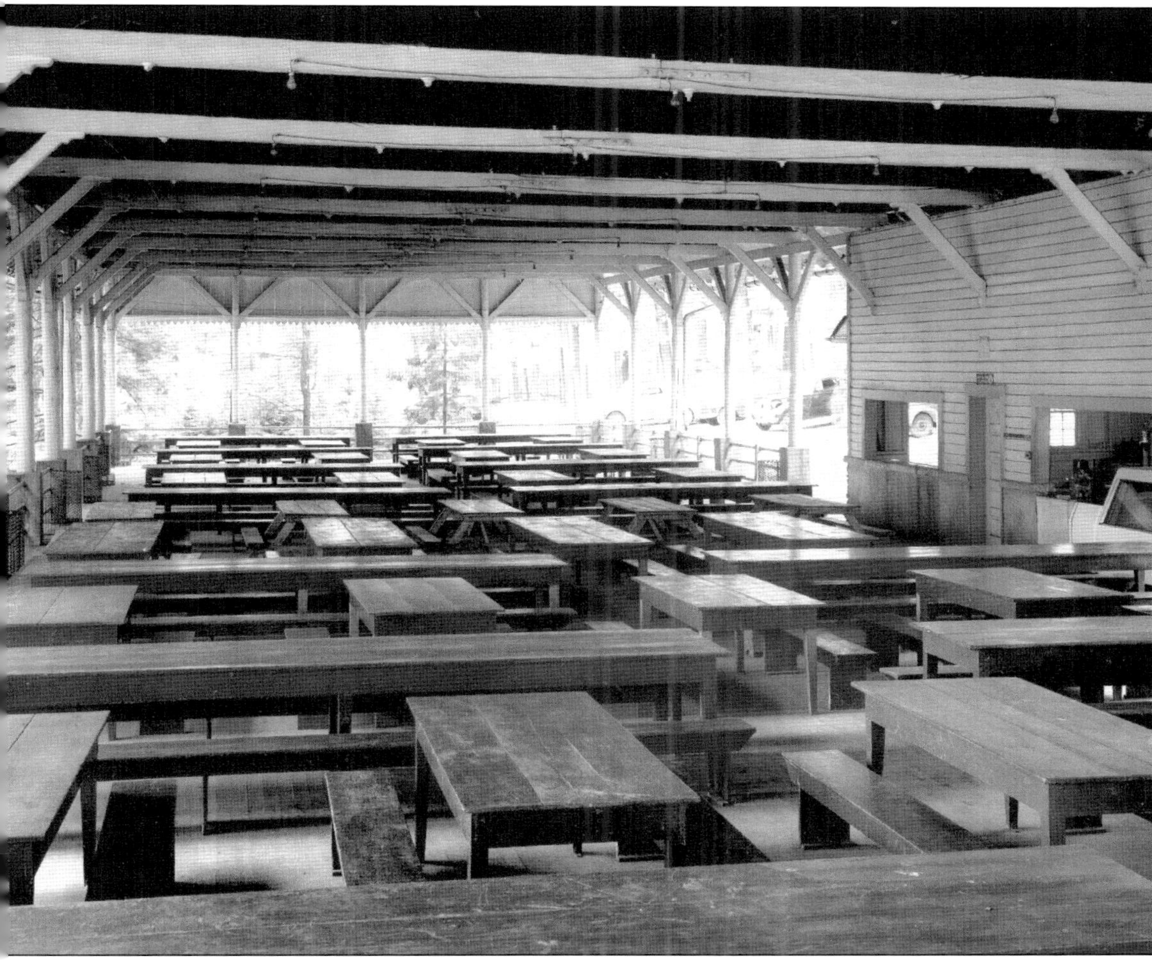

The interior of the dining hall could be set up to accommodate 1,000 people. It may have been tricky walking through the building, but there was a seat for everyone. The kitchen on the right featured the most modern equipment of the day. Note the abundance of wire baskets along the perimeter of the dining floor. Their presence throughout the entire park was a constant reminder to put litter in its place.

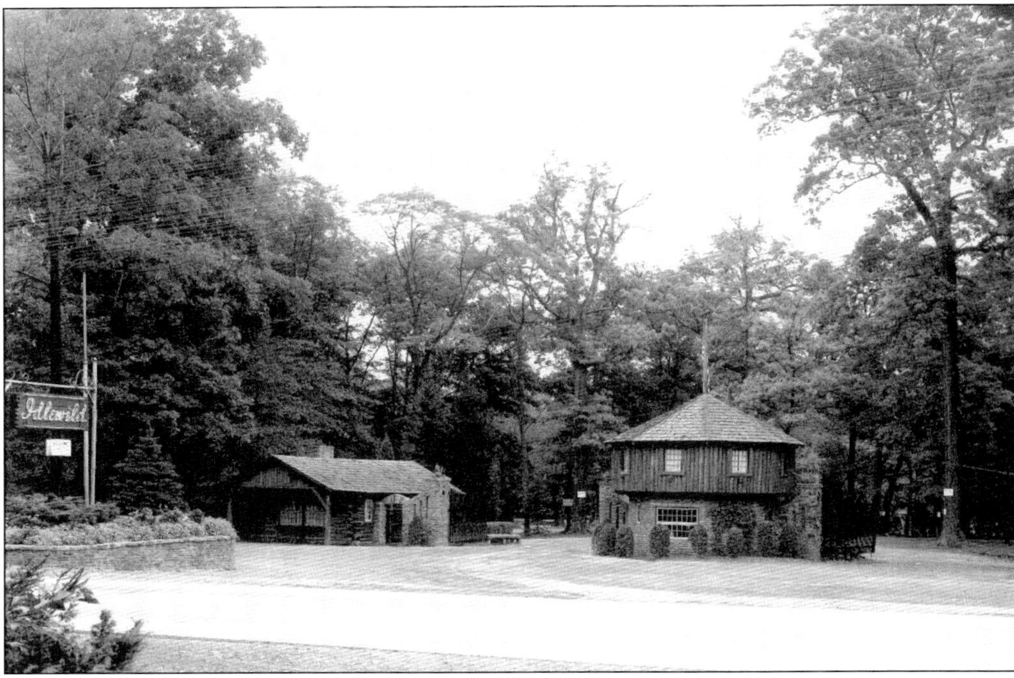

Modified from the earlier log entrance, the auto gate from the early 1950s no longer featured the Gulf Oil station or produce market. As seen from across the Lincoln Highway, this entrance featured a neon sign bearing the name of the park.

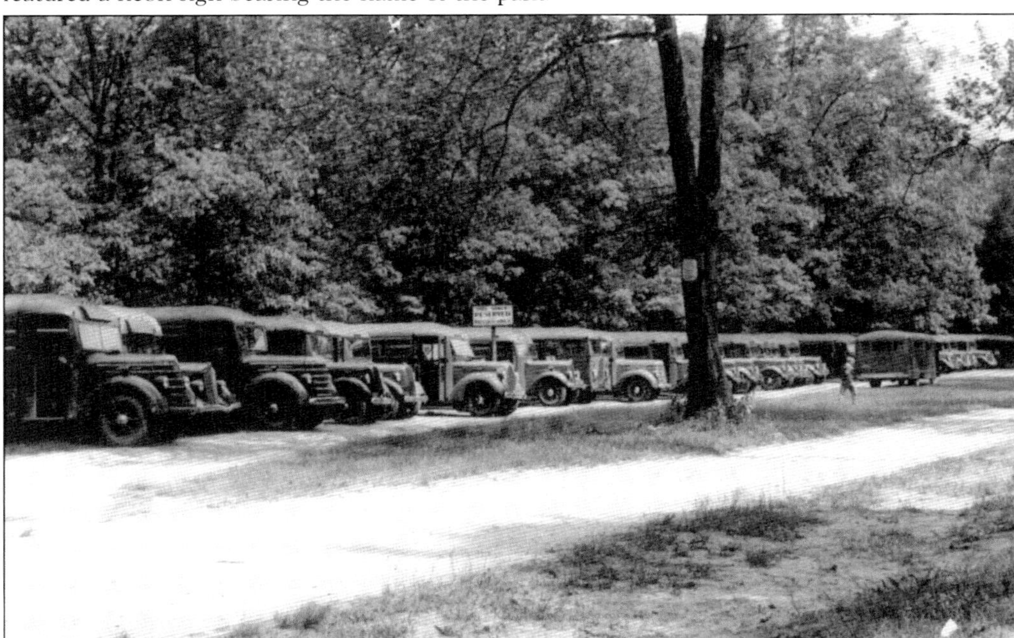

This 1940 photograph shows that many lots had been cleared to accommodate the increase in automobile traffic. On this day, the parking lot was reserved for buses, a popular mode of transportation for many school and community groups.

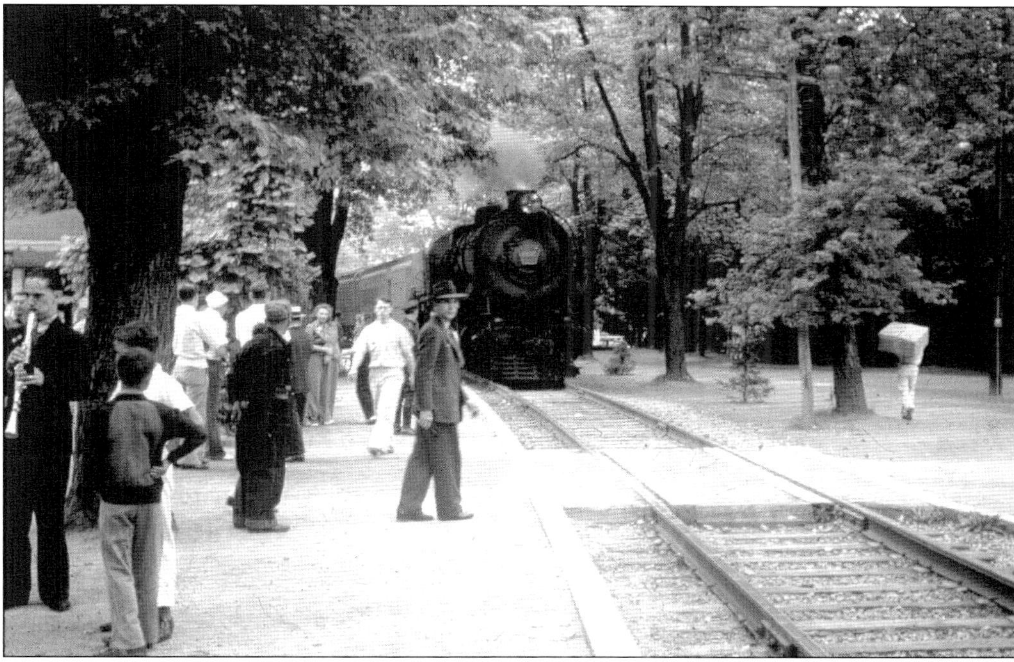

For almost three-quarters of a century, the trains of the Ligonier Valley Rail Road ran directly through the center of the park. In 1952, the year it ceased operations, the railroad listed its equipment as three locomotives, two gasoline cars, two gas electric cars (used for both passenger and freight), one coach car, and a caboose.

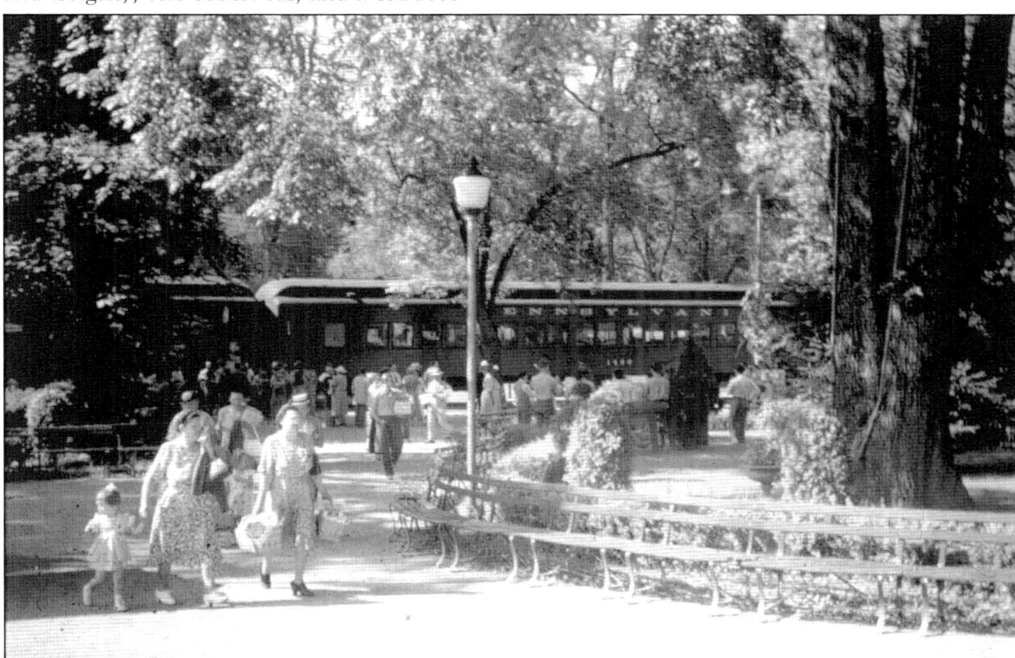

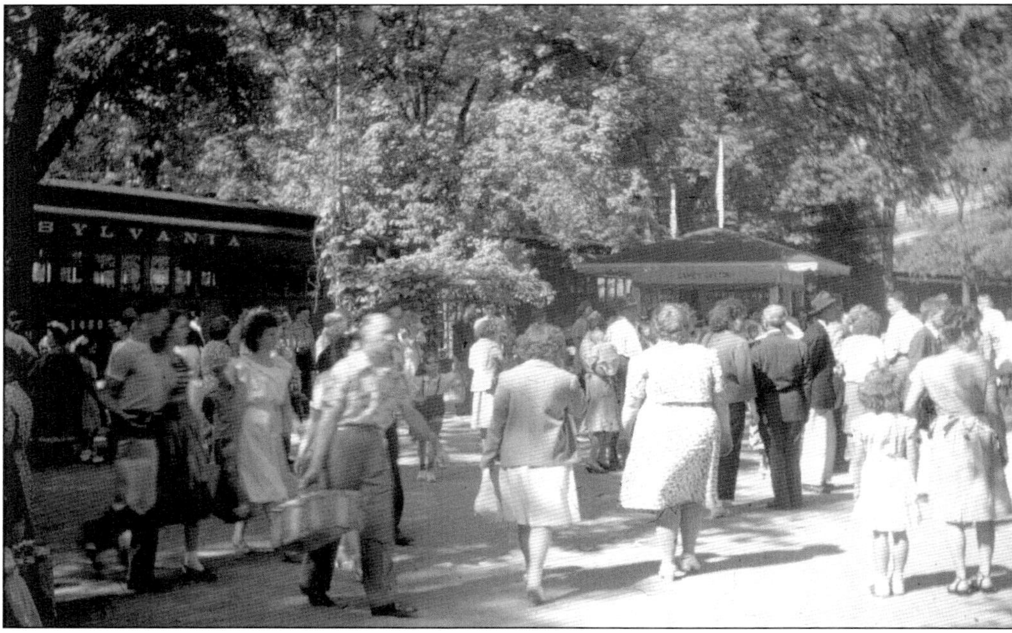

Although most picnickers were arriving by automobiles in the 1940s, there were still some picnics that drew large passenger service for the railroad. It was, however, not enough to justify the continued operation of the line. The final company picnics using the railroad included Koppers Incorporated with 3,000 passengers, Equitable Gas with 24 coach cars attached to two trains, and Duquesne Light with several thousand passengers.

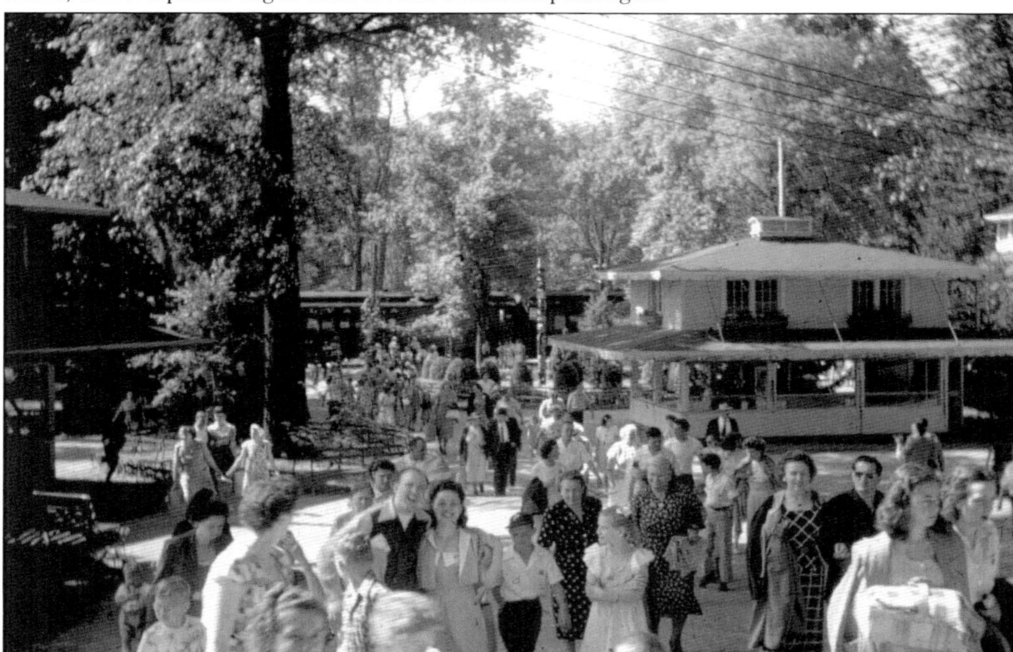

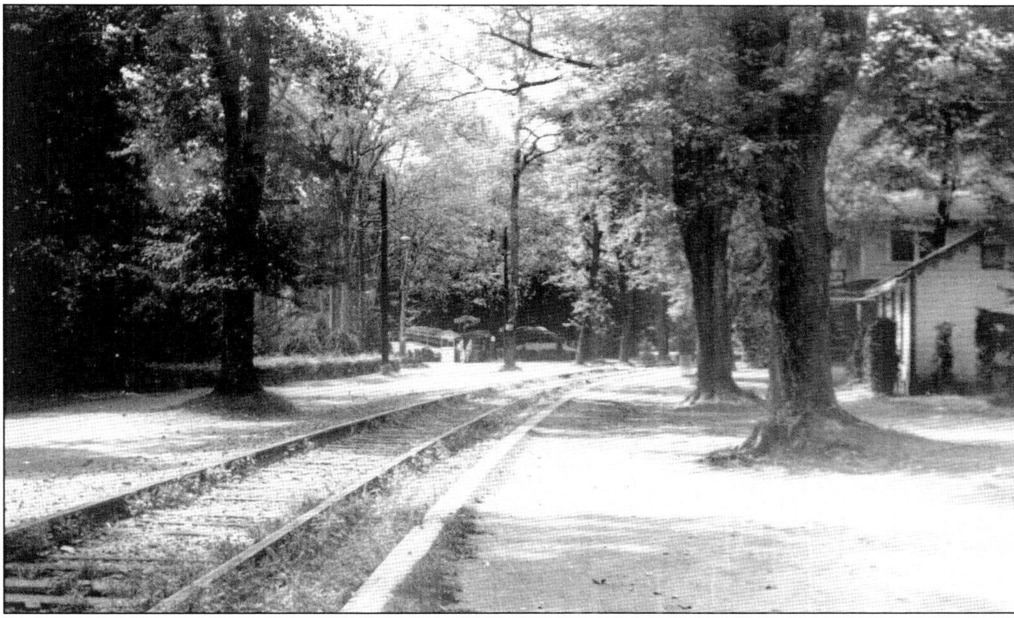

The Ligonier Valley Rail Road is shown here before the tracks have been lifted. The original depot building can be seen on the right with the two-story station located behind it. The Caterpillar is visible in the center of the photograph beyond the railroad tracks.

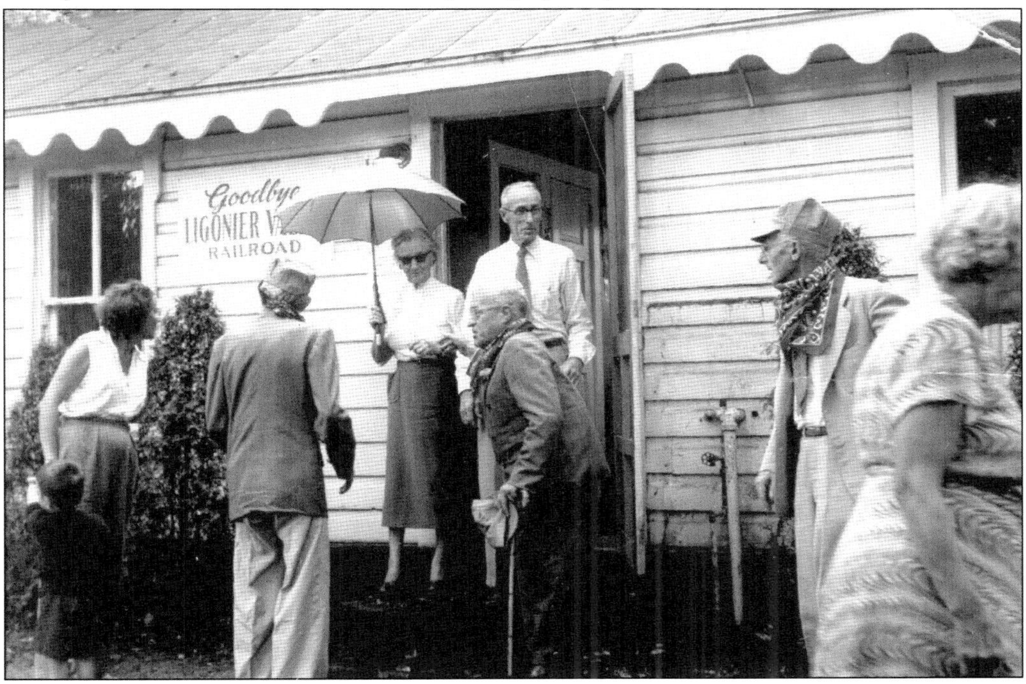

The last run of the Ligonier Valley Rail Road took place on August 31, 1952. Celebrations were held at the stations along the route. Here, Grace and C. C. Macdonald exit the original Idlewild depot to bid farewell to locomotive No. 807, which was adorned with 70 yards of black crepe to mark the abandonment.

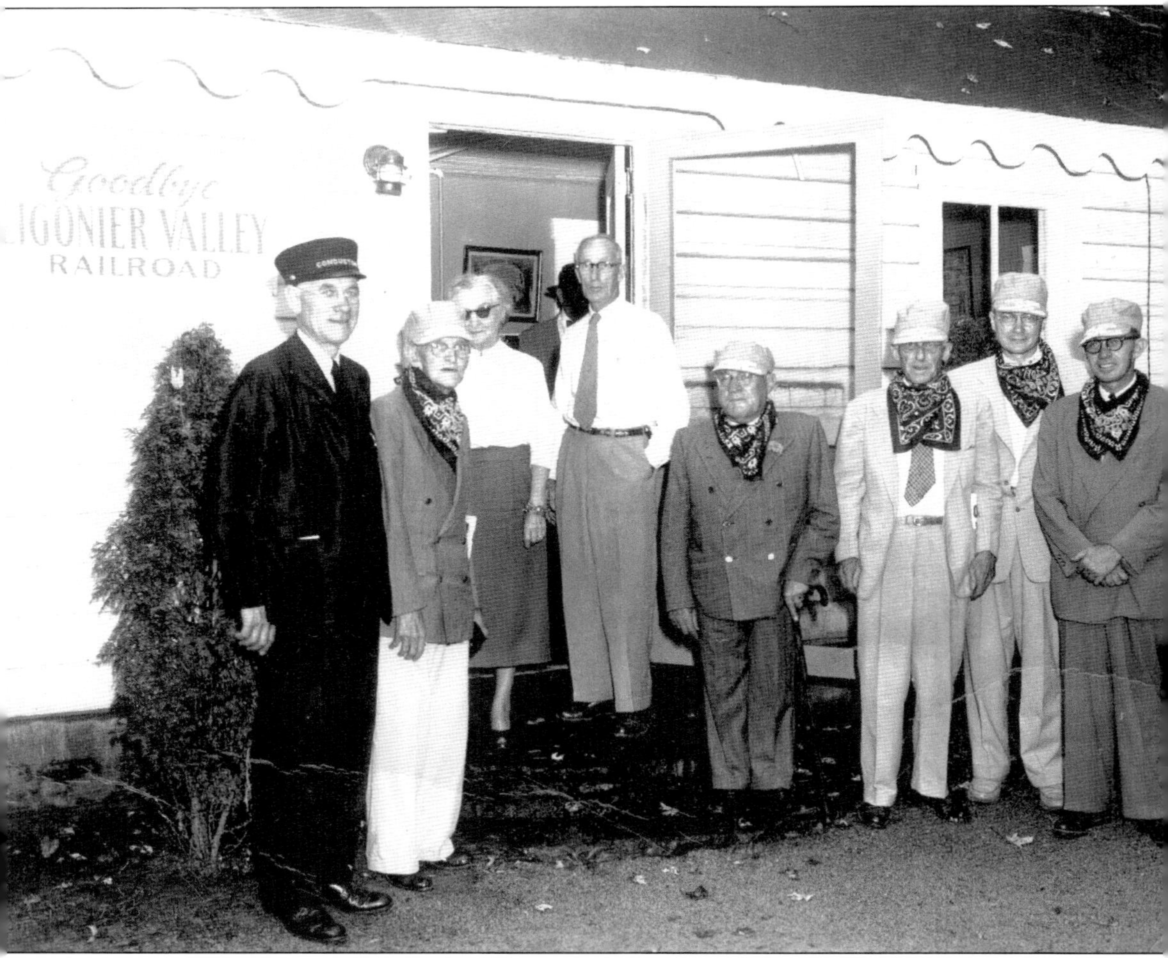

Saying goodbye to the railroad are, from left to right, as follows: conductor Denny Piper, unidentified, Grace Macdonald, C. C. Macdonald, Harry Whiteman from the Latrobe Bulletin newspaper, unidentified, chief burgess Vic Stader, and unidentified. (Courtesy R. Z. Macdonald.)

Three

YOU CAN'T BEAT FUN 1953–1982

Its days as a railroad park officially over, Idlewild in the mid-1950s began to distinguish itself as a premier location for family entertainment. The end of World War II had given rise to the baby boom, and the Macdonald family developed ways to appeal to the ever-increasing number of children who visited the park. C. C. Macdonald, who had managed the nation's first Kiddieland in San Antonio, Texas, decided to bring the concept to Idlewild. Situated between the former Ligonier Valley rail line and the Loyalhanna Creek, Kiddieland offered the finest in miniature amusement rides.

In 1956, Arthur Jennings, a performance clown at Idlewild, approached C. C. Macdonald with a proposal. The two gentlemen formed a partnership and began an expansion project on 17 acres of land adjoining the eastern edge of the park. For years, Jennings had dreamed of creating a theme park based on emotion rather than motion. With Macdonald's backing, he created a land of fairy tales known as Story Book Forest, featuring characters from children's stories and nursery rhymes. Jennings did much of the work himself—land survey, design, layout, and construction—with the aid of only a few local laborers. Appealing to children of all ages, Story Book Forest was an immediate success when it opened in June. Though they would operate as separate attractions, the two Macdonald-owned parks were marketed jointly, increasing attendance for both.

Also in 1956, the Lincoln Highway was expanded to a four-lane divided highway. The right-of-way for the new road passed through the northern edge of Idlewild's property, necessitating the removal of many trees and the old log automobile entrance. New attractive entrances were constructed for both Idlewild and Story Book Forest. The following year, the Macdonalds expanded across the new highway, adding the Timberlink Golf Course to further broaden the appeal of their parks to families.

Sadly, C. C. Macdonald passed away in 1957 leaving his sons, C. K. (Jack) and R. Z. (Dick), to take control of the family's interests. In 1959, they brought the Ligonier Highland Games to Idlewild. The Scottish event became a successful Idlewild tradition and attracted people from all over the country. During that same year, the brothers assumed complete control of Story Book Forest from Arthur Jennings. The Macdonalds continued improvements in the 1960s and 1970s with the addition of Frontier Safariland and the Historic Village, as well as many amusement rides.

Following the 1982 season, the Macdonald family decided to put the park up for sale. After 51 years of operating Idlewild, they can certainly be credited with much of the family atmosphere that generations of visitors have come to admire. Change, however, is inevitable, and the following year offered new owners who made Idlewild their own.

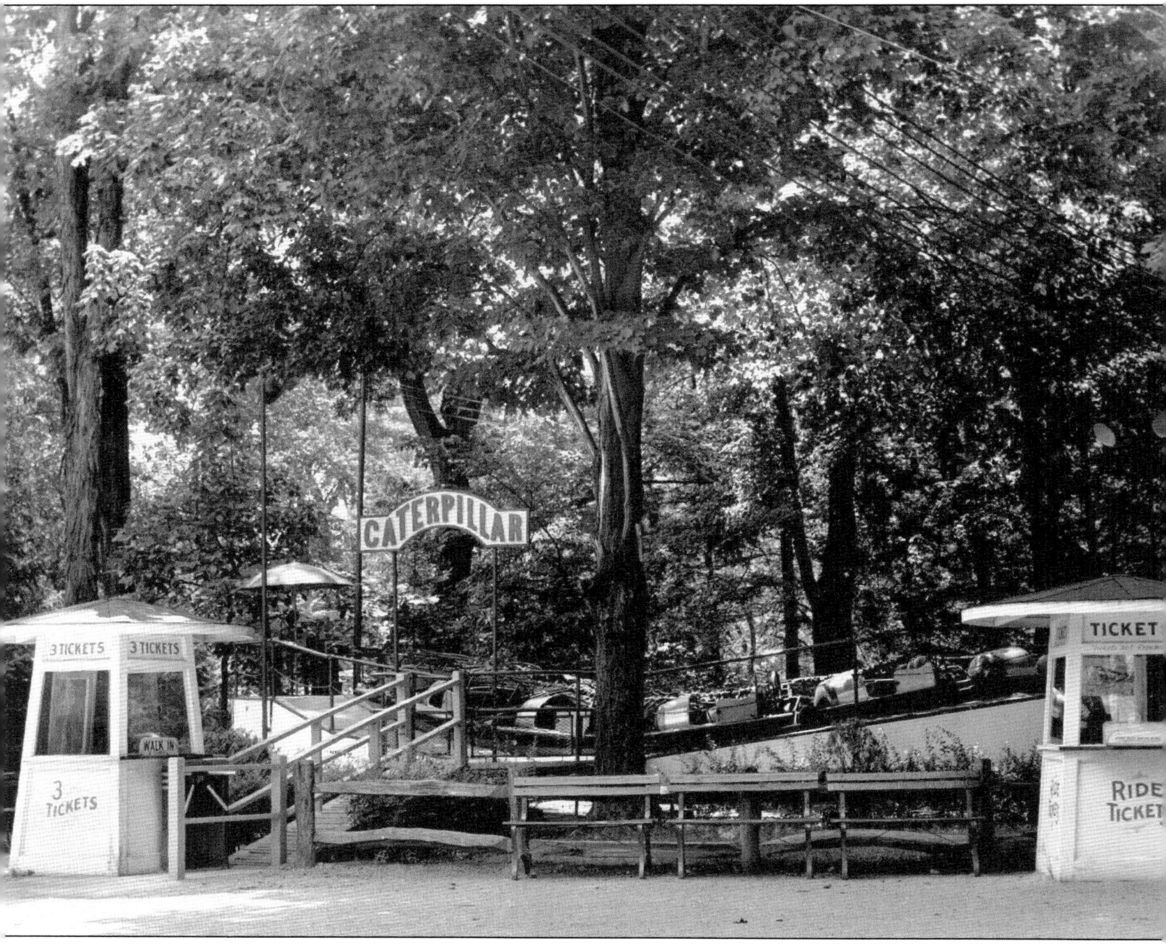

Designed by Hyla F. Maynes, the Caterpillar was once a very popular ride at many amusement parks. Sadly, the classic ride seems to be disappearing with less than 10 still in operation. Idlewild's 1947 Caterpillar, manufactured by the Allen Herschell Company, is pictured here in the 1950s. Many riders have been known to sneak a smooch with their sweetheart under the canopy top that springs up during the ride, encompasses the cars, and hides its riders.

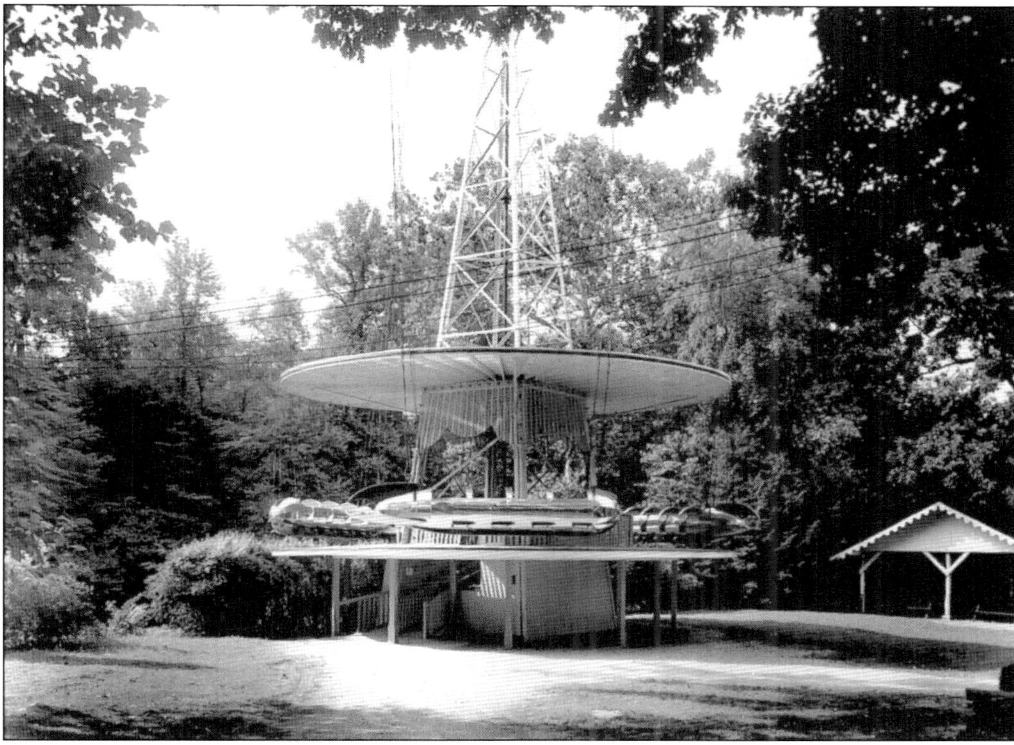

This modified circle swing first appeared at Idlewild in 1934. Originally, it swung airplanes out over the Loyalhanna Creek. These two photographs show the stainless steel rocket ships that replaced the airplanes in later years. The ride was removed in 1977.

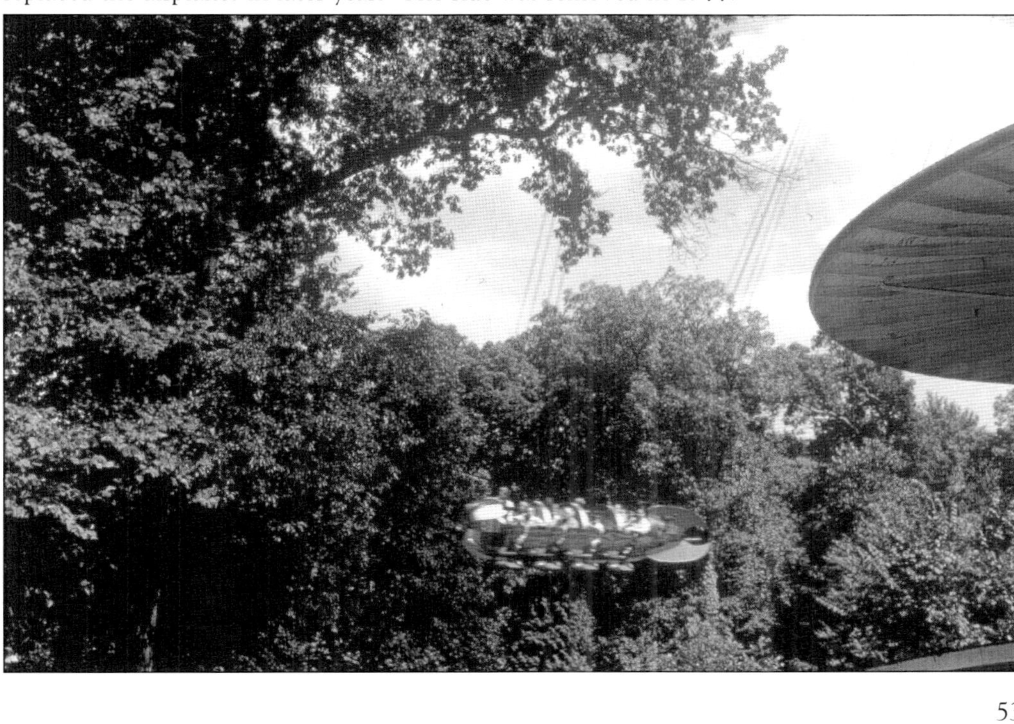

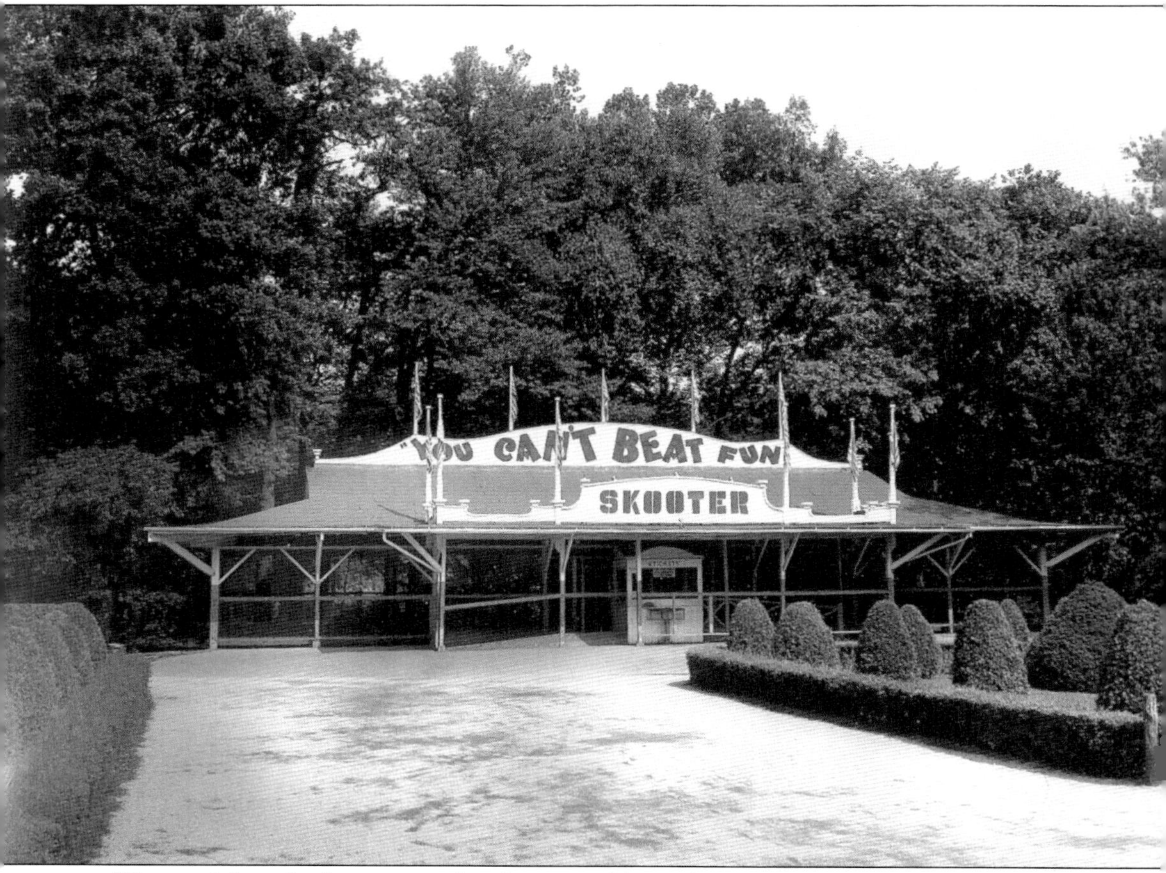

"You can't beat fun" was a popular slogan used by park management for marketing purposes in the 1950s. It was proudly displayed atop the Skooter building among the many flags. As you can also see, the Skooter admission was four tickets. Ride amusement tickets were sold in little booths throughout the park. That tradition continued until the 1980s, when a ride-all-day pass was instituted.

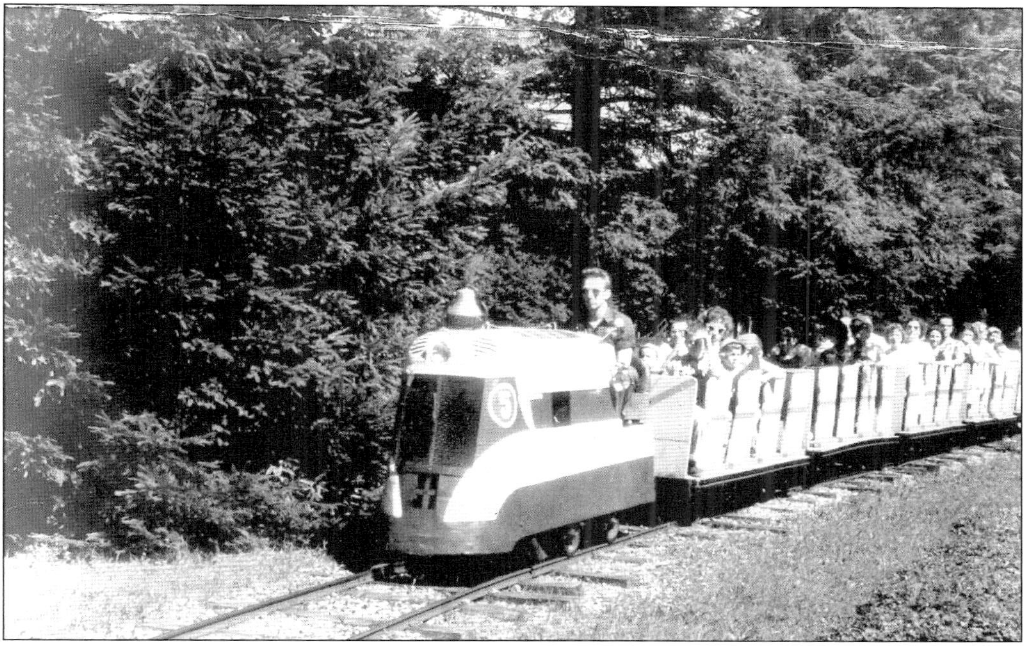

The Idlewild Express miniature railroad was built by the Dayton Fun House Corporation. The train ride passed by several thousand evergreens that were planted along the tracks, ran through a tunnel, and in later years traveled through a ghost town.

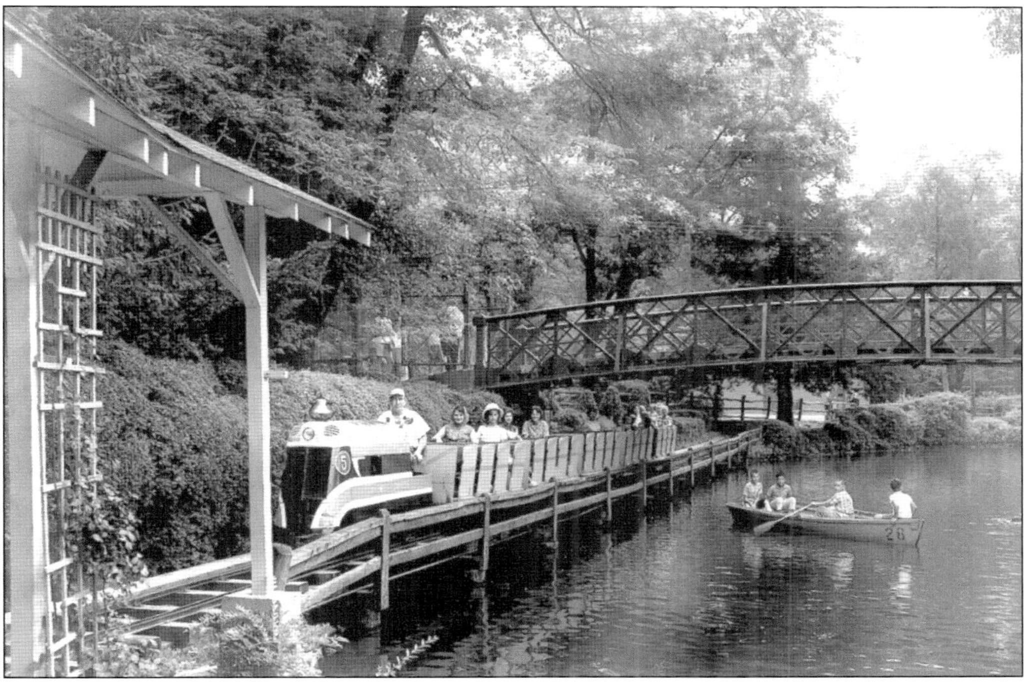

Two trains, each holding 40 passengers, ran on the Idlewild Express's tracks. In this image, one of the trains passes underneath the island bridge and pulls into the station. Years later, the name of the Idlewild Express was changed to the Lakeside Railroad.

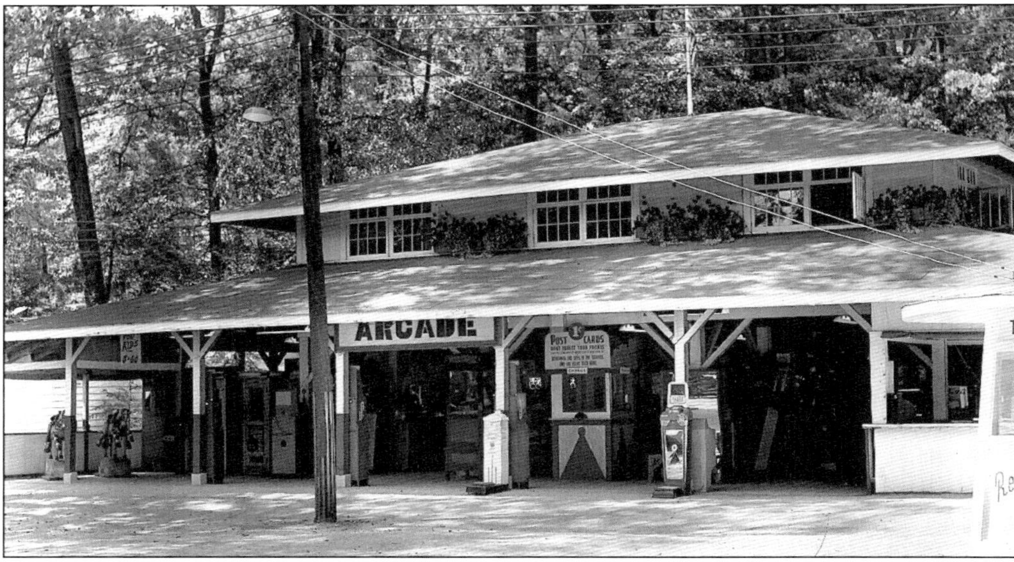

While the administration building had offices on the second floor, the ground floor was home to the arcade. It was filled with many penny games and Skee-Ball machines. Note the Grandmother's Predictions attraction located under the arcade sign. This seer offered fortunes and lucky numbers for nearly three-quarters of a century until the arcade was removed in 2002. Also, note the postcards sign reminding guests to "remember the boys in the service and the folks back home."

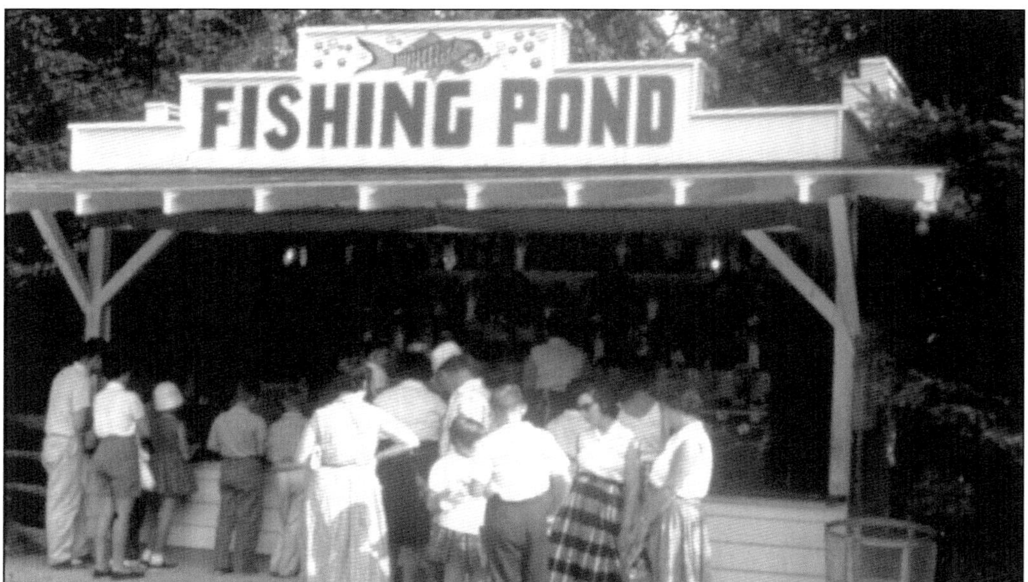

The fishing pond has delighted thousands of children since the 1940s. The popular game was actually designed and patented by C. C. Macdonald, with help from Charlie Presser, who operated nearby Oakford Park. In the beginning, the young ones caught a hand-cut plastic fish, but that was later updated to a more decorative molded model. The number etched on the belly of the fish corresponds with a certain prize that the child wins. Most fishers hope to catch fish No. 10, which offers the finest prize.

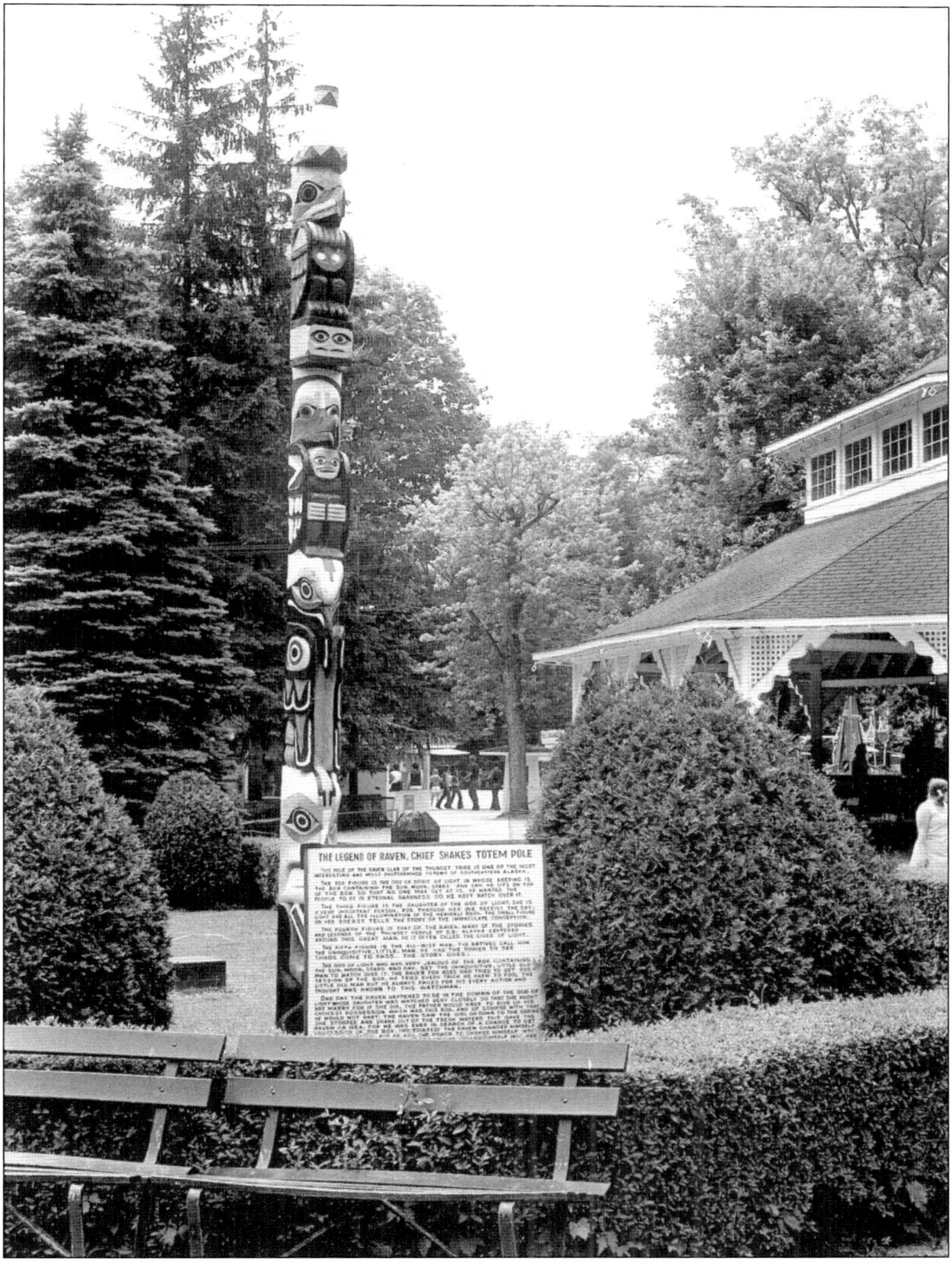

A product of the Raven Clan of the Tlinget tribe of Indians, the Chief Stakes totem pole was one of the most interesting and photographed of southeastern Alaska. Purchased and imported by the Macdonald family, the totem was placed near the carousel where it stood for more than 30 years. In 1984, it was moved to the Hootin' Holler area of the park where it remains today. The legend depicted by the figures on the pole is explained on the placard in front.

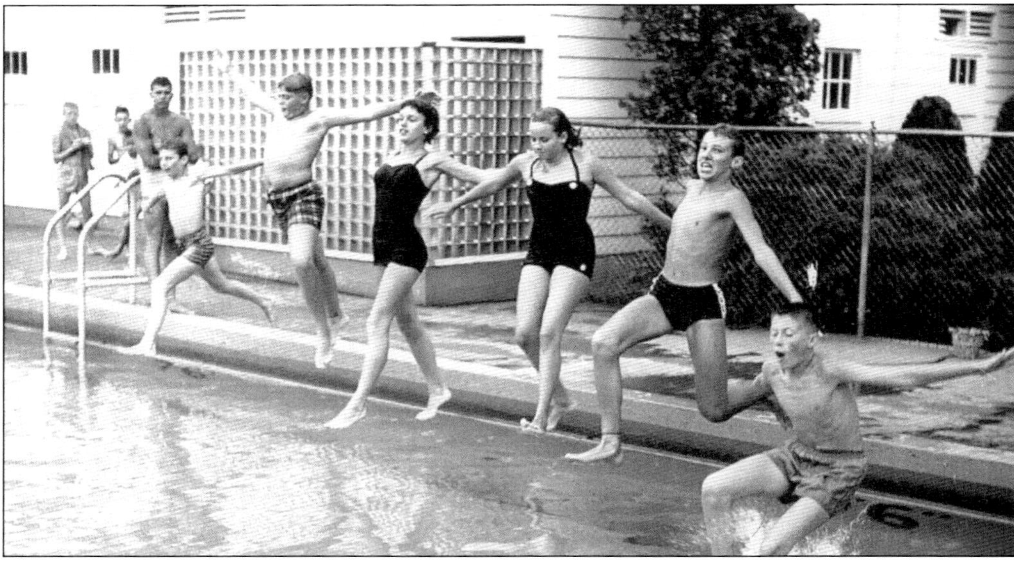

The youngsters shown here enjoy a skip into the swimming pool in this undated photograph. The pool traditionally opens with the rest of the park in May—regardless of the cooler weather—and remains in operation through Labor Day.

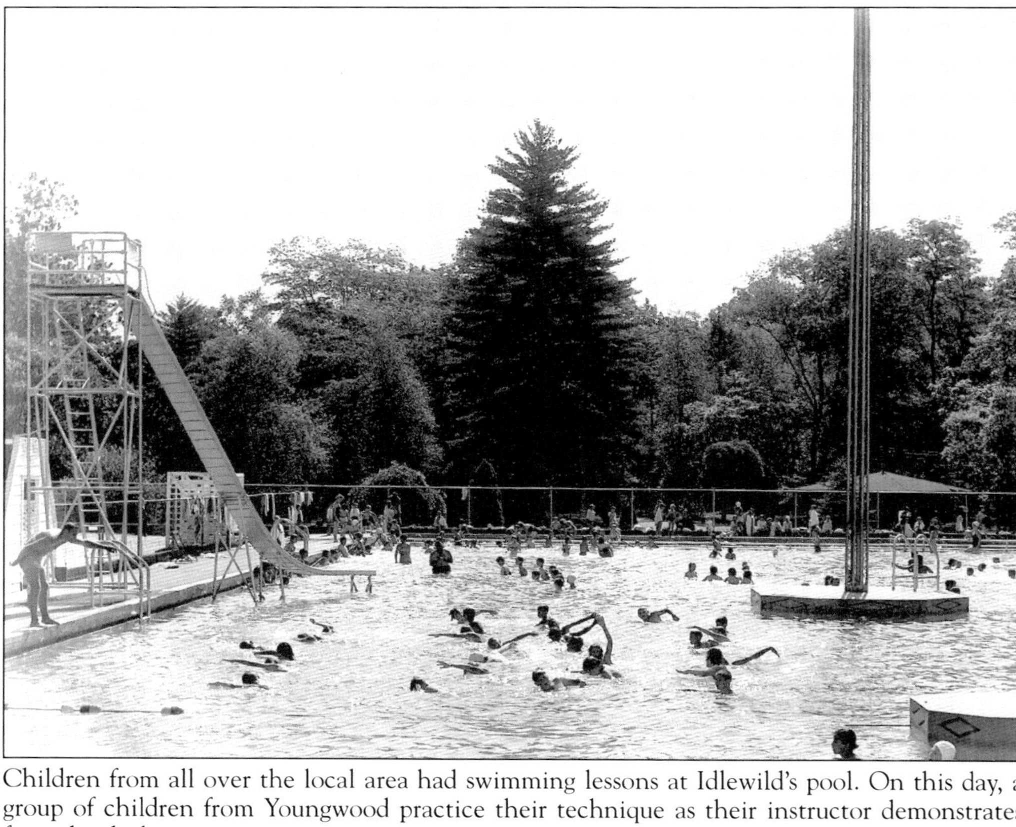

Children from all over the local area had swimming lessons at Idlewild's pool. On this day, a group of children from Youngwood practice their technique as their instructor demonstrates from the deck.

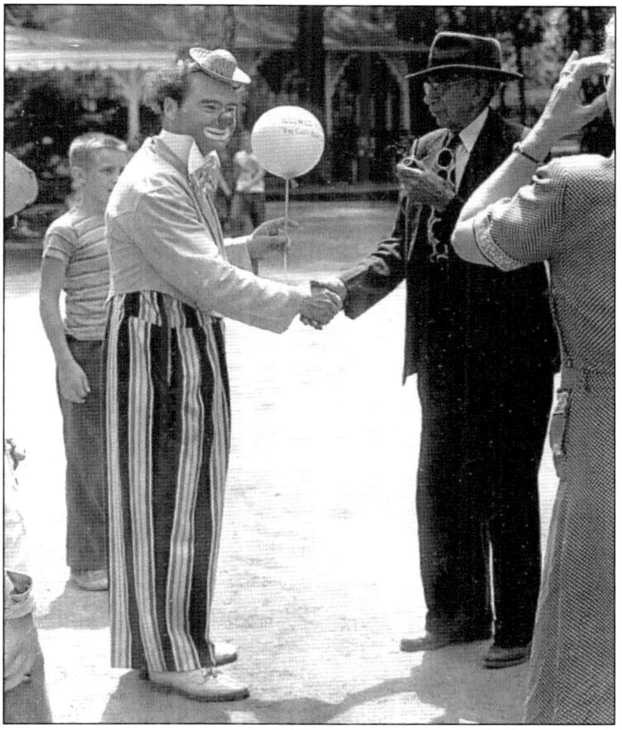

While Art Jennings's Happy Dayze clown performed throughout the park, he had special fondness for Kiddieland. Located on the north bank of the Loyalhanna where the Rumpus once stood, Kiddieland was built between 1954 and 1956. Welcoming the children to their specially designed area was another clown, pictured below, who stood for more than 35 years.

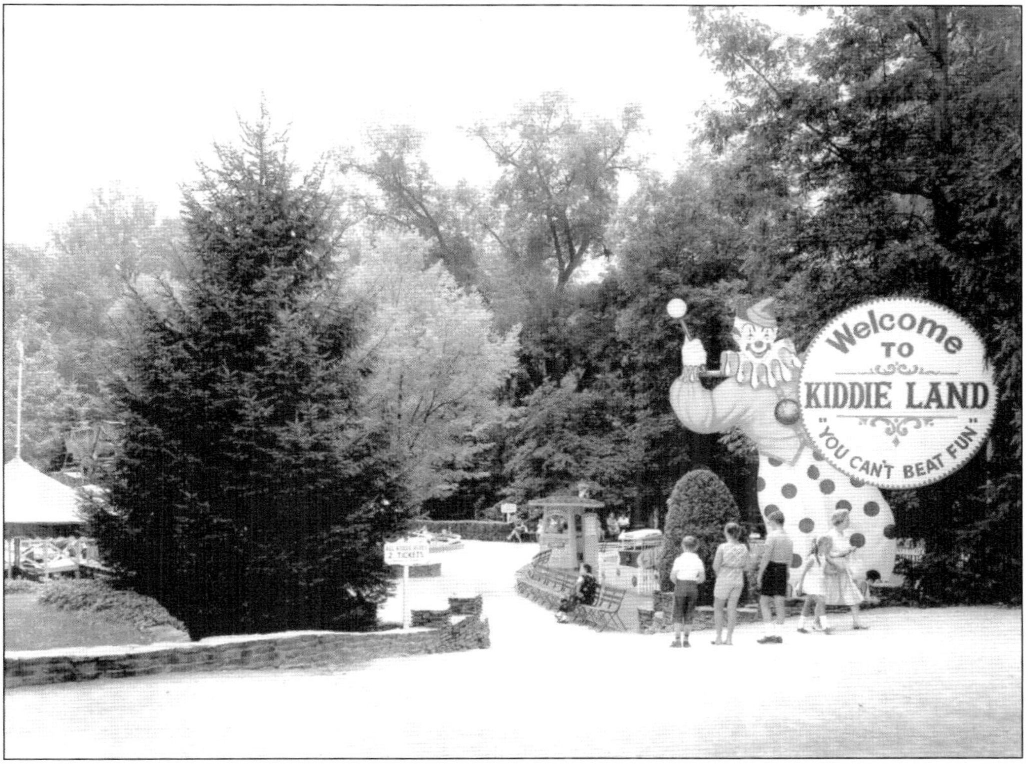

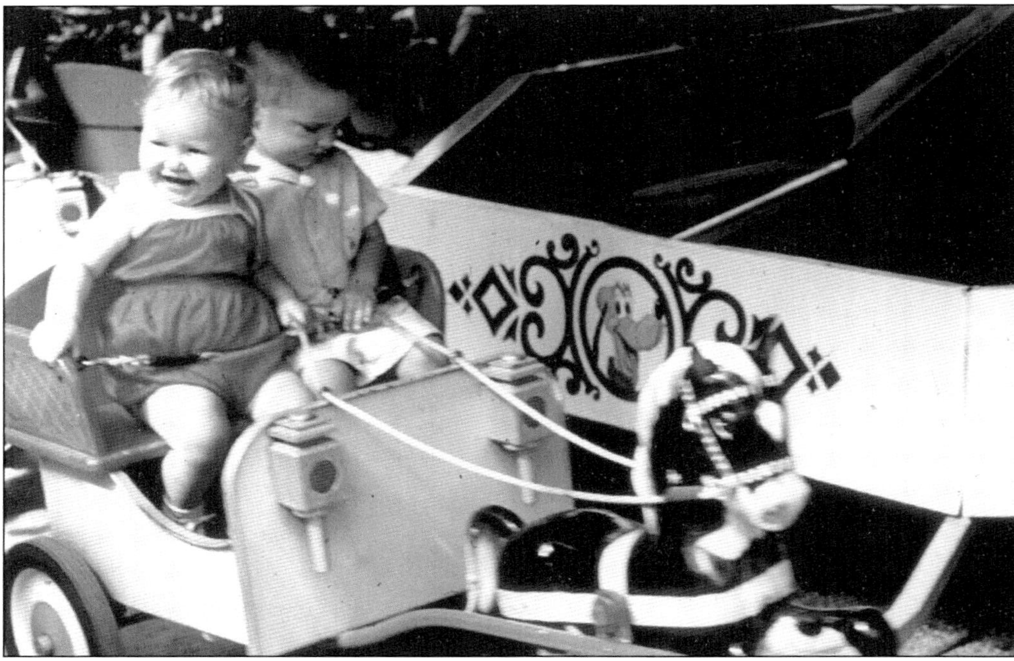

Every child loved to grab the reins of a horse and go for a ride. The pony carts were a fixture of Kiddieland from the 1950s until the early 1980s.

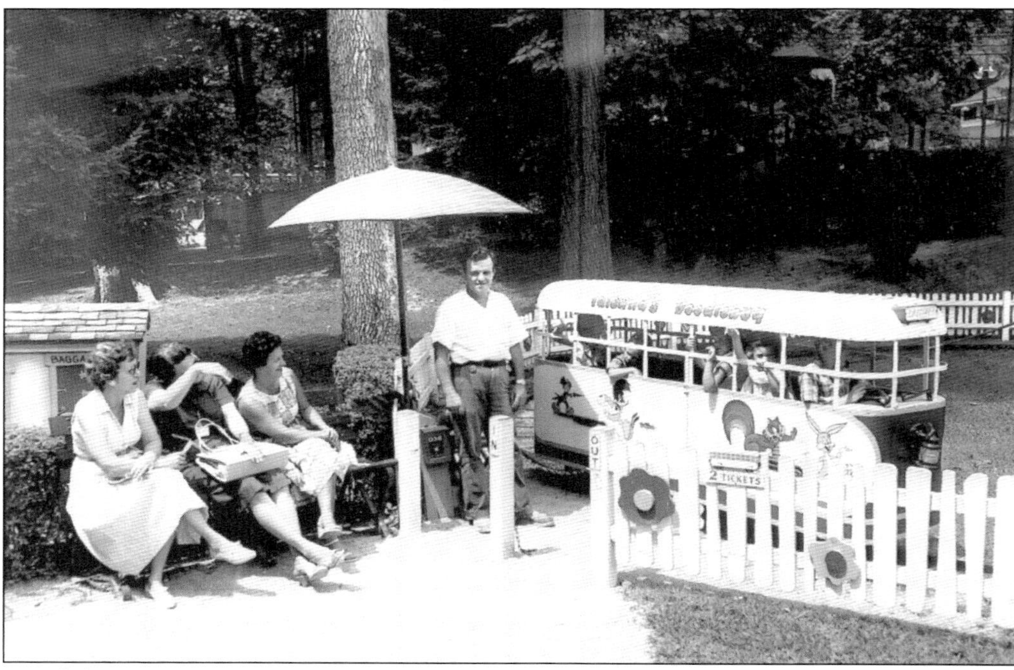

Doodlebugs were gas-electric train cars commonly used on railroads in the early- to mid-1900s when traffic was not heavy enough for the use of locomotively hauled trains. While Idlewild's doodlebug runs along a simple circular track, it still provides plenty of excitement to its half-pint riders.

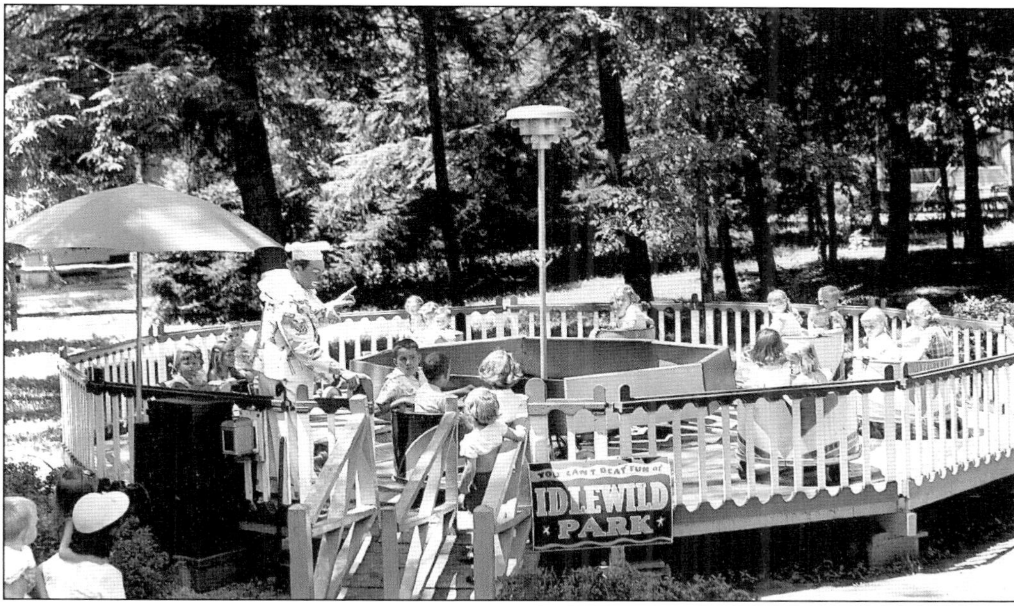

The miniature Whip was an added attraction for the 1941 season. Pictured here at its Kiddieland location in the 1950s, the ride was operated by Happy Dayze.

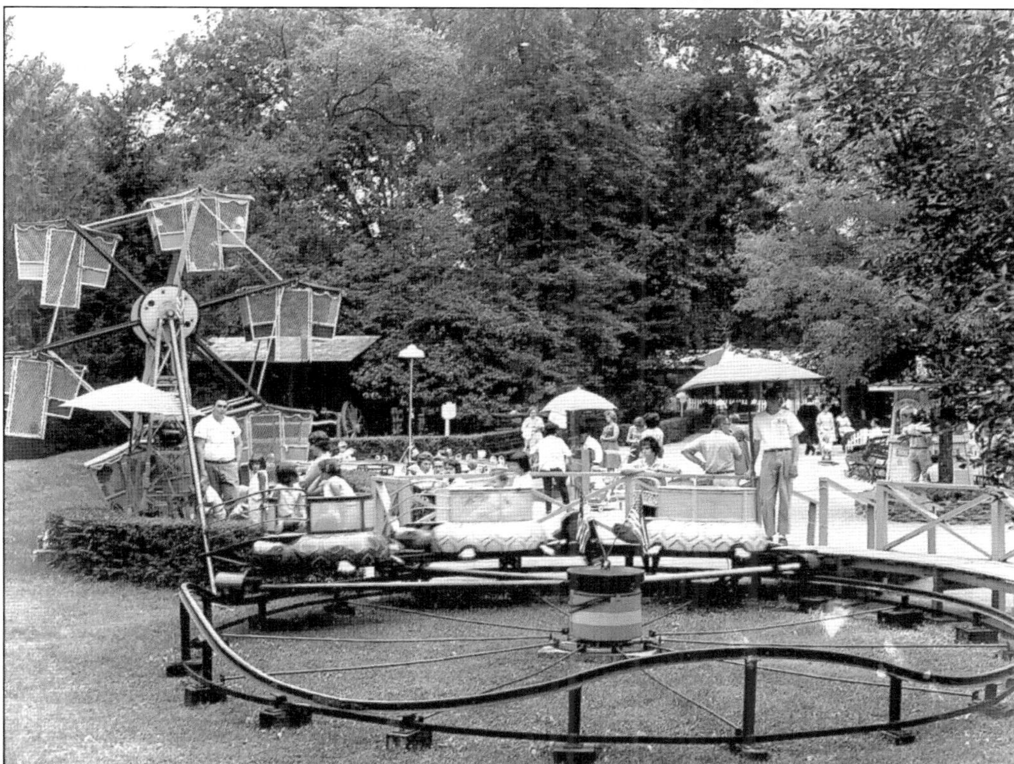

The miniature Ferris wheel and the Turtle were added to the park's lineup in 1955 and 1956 respectively. Both rides still operate at Idlewild.

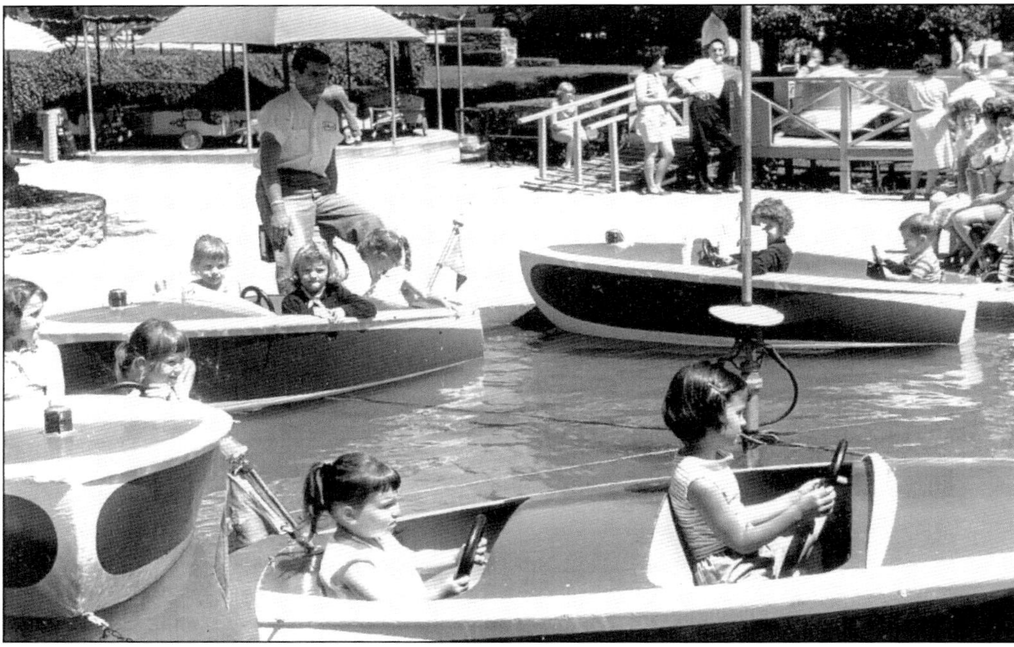

The miniature boat ride was popular with the children who visited Kiddieland from the 1950s to the 1980s. When Raccoon Lagoon opened in 1990, the boats sailed out of their small, concrete pond and into the new themed area.

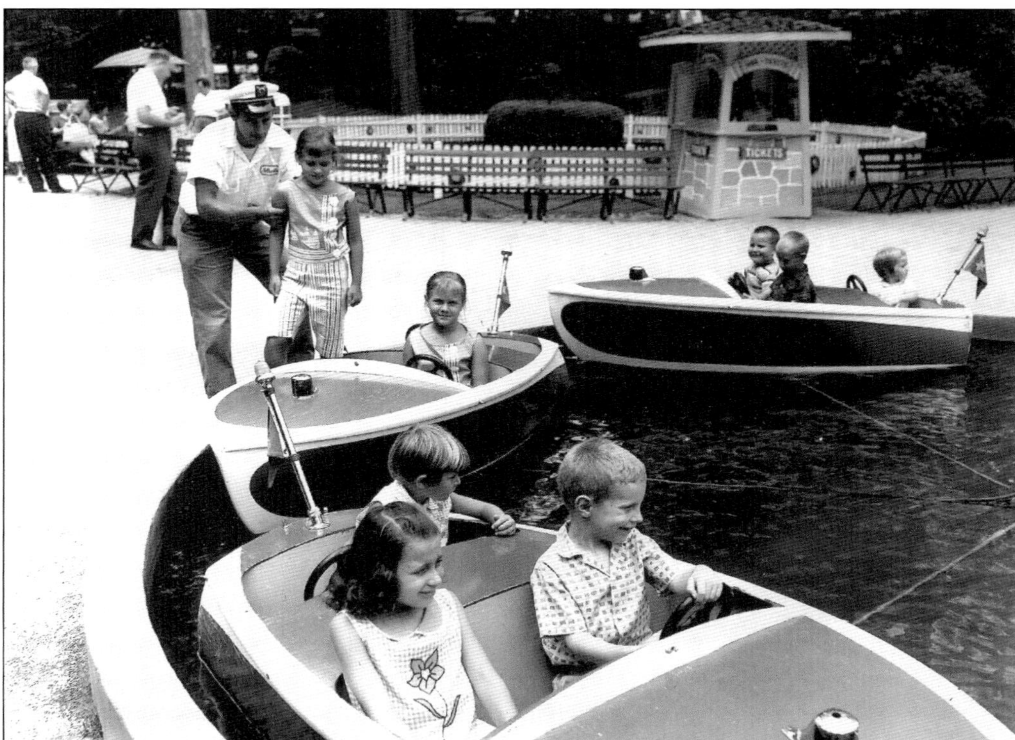

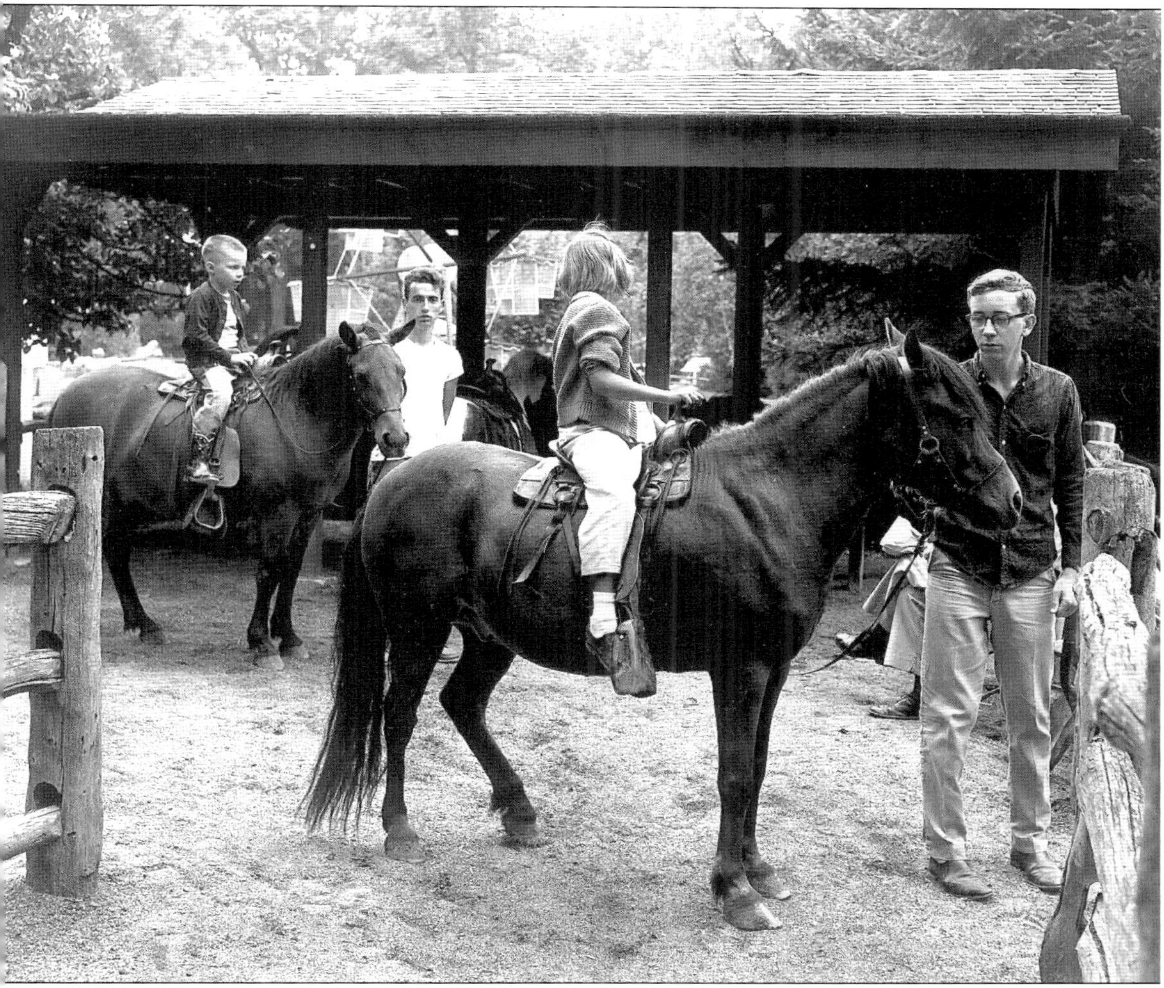

After riding the carousel and the pony carts, children had the chance to ride a real "horsey" at the pony rides near Kiddieland. These two little ones saddled up for their trot around the track in the late 1950s. In 2000, pony rides returned in a new location on the opposite side of the Loyalhanna.

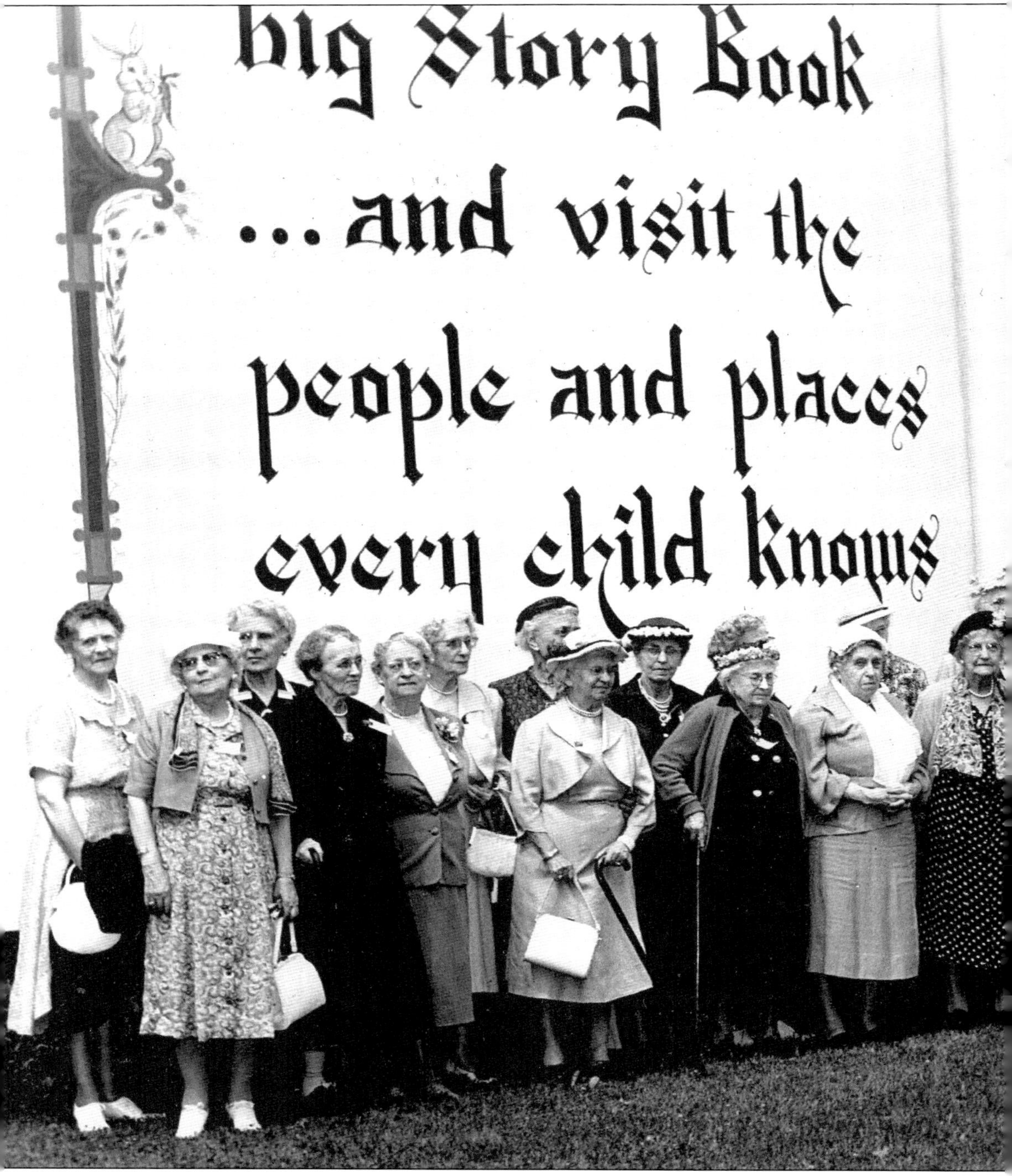

Arthur Jennings's dream of building a park based on fantasy and emotion was realized when Story Book Forest opened in June 1956. After appearing in a full-color feature in the *Pittsburgh Press* during August of that year, its popularity really took off. Visitors to the forest were not just children, as is evident in this photograph. On June 19, 1958, ladies from the Presbyterian Home in Oakmont were transported to Idlewild for an all-day outing. Following a scrumptious

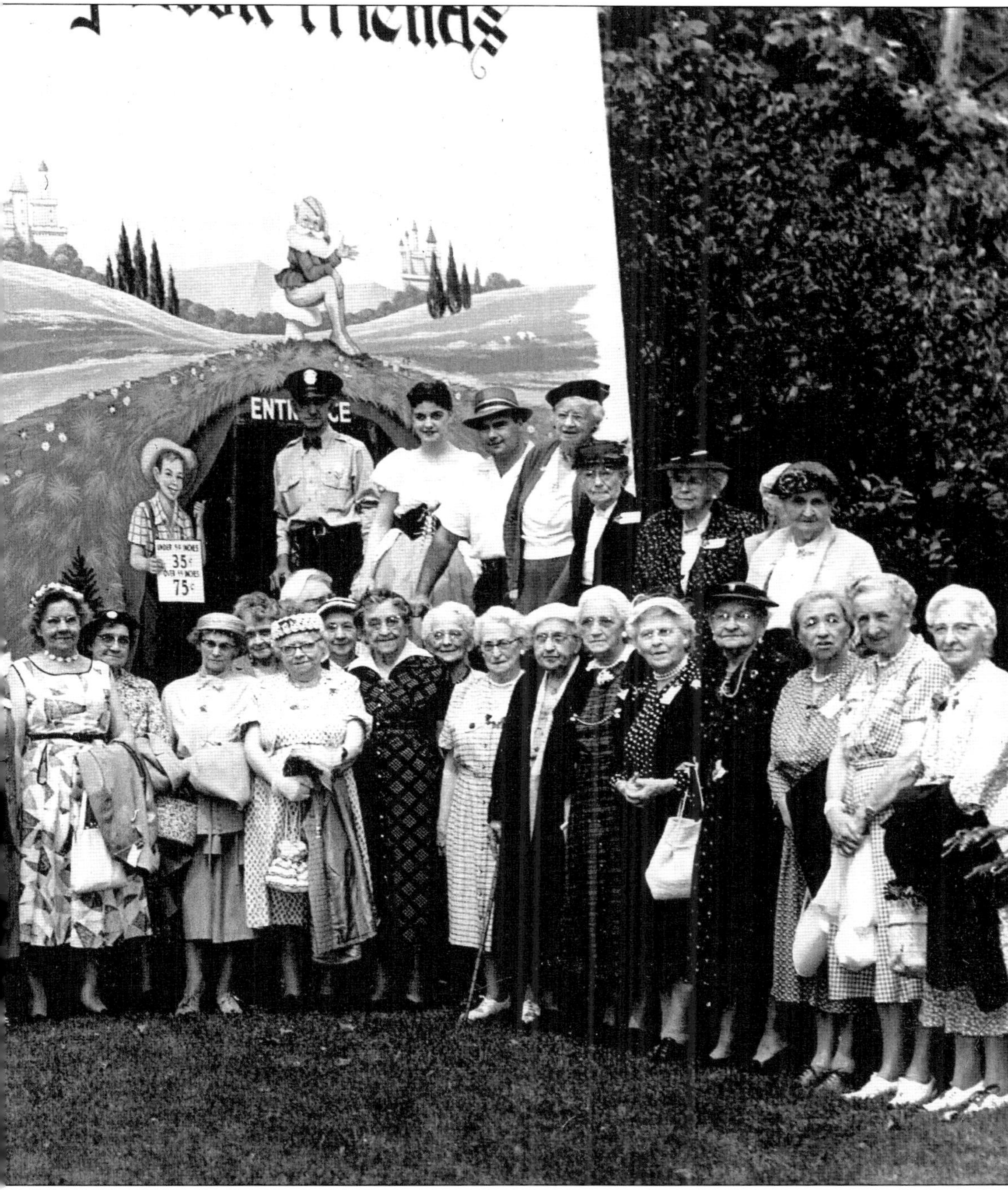

chicken dinner, the group toured Story Book Forest, where everyone enjoyed their journey back to childhood fantasy. The entrance to the fairy tale land is through the pages of a giant story book. The words on its pages read, "Here is the Land of Once upon a Time . . . Step through the pages of this big Story Book . . . and visit the people and places every child knows . . . and Loves. Here dreams are real . . . and so are your Story Book friends."

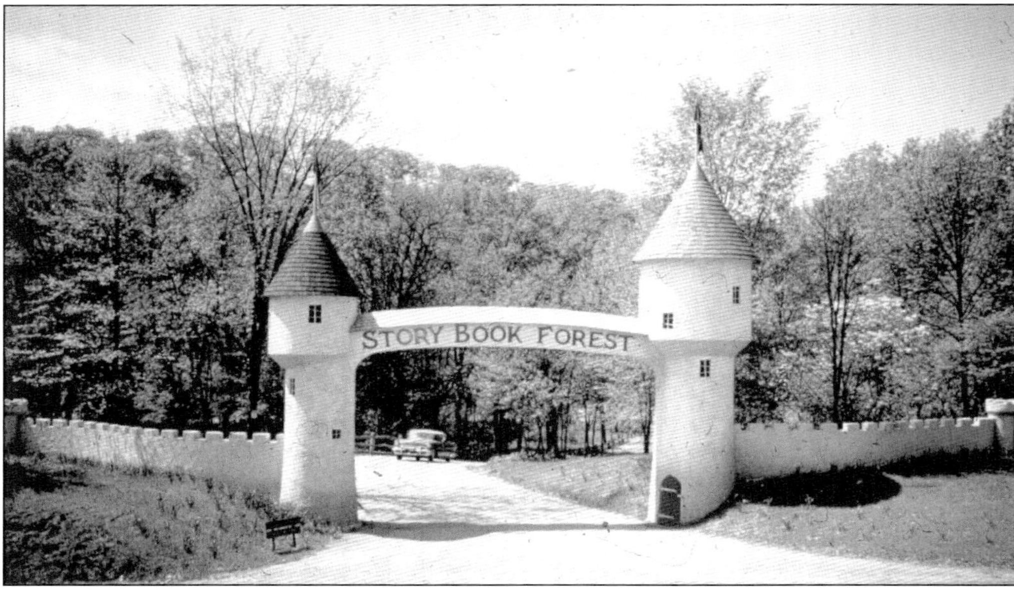

The automobile entrance to Story Book Forest was modeled after a castle's tower. Quite visible from the Lincoln Highway, Story Book Forest remains one of its most popular roadside attractions.

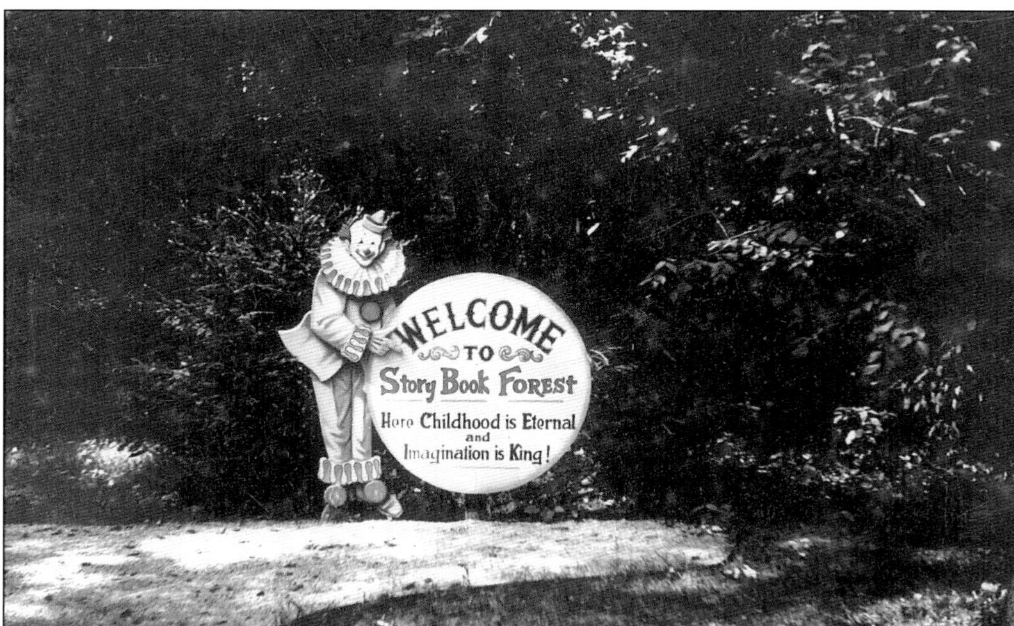

Greeting guests to the park was this wooden model of Arthur Jennings's alter ego. Happy Dayze proudly displayed the motto of Story Book Forest: "Here Childhood is Eternal and Imagination is King!"

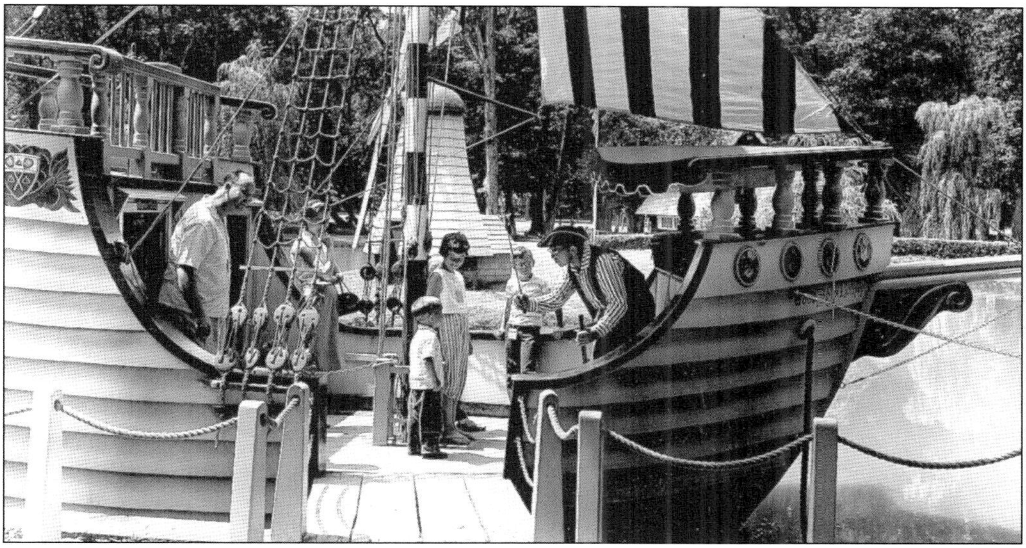

Children usually love their visit to the Good Ship Lollipop because Captain Candy is a very friendly pirate. He even shares a piece of his treasure with the guests that come aboard. The vessel was originally intended to float around the pond in Story Book Forest. However, too much governmental red tape forced Arthur Jennings to permanently dock the ship on concrete pillars below the water's surface.

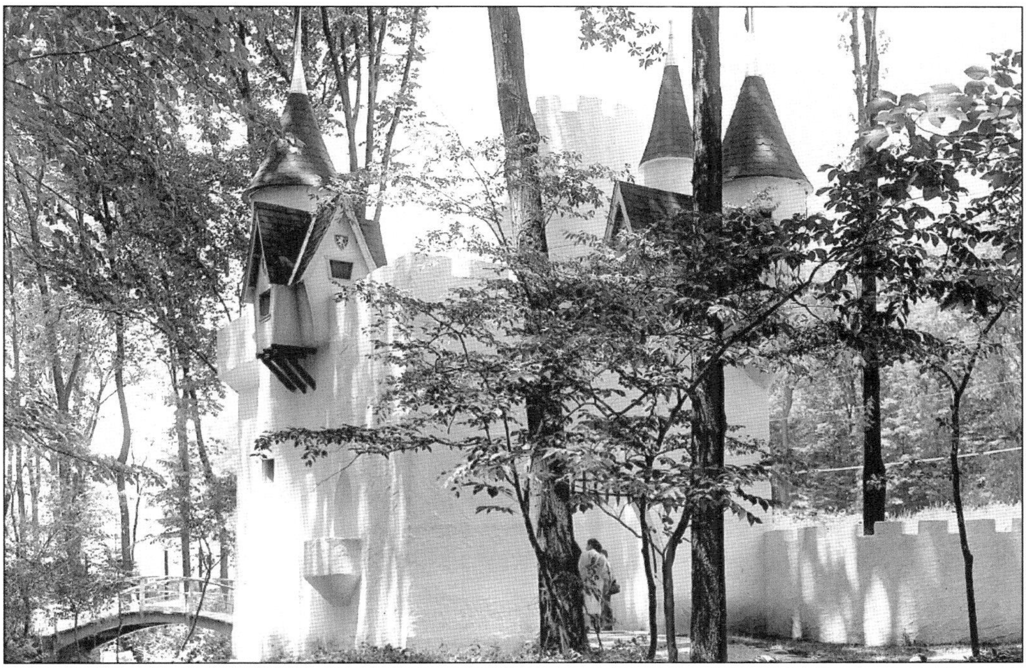

King Arthur's castle, built in 1956, stood for more than 40 years. Initially a walk-through attraction, the castle was converted to a tunnel in 1986, when a new auto entrance was constructed at the east end of Story Book Forest. In 1997, park management made the difficult and controversial decision to remove the aging castle for the expansion of the entrance road, increasing its capability to two-lane traffic.

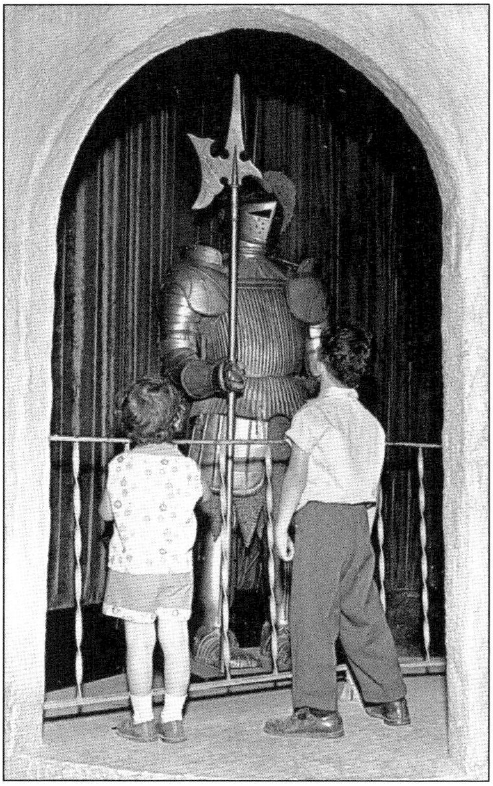

The Golden Knight stood proud and tall within the castle walls. He spoke to the visitors from his tower alcove. The talking statue once stood in a famous Chicago restaurant. However, when the restaurant closed, the statue was moved to Story Book Forest. Once they exited the castle, children could try and pull out King's Arthur's sword from the stone.

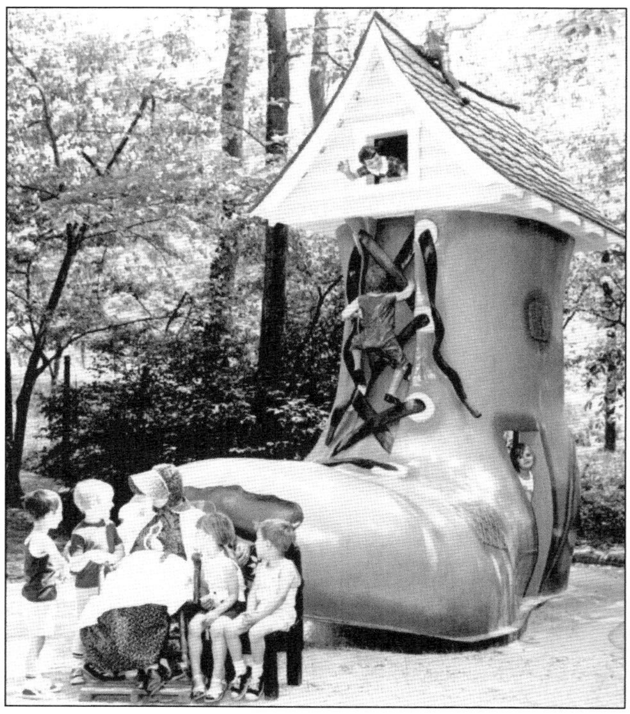

Live character actors were used to enhance the charm of Story Book Forest. Generations of children have visited the Old Woman Who Lived in a Shoe. Some of her many children can be seen climbing all over their abode. The children are actually figurines created by a talented local artist named Tony Diminno. His works, which can be seen all throughout the forest, are very detailed and lifelike. In fact, other story land parks have even visited Idlewild to study the artistry of the attraction.

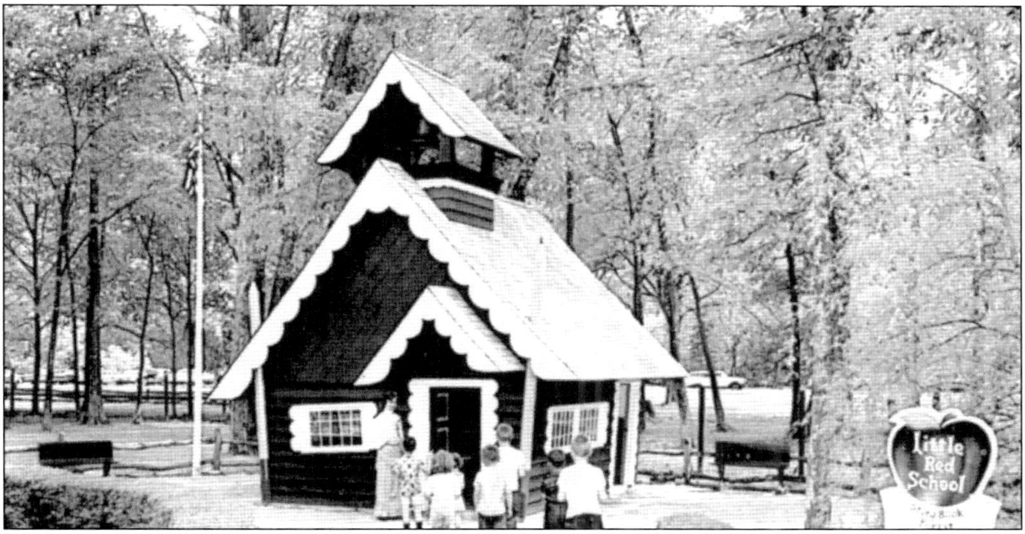

Children do not complain about going to school when it means visiting the Little Red School in Story Book Forest. The interior is complete with artifacts reminiscent of a one-room schoolhouse, including antique desks, a chalkboard, a portrait of George Washington, and the resident "dunce" sitting in his corner, punished for his naughty behavior. The alphabet is displayed across the front of the room and schoolbooks are located on the shelves. Children are encouraged to leave their names on the chalkboard in front. Here, the teacher rings her bell to begin class.

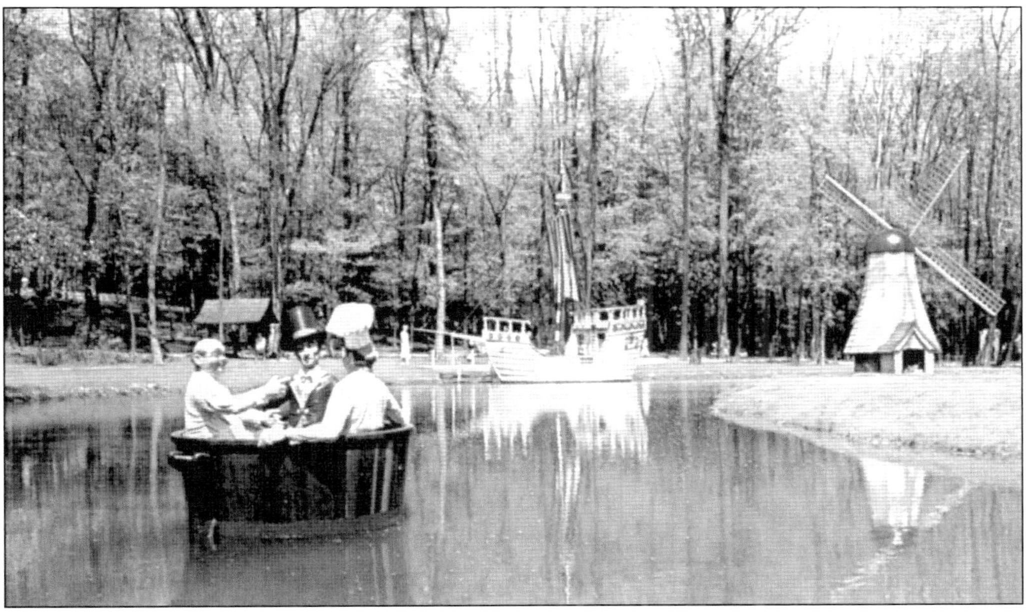

The pond in Story Book Forest was dug using a mule dragging a hand pan. This 1960s postcard depicts the "aRub-aDub-Dub" gang floating in their tub. Artist Tony Diminno fashioned the trio after Arthur Jennings and two Pittsburgh radio personalities, Rege Cordic and Ed Shaunessy. The Good Ship Lollipop and the Story Book Windmill are in the background.

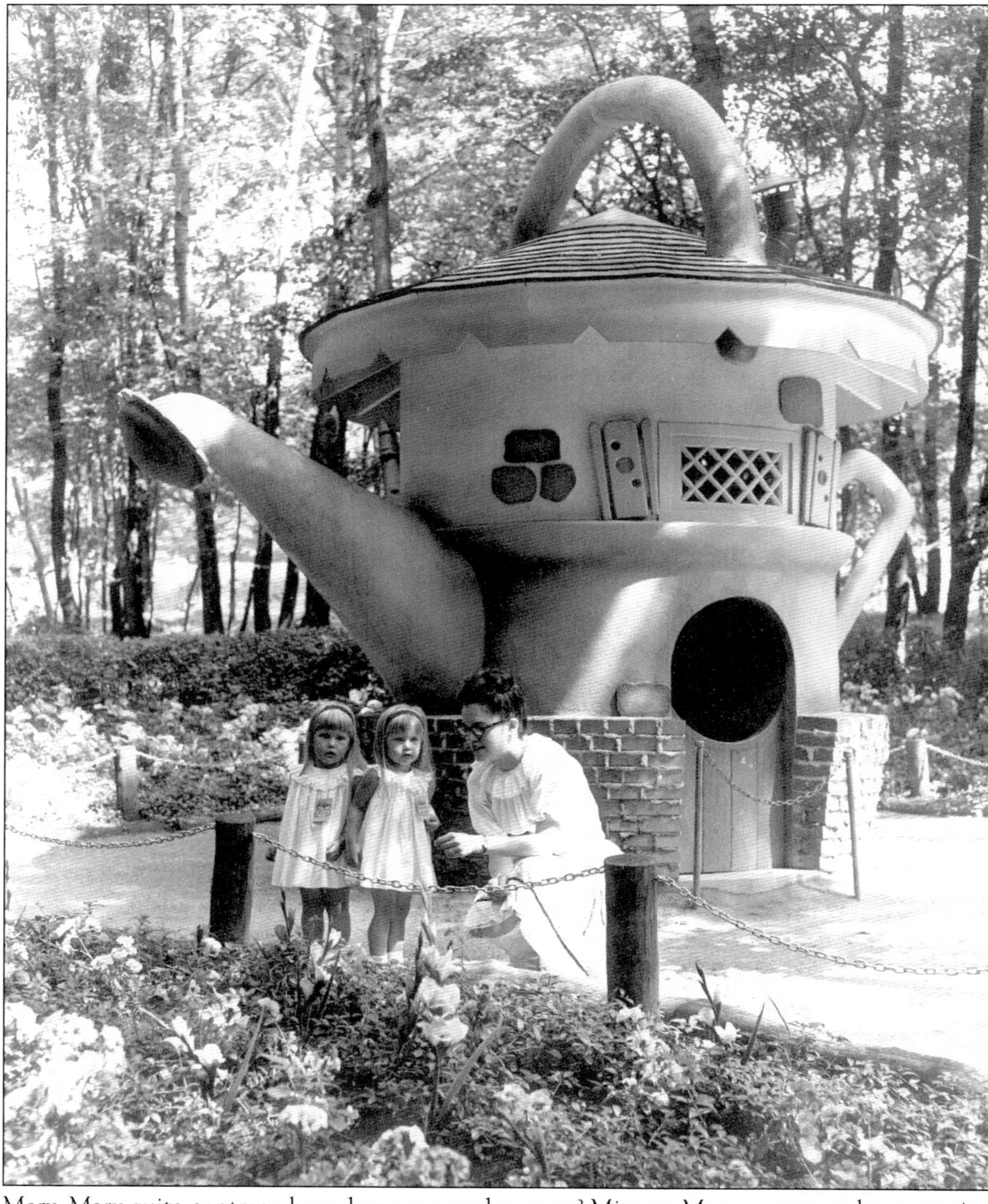

Mary, Mary quite contrary, how does your garden grow? Mistress Mary appears to be answering that question for these two young guests visiting the forest. Jay Schrader, a local engineer who took over design and construction duties at Story Book Forest from Arthur Jennings, designed the giant watering can and many other buildings currently in the park. He wanted a beautiful live flower garden as part of the Mistress Mary attraction, but the tall trees kept the area well shaded. When he found some greenery that grew in the location, he mixed in artificial flowers made of clay for the appearance of a lush garden.

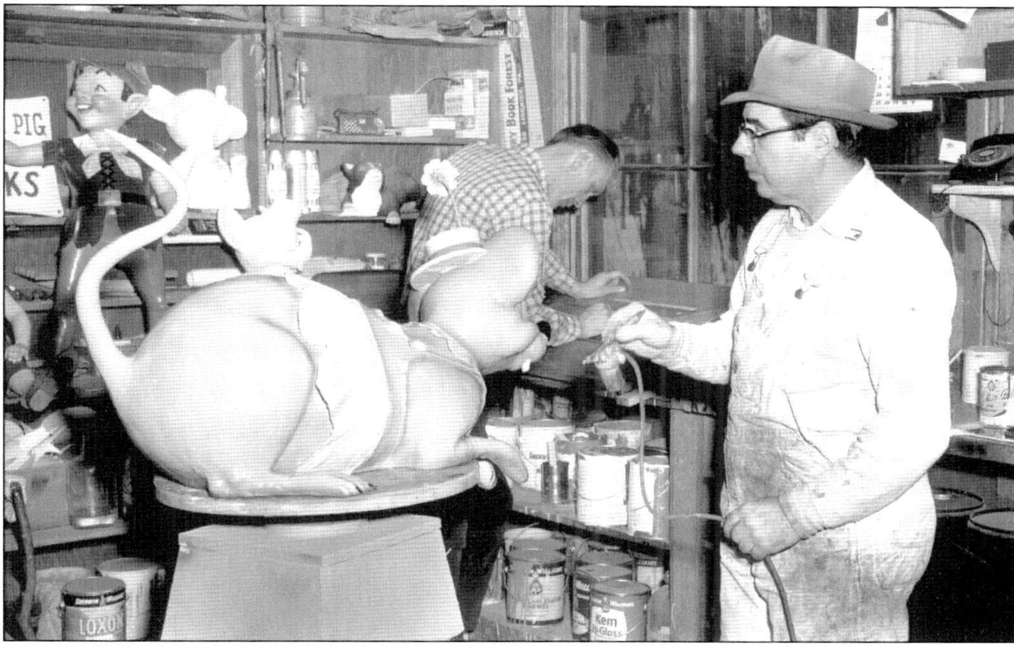

Many talented artists helped to make Story Book Forest become a fantasy wonderland. In this 1960s photograph Tony Diminno touches up one of the figurines, while Jay Schrader does some design work in the Story Book Forest paint shop.

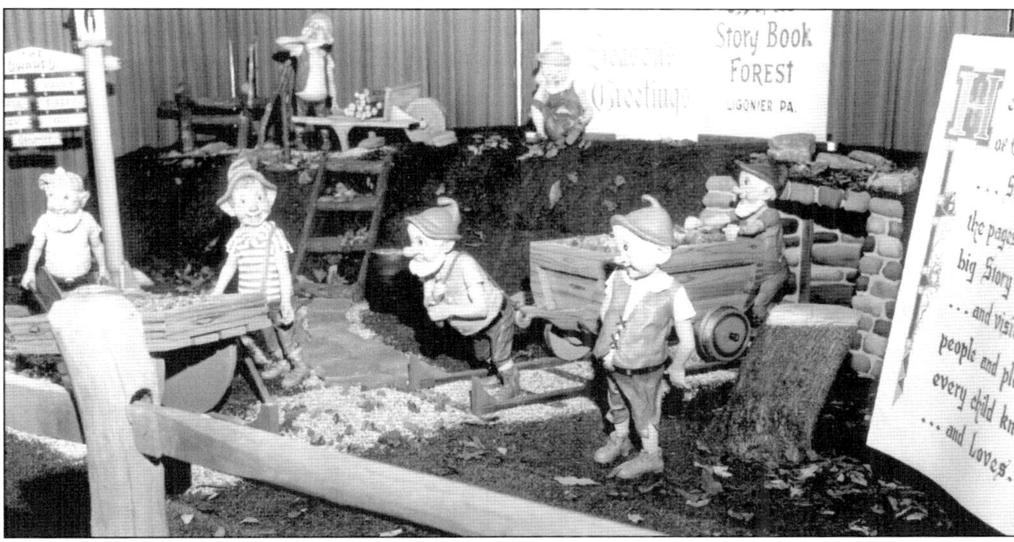

Story Book Forest has become so popular that during the off-season many of its characters make personal appearances outside of the park. The seven dwarfs posed for this photograph during a travel show, promoting the attraction. Through the years, various characters have visited hospitals, marched in parades, or appeared at grand-opening celebrations. Many of these promotional tours were planned by Miles Buell, who served for many years as promotion and advertising director for Story Book Forest and Idlewild. R. Z. Macdonald credits Buell for much of Story Book Forest's success; Buell traveled the whole eastern half of the United States touting its charm.

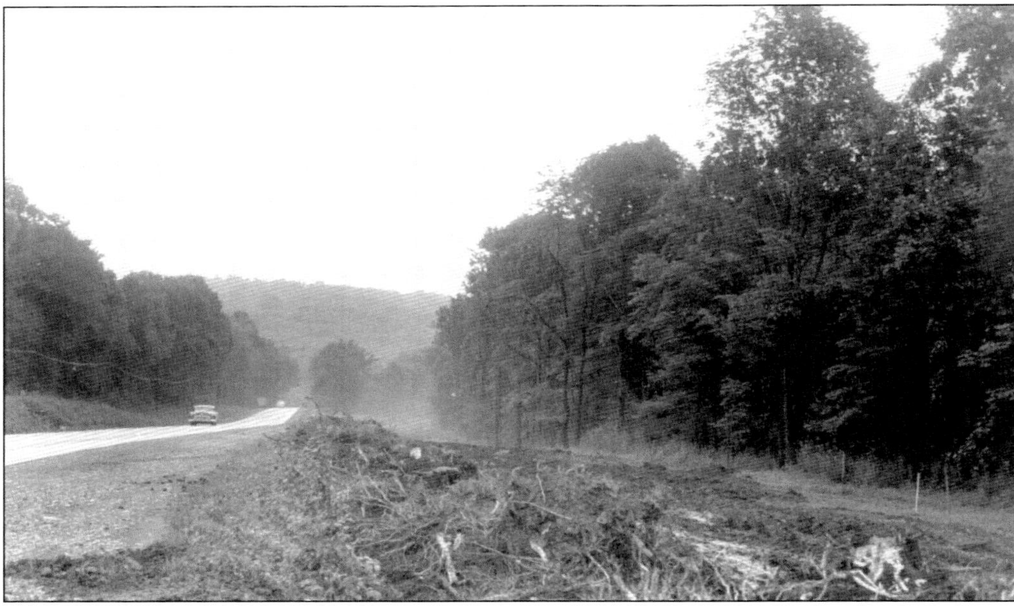

For more than 75 years Idlewild management followed the tradition set forth in the initial letter by William Darlington to not cut or harm any trees. However, when the Lincoln Highway (U.S. Route 30) expanded to four lanes in 1956, 14 acres of the park's frontage had to be cleared of timber. Originally, the plans for the new highway called for it to follow the exact path of the former Ligonier Valley Rail Road. This would have put the eastbound lanes directly through the center of the park, thus putting an end to Idlewild. Thankfully, the Macdonald family convinced the state highway department to follow an alternate route. Besides the 14 acres, the old log entrance was lost as well. The stone entrance constructed to take its place currently serves as the park's exit gate.

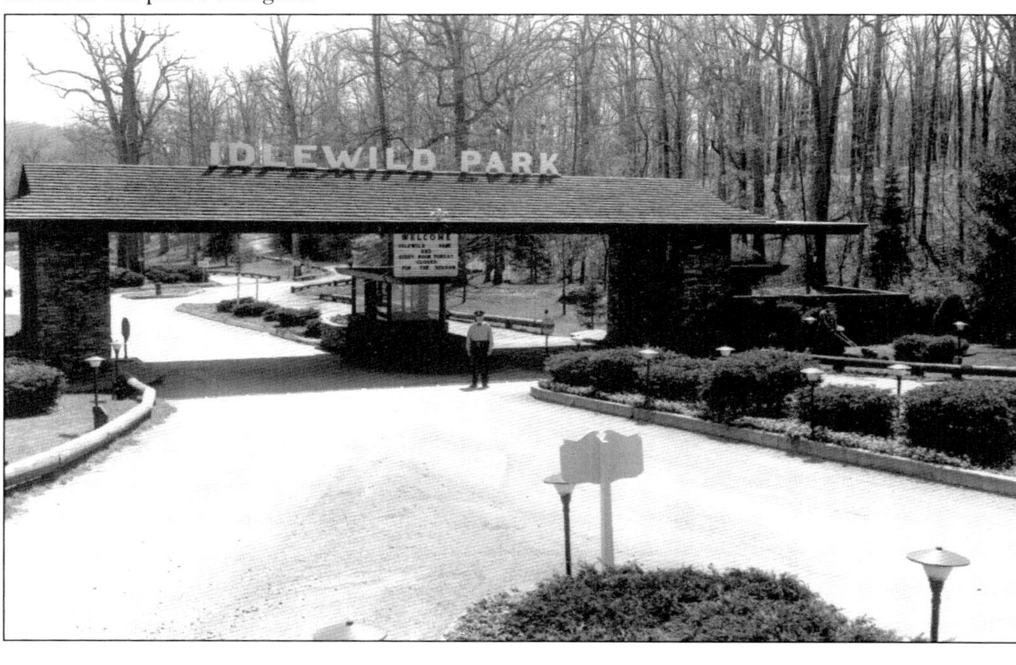

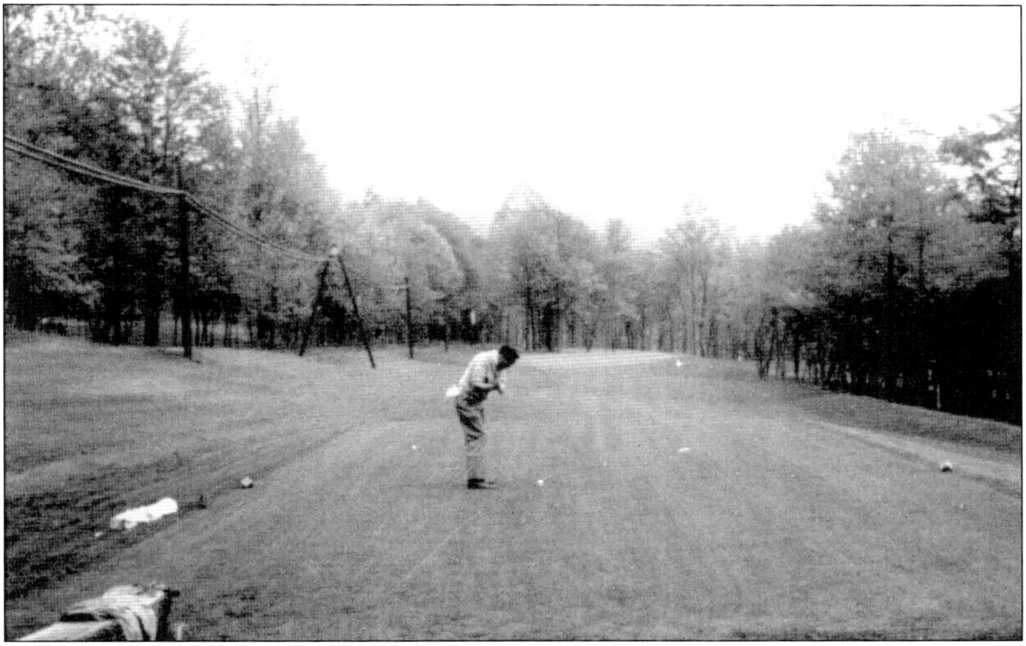

To further enhance Idlewild as a family entertainment complex, the Timberlink Golf Course was added in 1957. It is located on the northern side of the Lincoln Highway, across the road from Idlewild and Story Book Forest. While still owned by the park's current management, Kennywood Entertainment Partners, another party operates the golf course.

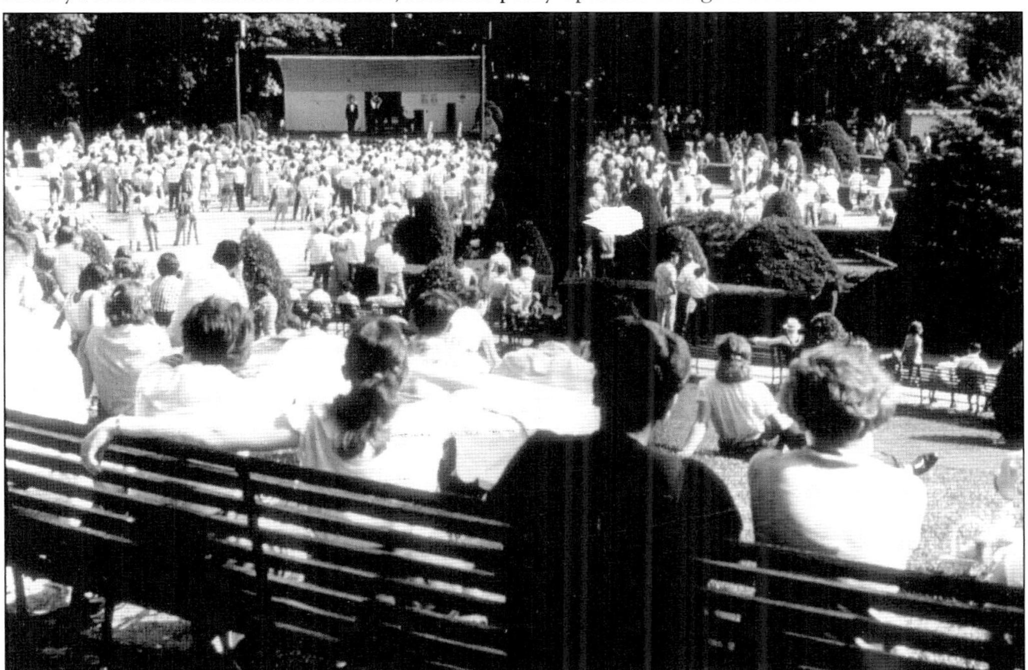

Here an act performs for the crowd on the parks main stage, while many watch from the benches on top of the hillside.

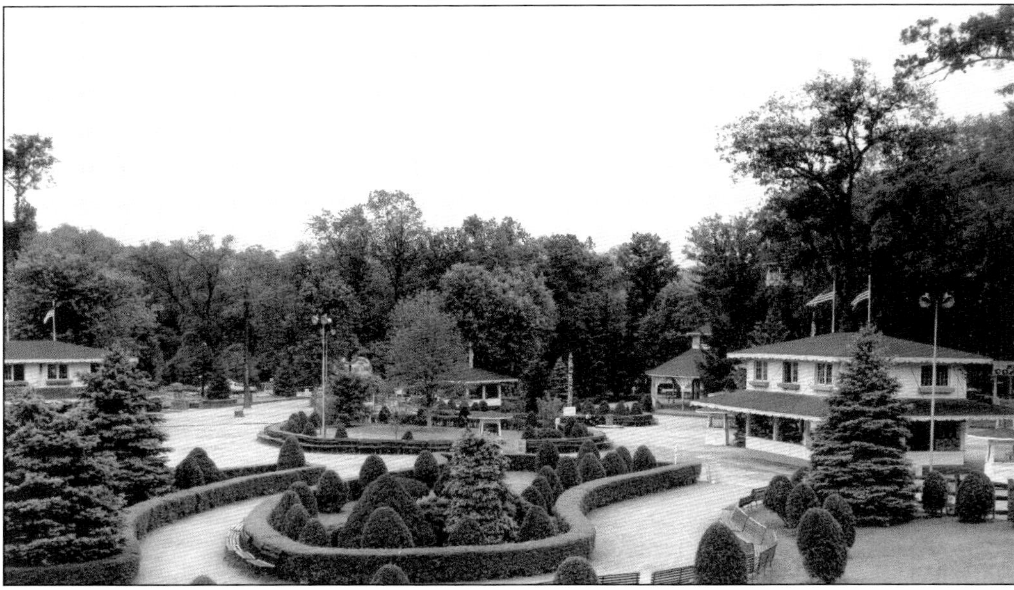

Fairly mature by the 1950s, the formal arrangement of hedges and shrubs made for fascinating geometric displays amid Idlewild's midways. R. Z. Macdonald credits two park superintendents for keeping the park in top-notch shape throughout the Macdonald years: Walter Anderson in the 1940s and William Luther who served in the position from the late 1940s through the mid-1980s.

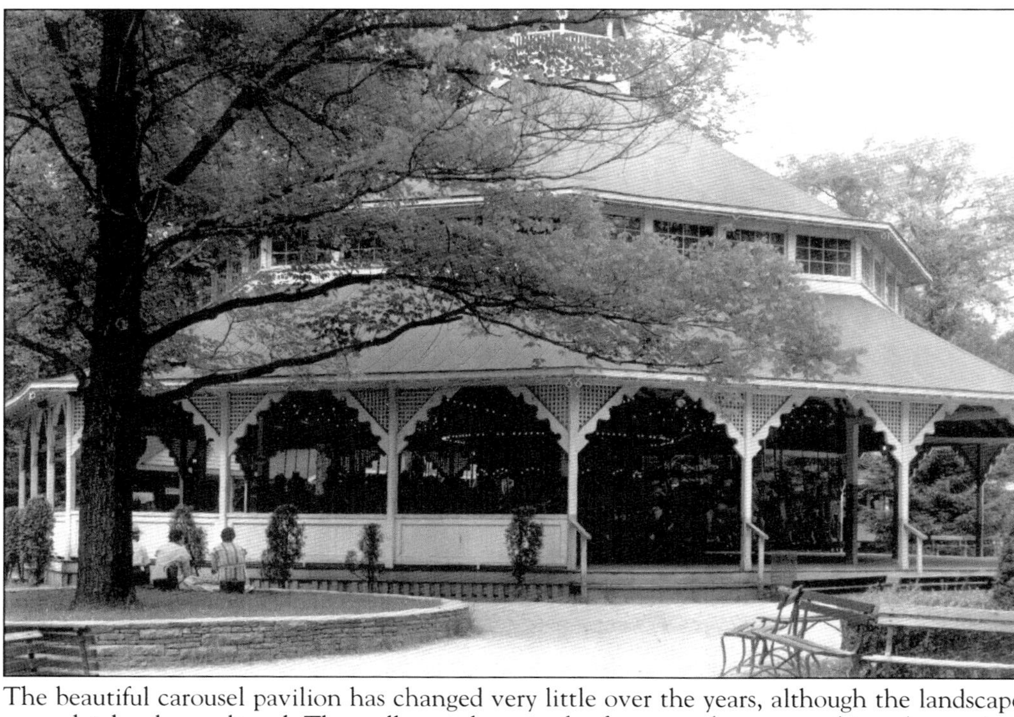

The beautiful carousel pavilion has changed very little over the years, although the landscape around it has been altered. The walk seen here in the foreground was turned into lawn when the park added two new game buildings to the midway in 1998.

Traditional Scottish athletics, such as the caber toss, are a highlight of the Ligonier Highland Games, which have been held at Idlewild each September since 1959. The festival also features Scottish merchants, authentic food, dancing, and music.

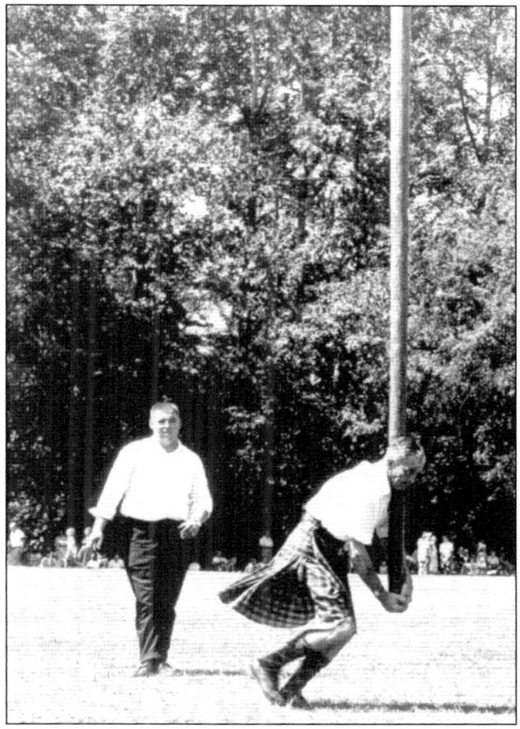

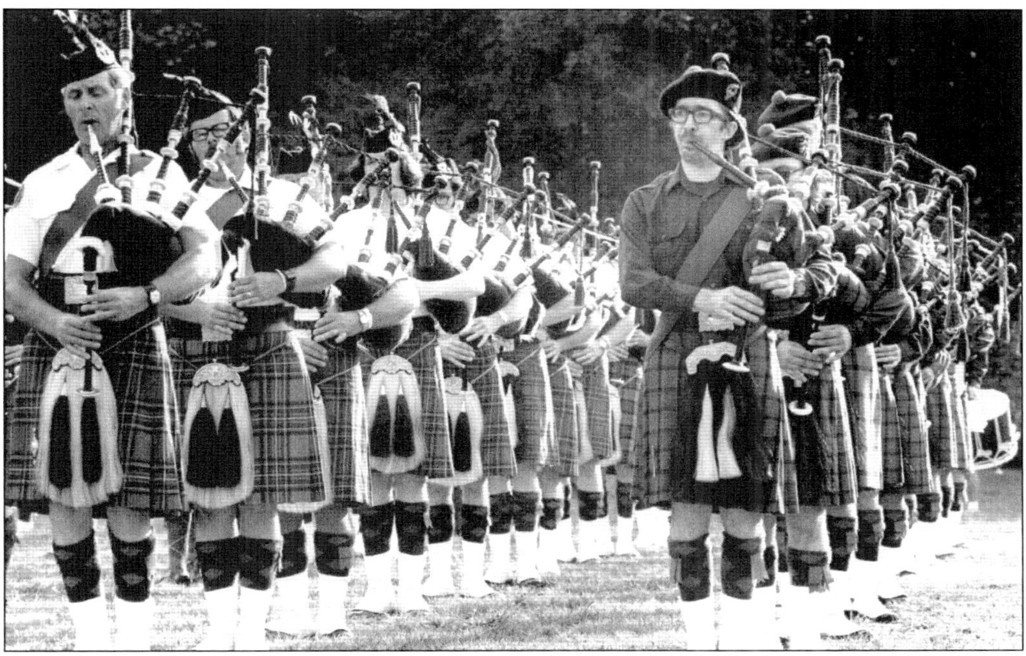

Each year at the close of the games there is a final mass of bands. The ceremony, featuring hundreds of musicians, takes place at the game field following the award ceremony. Visitors from several states attend the event year after year. The experience of the closing ceremonies is indeed powerful to all who witness it.

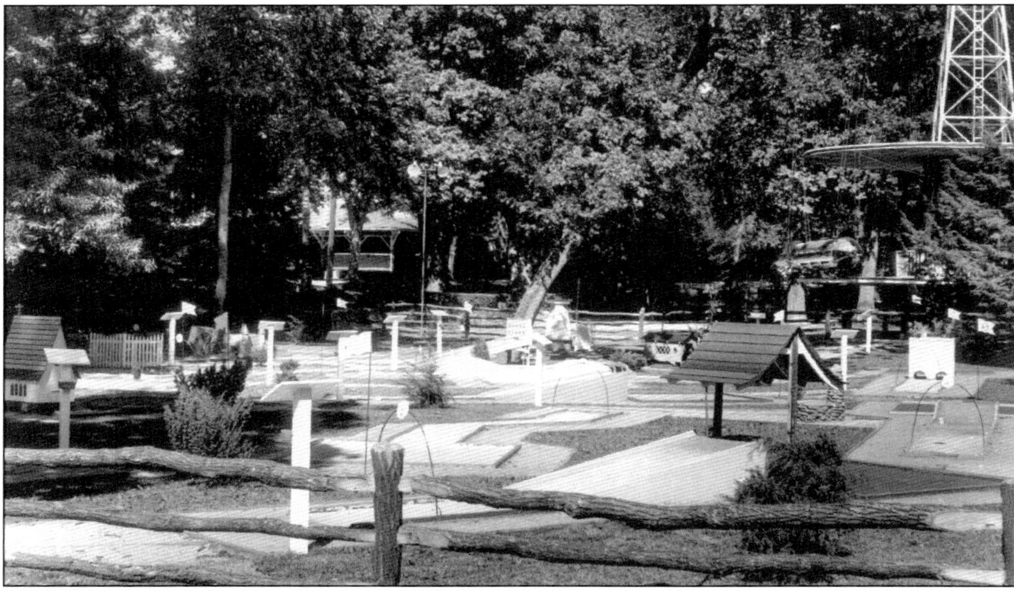

Miniature golf came to Idlewild in 1959, when this challenging course was built along the banks of the Loyalhanna Creek. The rocket ships of the circle swing, seen to the right, swung out over the golfers as they played. The course was slightly redesigned in the 1980s and operates today under the name Goofy Golf.

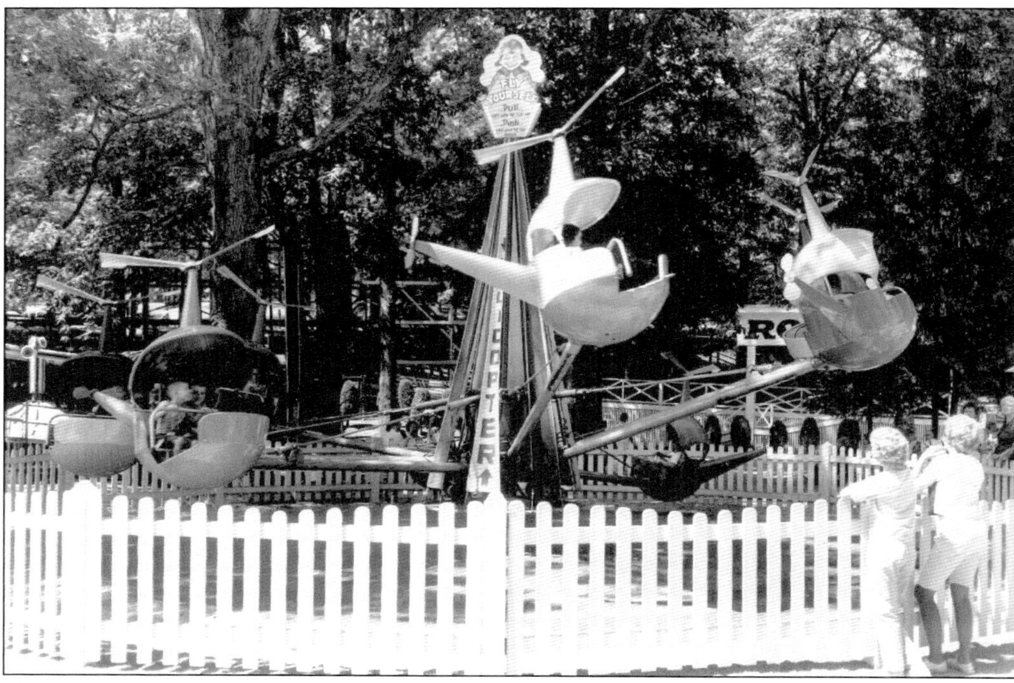

Flying yourself around in a helicopter sure was fun! The best part of the flight was that the rider actually controlled the height of their copter by pushing and pulling their lap bar. The amusement ride, manufactured by the Allen Herschell Company, was a fixture at Idlewild from the 1960s until it was removed in 1987.

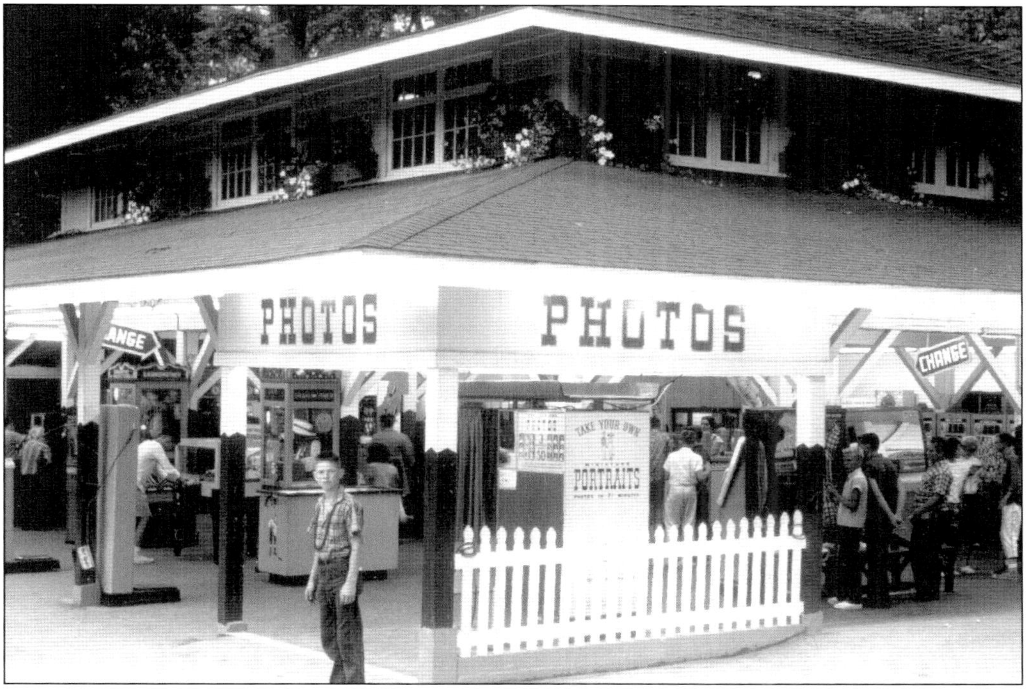

The Idlewild arcade saw many changes during more than 50 years of existence. This is how it appeared in 1962. The photograph booth, which advertises, "Photos in 2½ minutes," was high-tech at the time.

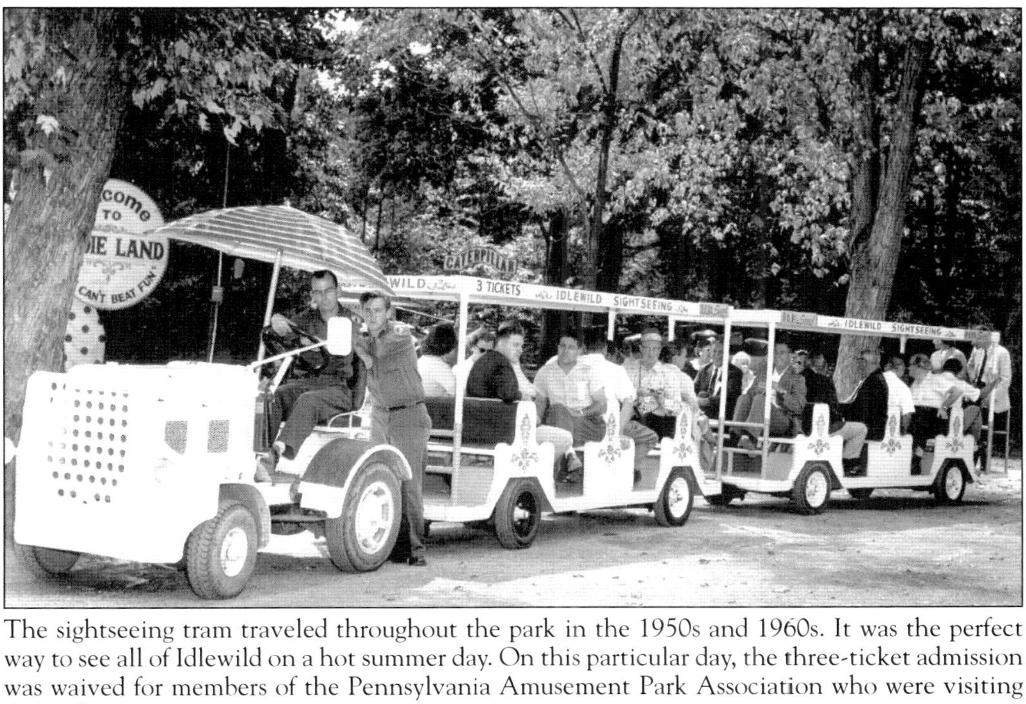

The sightseeing tram traveled throughout the park in the 1950s and 1960s. It was the perfect way to see all of Idlewild on a hot summer day. On this particular day, the three-ticket admission was waived for members of the Pennsylvania Amusement Park Association who were visiting the park.

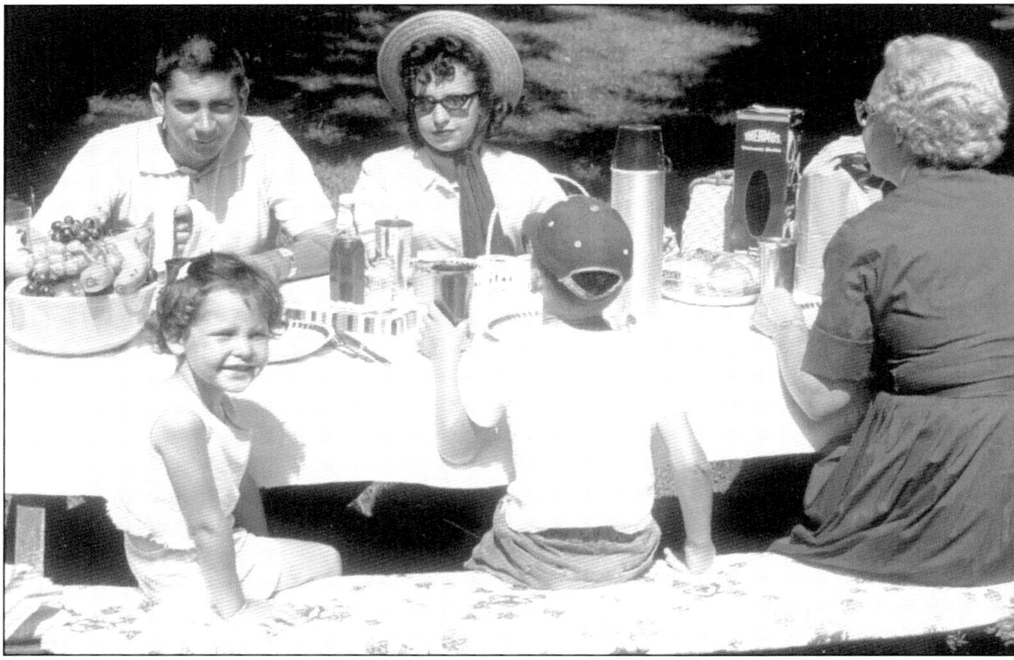

Nothing beats taking a time-out to enjoy lunch with the family in one of Idlewild's shady picnic groves.

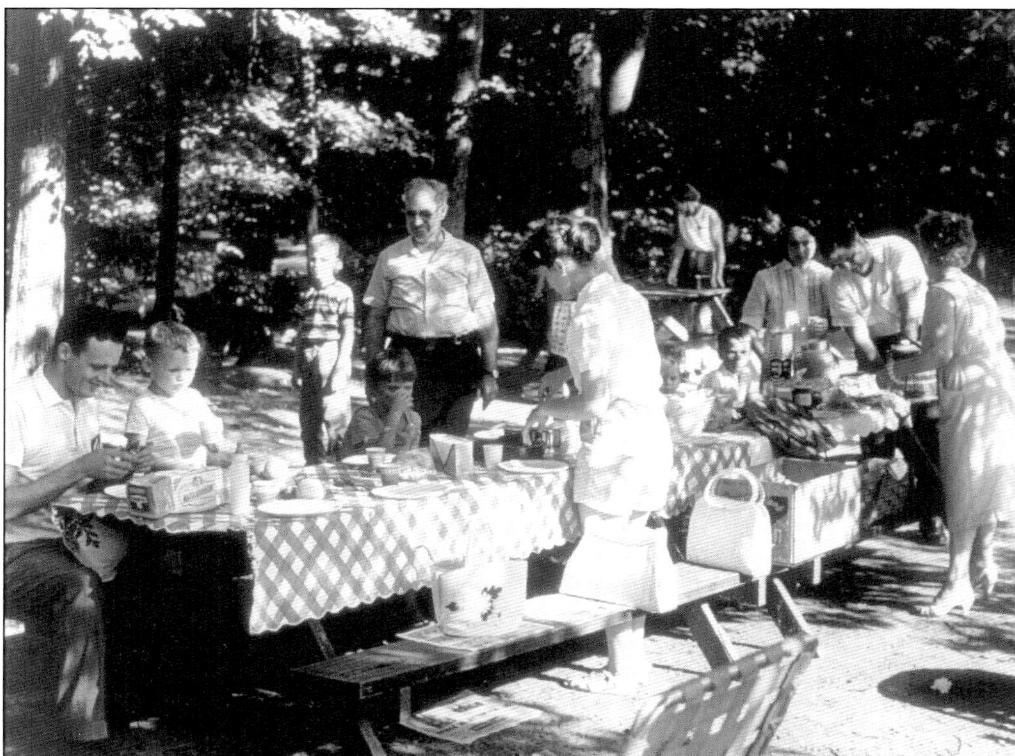

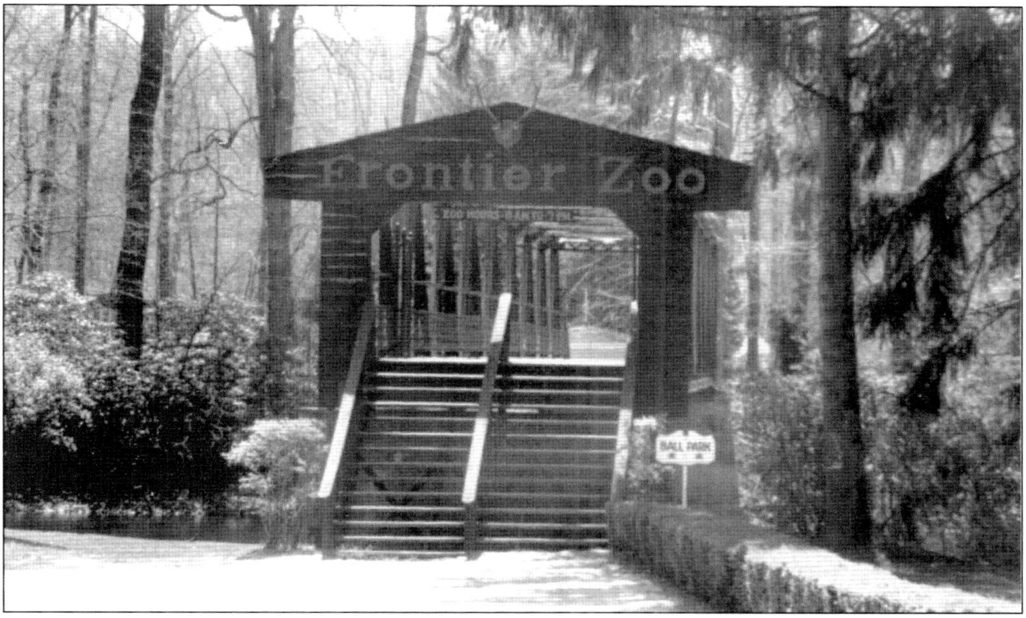

In 1965, Frontier Safariland opened. The small zoo featured North American animals such as foxes, wolves, raccoons, seals, and porcupines. In the early 1970s it became known as the Frontier Zoo and featured a mule-train ride through the woods. The bridge crossing the Loyalhanna led to the zoo, which occupied a portion of the former Woodlands.

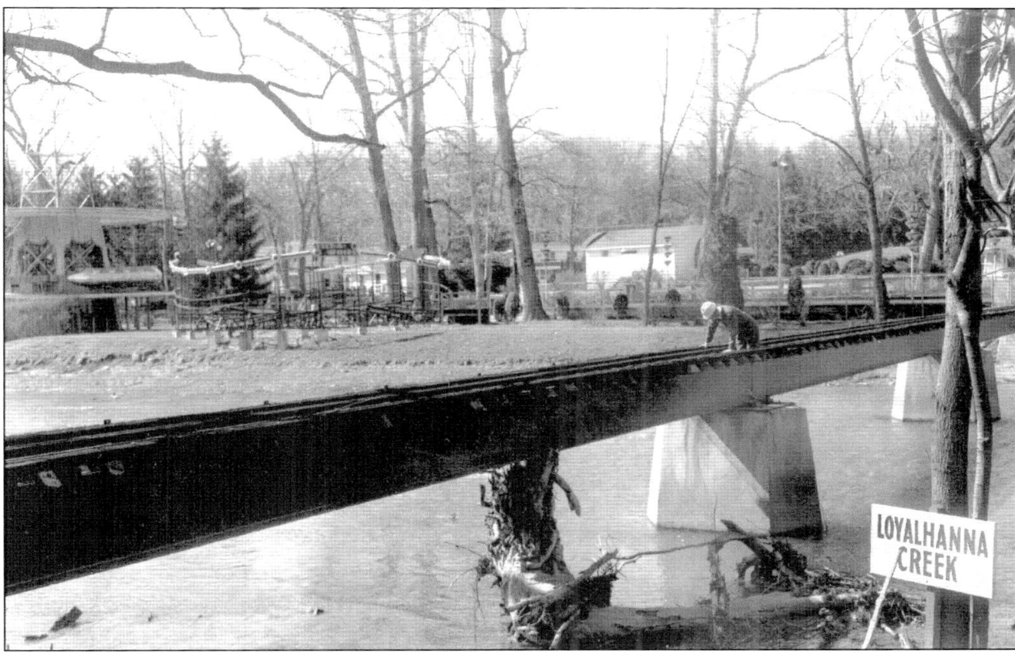

A miniature railroad (the park's second) was constructed to transport guests across the Loyalhanna Creek once the south side of the property began to be developed. In this photograph, construction is progressing on one of two new bridges that eventually carried the Loyalhanna Limited across the water.

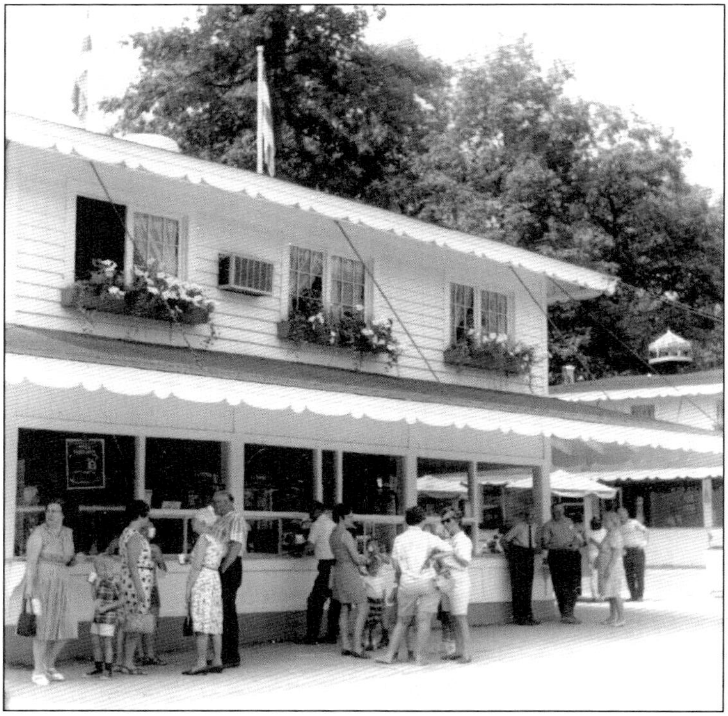

Here a small crowd gathers in front of the lunch stand on a sunny afternoon in 1969. The ice cream stand, located in the background, was designed to match the exterior of its neighbor. The decorative ice-cream-cone carousel on its roof once rotated but now serves solely as an ornamental fixture.

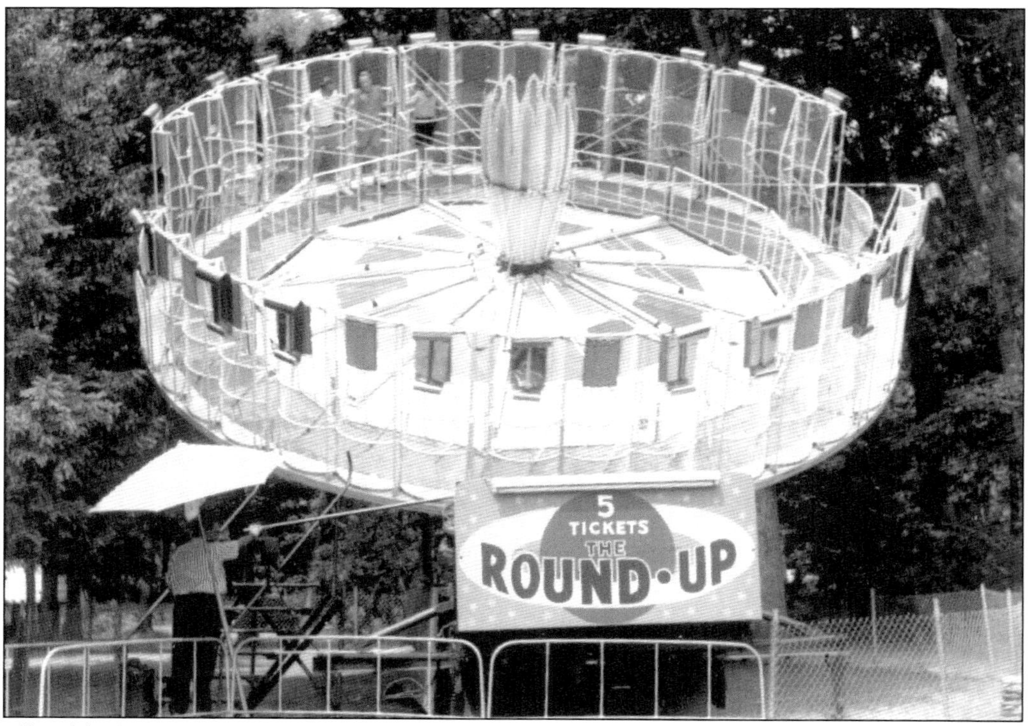

Idlewild's first Round-Up was added in the 1960s and remained until 1984. It had a capacity of 30 riders per cycle.

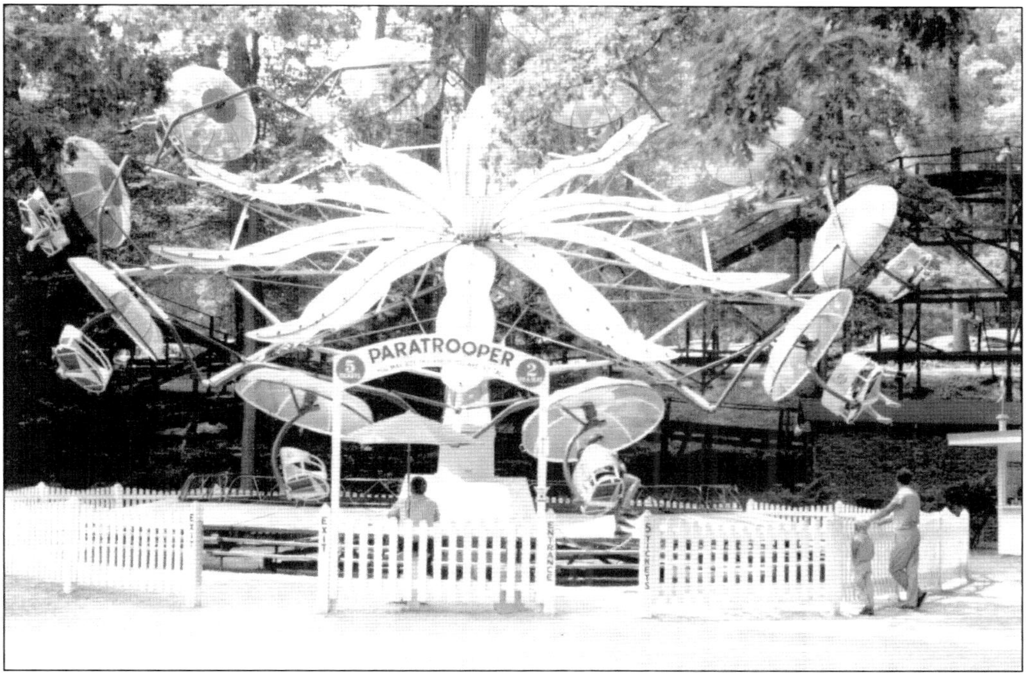

Taking a high-flying trip on the Paratrooper is always an easy way to cool off on a hot summer day. The ride's location near the Rollo Coaster, as seen here in 1969, was situated so closely to some tall trees that riders often felt they could grab a leaf. Made by Frank Hrubetz and Company, the Paratrooper was relocated in 1998 near the Skooters to make room for the Trinado.

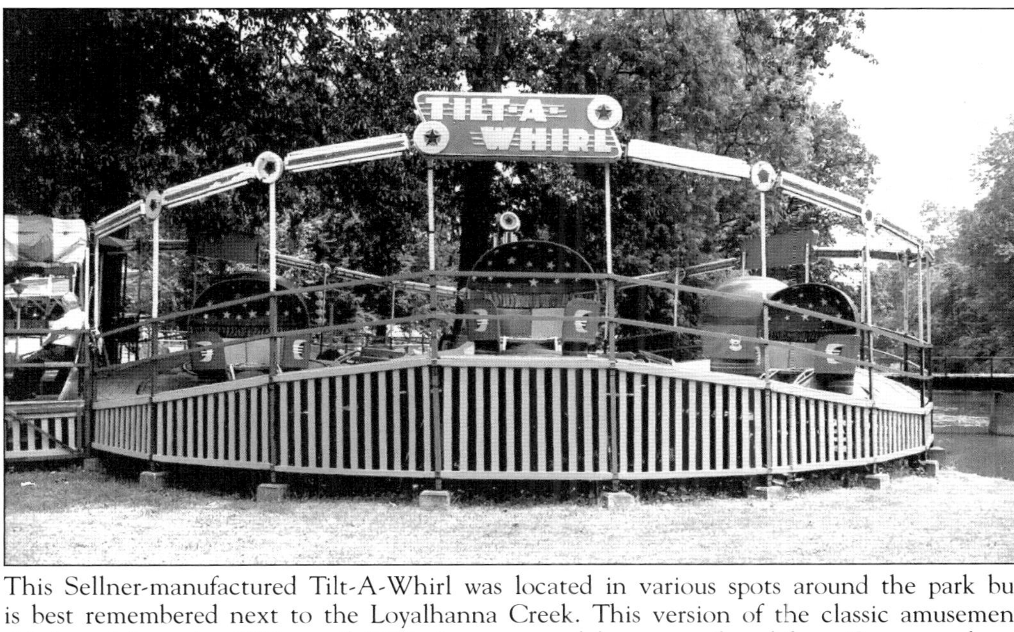

This Sellner-manufactured Tilt-A-Whirl was located in various spots around the park but is best remembered next to the Loyalhanna Creek. This version of the classic amusement ride lasted from the 1960s until 1989. A newer model was transferred from Kennywood and replaced it.

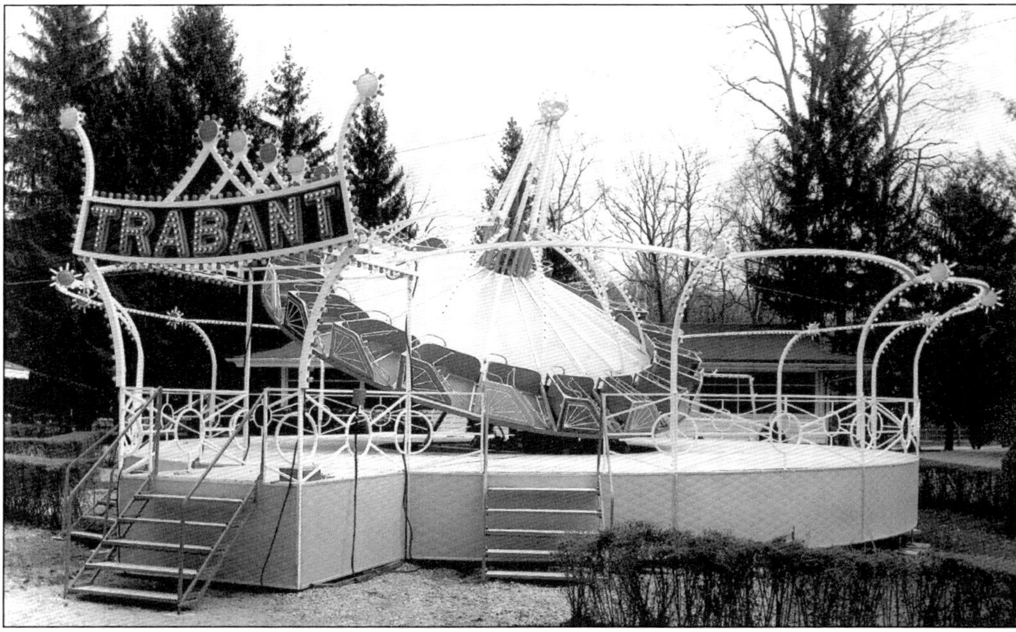

The Trabant was added to the park's ride lineup in 1971. Pictured here in the off-season near the park's restaurant, it was also once located at the site currently occupied by the Spider. The ride was removed in 1983.

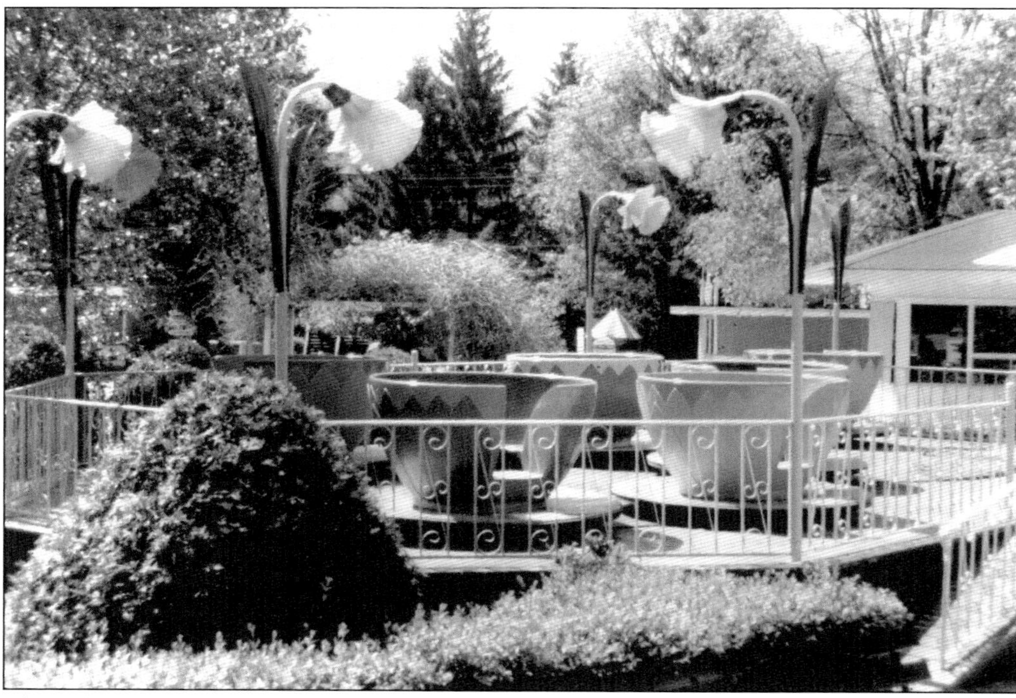

The colorful Crazy Dazy, manufactured by the Philadelphia Toboggan Company, spun into Idlewild in 1974. It remained at its location, the spot currently occupied by the Scrambler, until 1985.

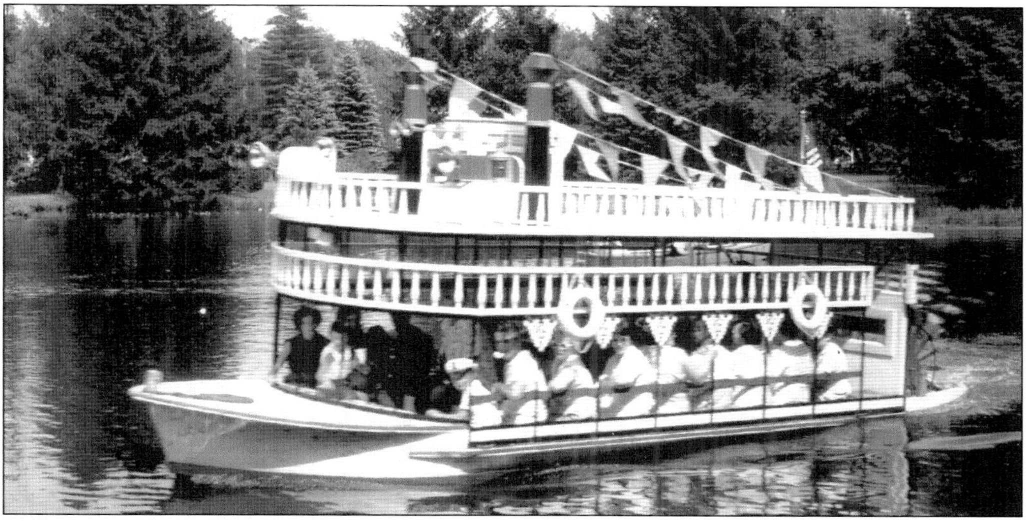

The Showboat replaced the motor launches of earlier years. The paddle wheel propelled patrons around scenic Lake Bouquet, beginning in 1948 and lasting until 1987. After the Showboat was retired, the boathouse was turned into a picnic pavilion.

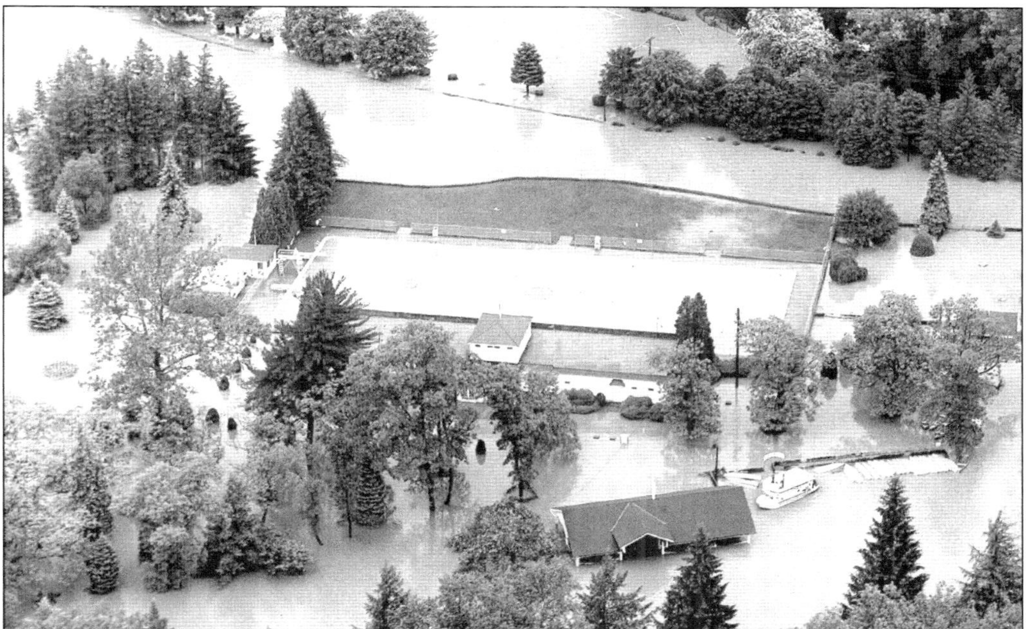

When the remnants of Hurricane Agnes stalled over Pennsylvania in 1972, it dumped 14 inches of rainfall in a 24-hour period. Idlewild was still feeling the effects of the floodwaters that resulted from the storm when this aerial photograph was taken. Lake St. Clair and Lake Bouquet, previously separated by Deemer Lane (the name given to the old rail bed of the Ligonier Valley), appeared as one. The boathouse, in the foreground was significantly underwater, whereas the swimming pool narrowly escaped major damage. Elsewhere in the park, the track of the Loyalhanna Limited needed extensive repairs after being lifted and twisted by the raging floodwaters.

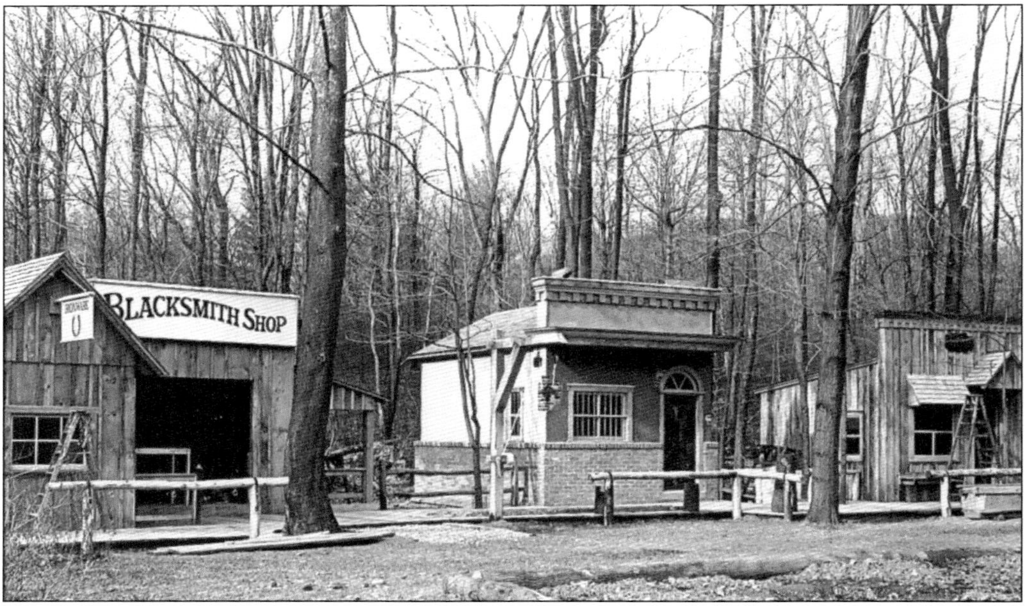

The Historic Village was built to commemorate the country's bicentennial in 1976. Modeled after a typical town of the 1800s, it included a general store, blacksmith and woodcrafter shops, sheriff's office, newspaper office, saloon, and the Feed Box restaurant. In the image below, Jay Schrader locks up an "inmate" in the Historic Village's jail. (Both images courtesy R. Z. Macdonald.)

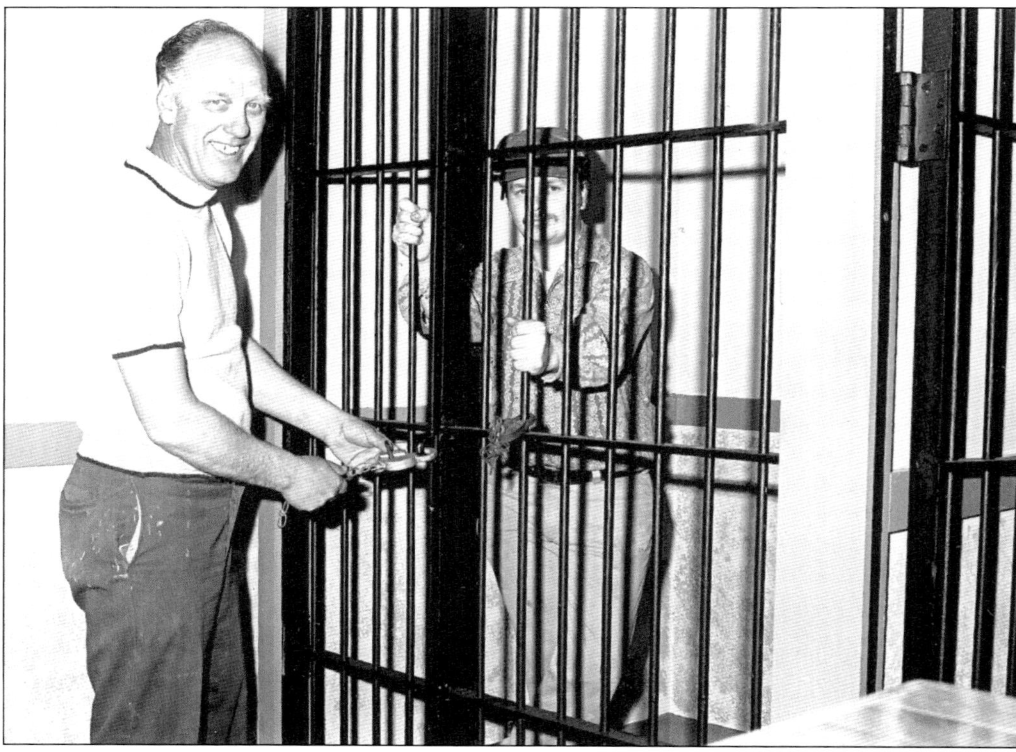

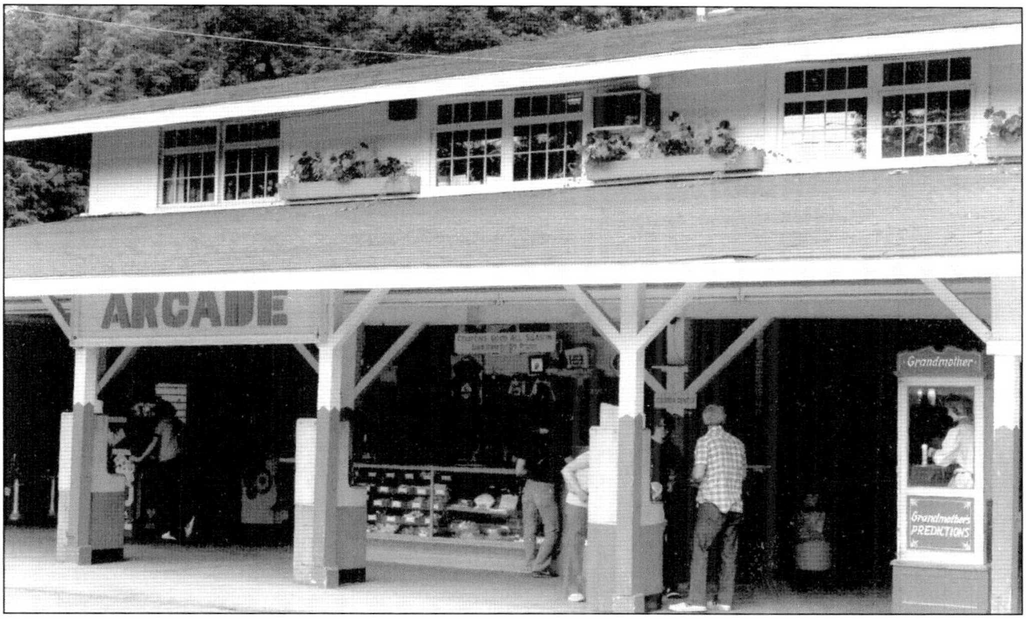

In 1980, the arcade was still very popular. Video games sat alongside the penny games of yesteryear. Redemption games, such as Skee-Ball and Three In A Line, offered guests a chance to take home anything from a pencil to a set of dishes.

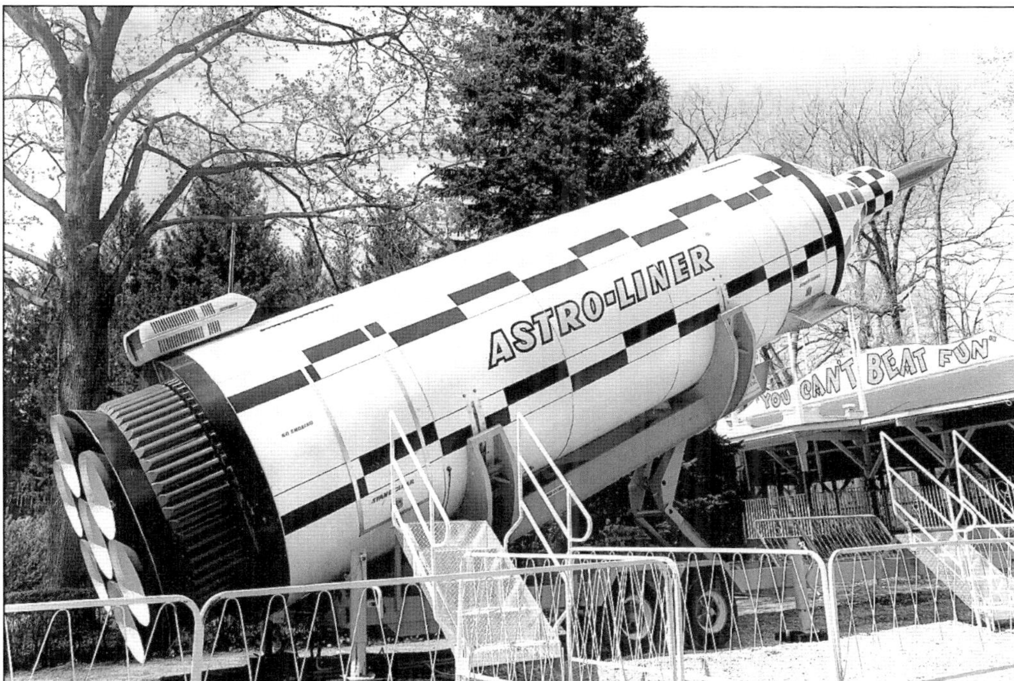

Welcome aboard the Astro-liner. This space flight featured the realism of the space shuttle and all the fantasy of *Star Wars*. The space-age adventure helped Idlewild launch its second century in 1978 and remained in the park through the 1983 season.

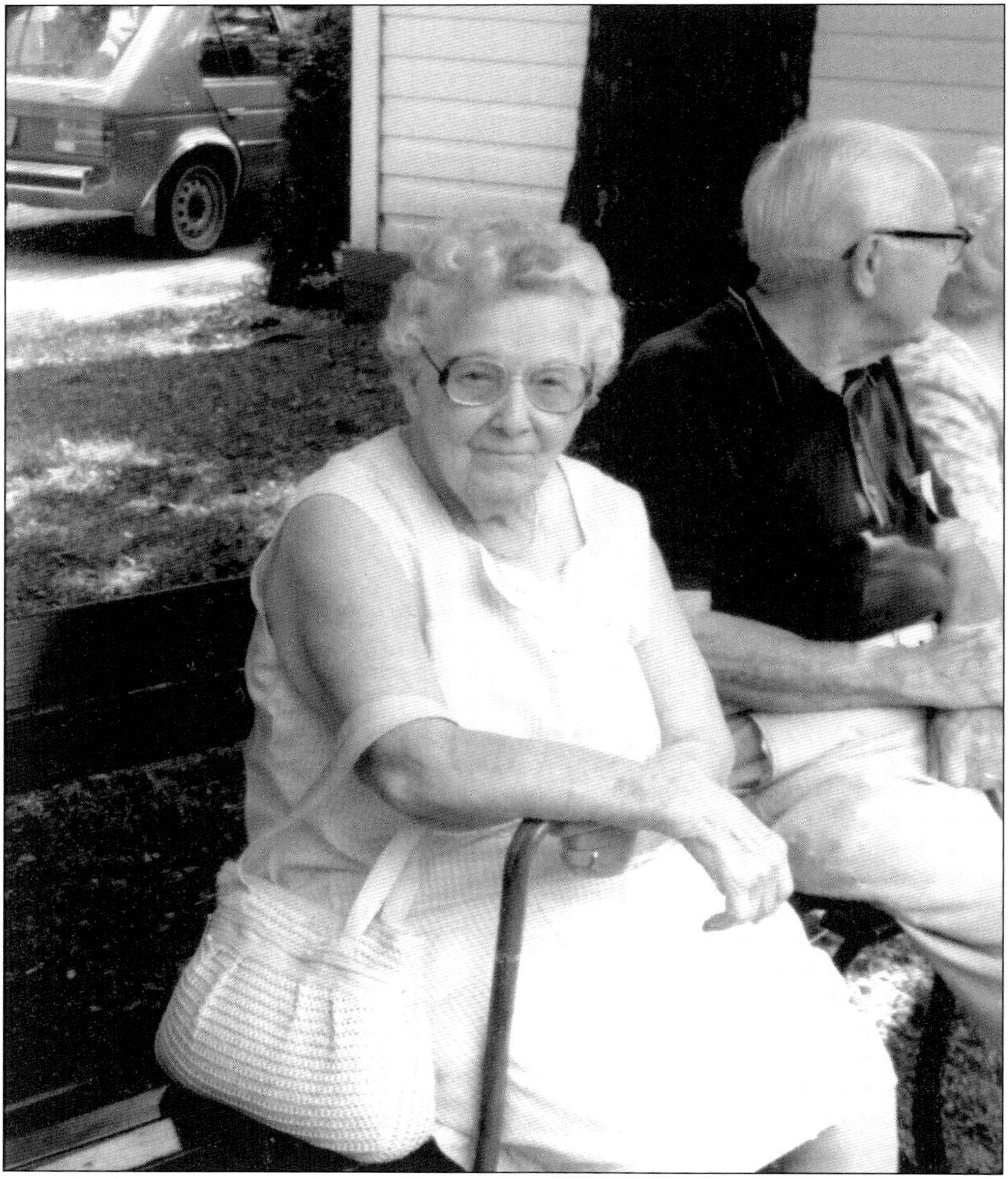

As a child, the author attended the annual Norwin Community picnic with four generations of his family. His brother, cousins, and he were always running off to the next ride or the next game of chance. His parents and grandparents were always interested in the musical shows or what delicious food they could try next. His great-grandmother, who was elderly and had trouble walking, simply picked a shaded green bench in the center of the park and planted herself there for the day. As she remained in place, all of her friends and neighbors from the community eventually passed by, engaged in conversation, and then continued on. For the author's family, "grandma's bench" became their meeting place. This is a photograph of the author's great-grandmother Edith Lindh, seated on a green bench near the old Idlewild depot. (Courtesy Carol Croushore.)

Four

The Finest in Family Fun 1983 and After

In February 1983, the MacDonald Family sold the park to the Kennywood Entertainment Corporation, operators of Kennywood amusement park in West Mifflin. Born much the same way as Idlewild, Kennywood was built in 1898 as an amusement resort alongside the trolley line of the Pittsburgh Street Railway Company. In 1906, the railway company designated the park's lease to A. S. McSwigan and Frederick W. Henninger, whose families continued to operate Kennywood for four generations. By 1983, it was widely known as one of the finest traditional amusement parks in America.

From early on, the new management made it clear that there would be no major overhaul to Idlewild. They improved and expanded, but Idlewild's family atmosphere and natural beauty remained intact. Jumpin' Jungle, a soft play area, was added for the 1983 season and Hootin' Holler opened the following year. The additions of these two themed areas filled the land gap that existed between the amusement rides and Story Book Forest. The latter would no longer be operated as a separate attraction but as one feature of Idlewild.

The H2Ohhhh Zone (a water slide complex) debuted in 1985, and a new 14-gate automobile entrance was built the following year. Concentration was also given to develop the park's midways with popular games of chance, new food stands, and restaurants. Rafter's Run, a Ferris wheel, and a new Tilt-A-Whirl were added by the end of the 1980s, as was Mister Rogers' Neighborhood of Make-Believe. Based on the popular children's television series and created especially for Idlewild by Fred Rogers, it features a trolley ride where guests can interact with their favorite Neighborhood characters. Following that, a new children's area across the Loyalhanna Creek, named Raccoon Lagoon, replaced Kiddieland.

In the 1990s, the central midways were redesigned and paved, and the Hillside Theater was constructed, providing a spacious stage for performances. A new steel coaster, the Wild Mouse, was built on the old Kiddieland site, and three more rides were added. Kennywood Entertainment also presented free acts—reminiscent of the Macdonald era—such as circus, lumberjack, and acrobat shows. In 1999, a new picnic grove, featuring beautifully hand-carved log pavilions and game fields, was created. The H2Ohhhh Zone gave way to the SoakZone, an expanded water park with additional water slides, water cannons, tipping cones, and a giant tipping bucket. In 2001, the popularity of the new area led the park to adopt a new name: Idlewild and SoakZone.

The owners, Kennywood Entertainment Partners, have remained committed to preserving the ideals of the Mellon and Macdonald families. Once named "America's Most Beautiful Theme Park," Idlewild continues to offer the finest in family fun and entertainment.

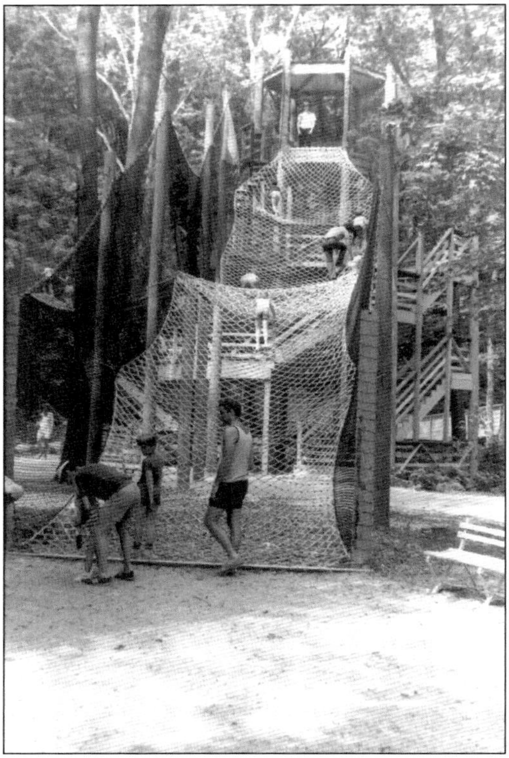

Jumpin' Jungle was the first attraction added by the Kennywood Corporation in 1983. It was built between Story Book Forest and the Idlewild amusement rides. The centerpiece of Jumpin' Jungle is the towering tree house, accessible by the net climb. In the company's premiere year, other elements included slides, a ball crawl, a punching-bag maze, a roller race ride, and a raft ride. In following years, a serpentine slide, tarzan swings, jungle phones, ball blowers, and a jungle organ were added.

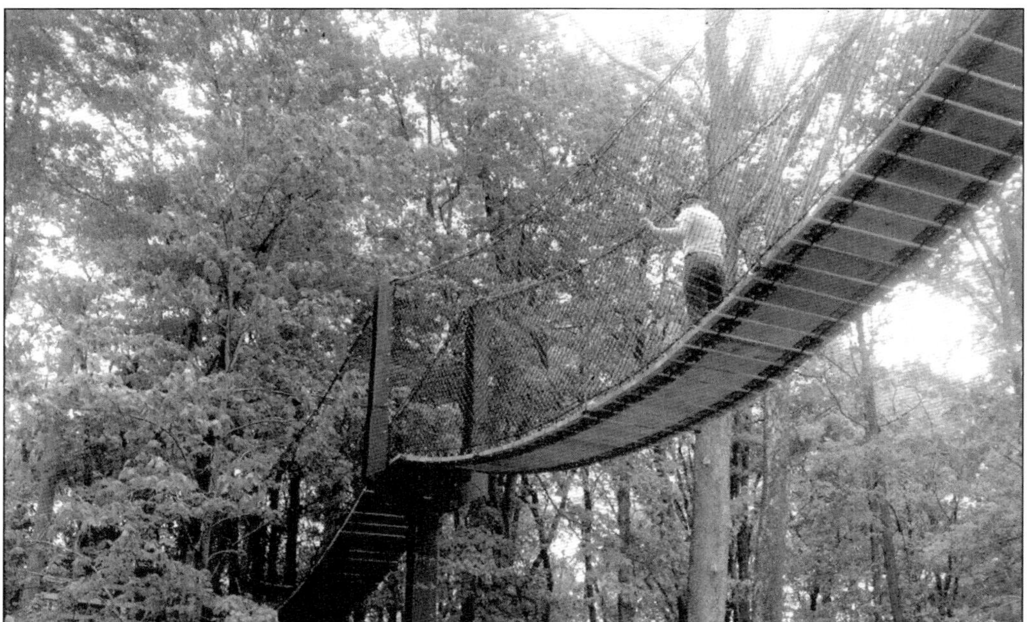

The suspension bridge hangs high above the Jumpin' Jungle floor. For those who climb the giant net to the tree house, the bridge serves as a way back down. For the faint of heart, a set of stairs is also offered as an alternate route.

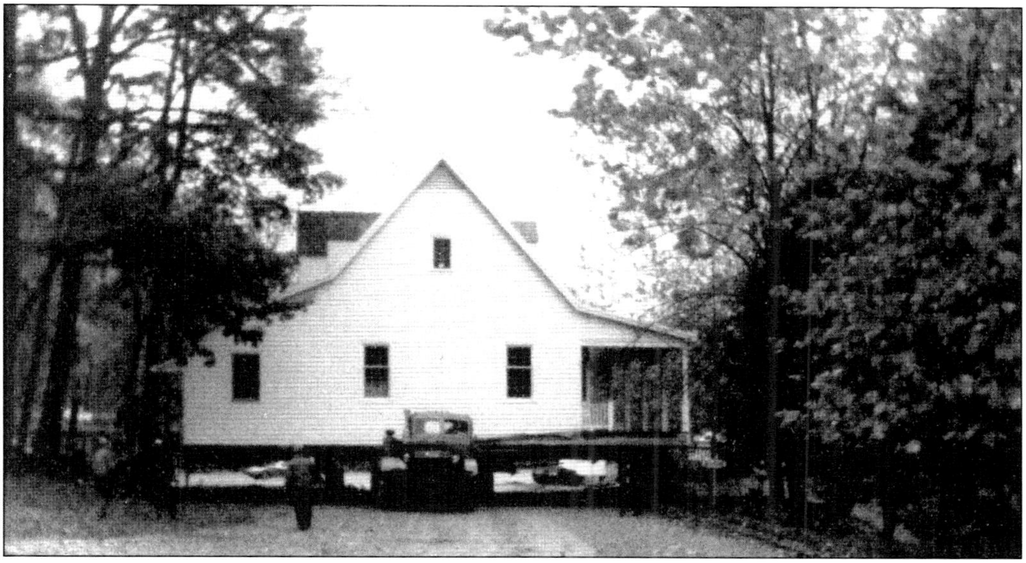

In 1984, in an effort to further bridge the gap between the amusement rides and Story Book Forest, management created Hootin' Holler. This area, featuring eateries, gift shops, games, and performance stages, is themed after a mining town of the Wild West. The design called for the relocation of many buildings that made up the park's former Historic Village. The largest of these structures was the General Store, pictured here on a flatbed truck en route to its new location.

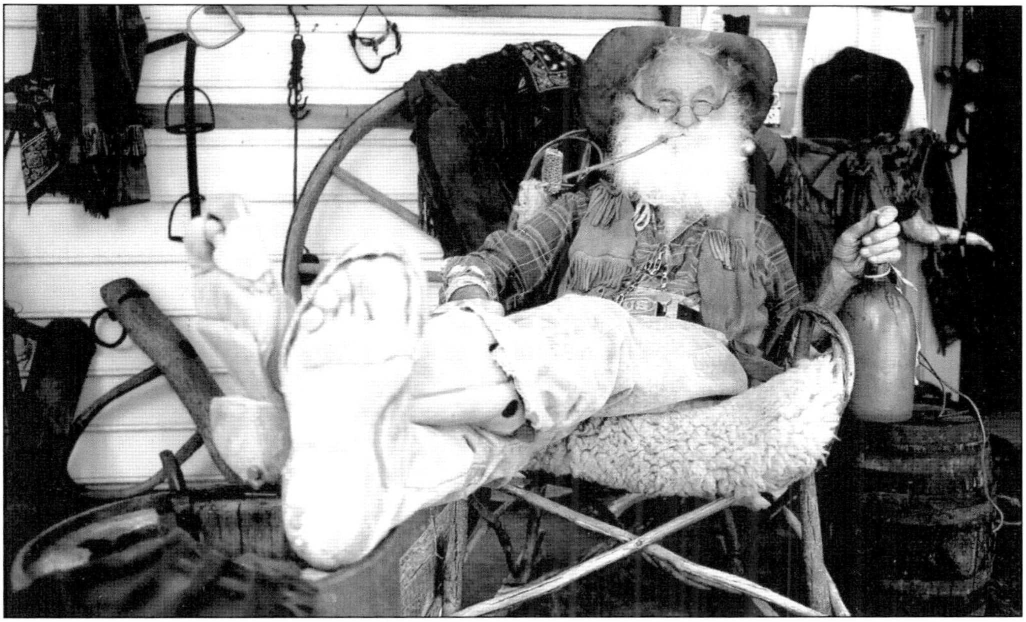

Idlewild "struck gold" when they opened the new western mining town and hired Steven Tomasic to portray the settlement's old-timer. Tomasic, who had performed blacksmith demonstrations at the park prior to the creation of Hootin' Holler, brought with him many antiques to decorate the area's buildings. The popular character could often be found close to Hootin' Holler's resident quilter, portrayed by his wife, Eunice.

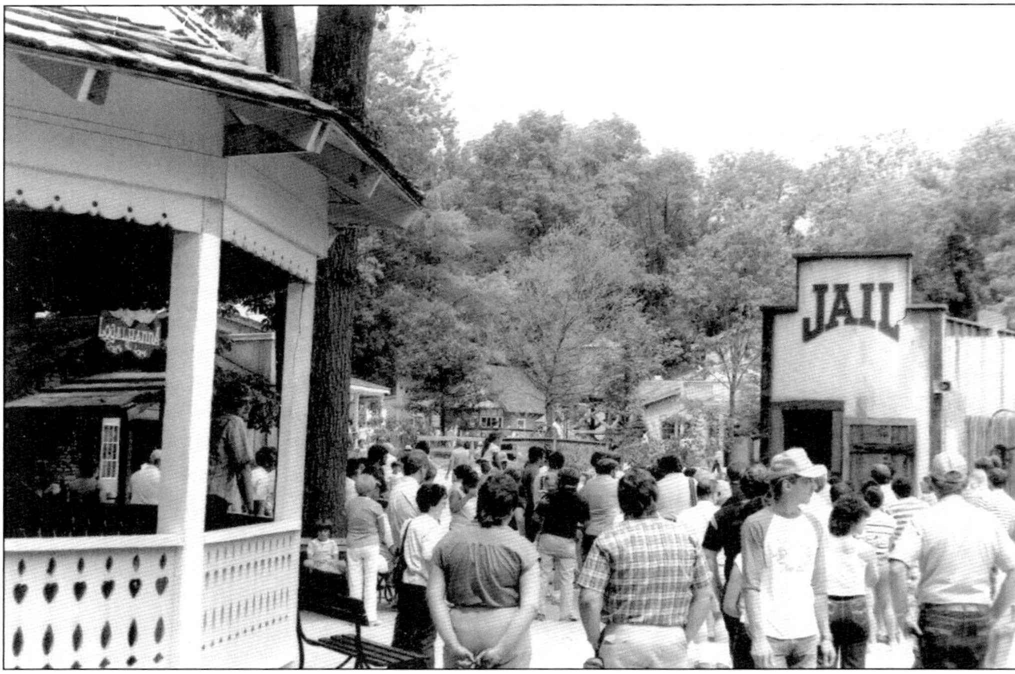

The Hootin' Holler jail, shown above, was the scene for street theater performances and puppet shows. The themed area is beautifully landscaped, with a babbling brook flowing throughout. The Wild Horse Saloon, below, was a restaurant featuring stage shows. It was removed in 1994.

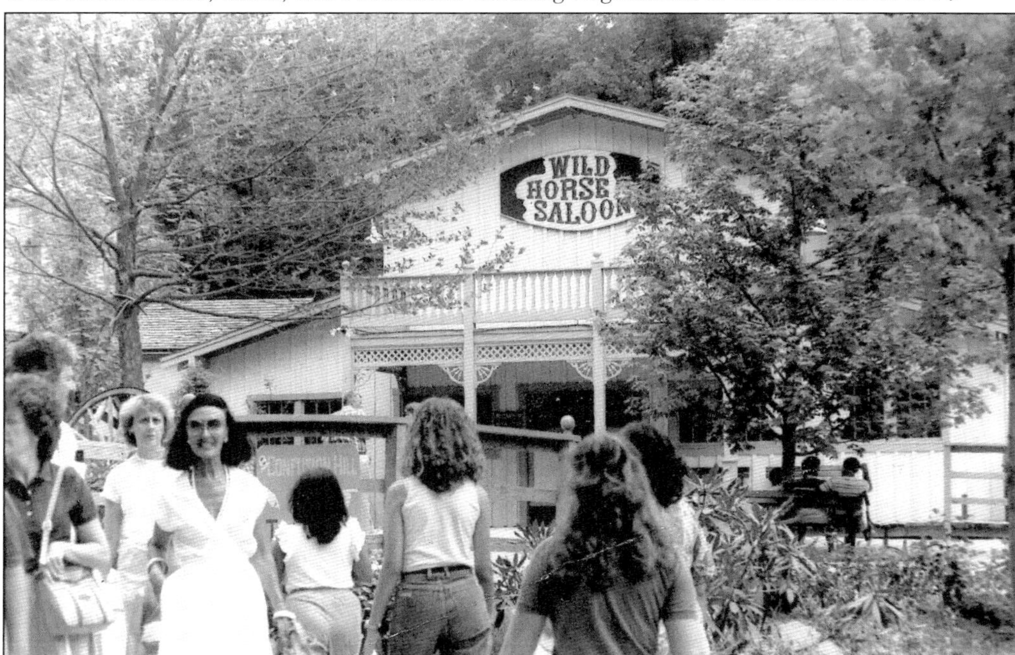

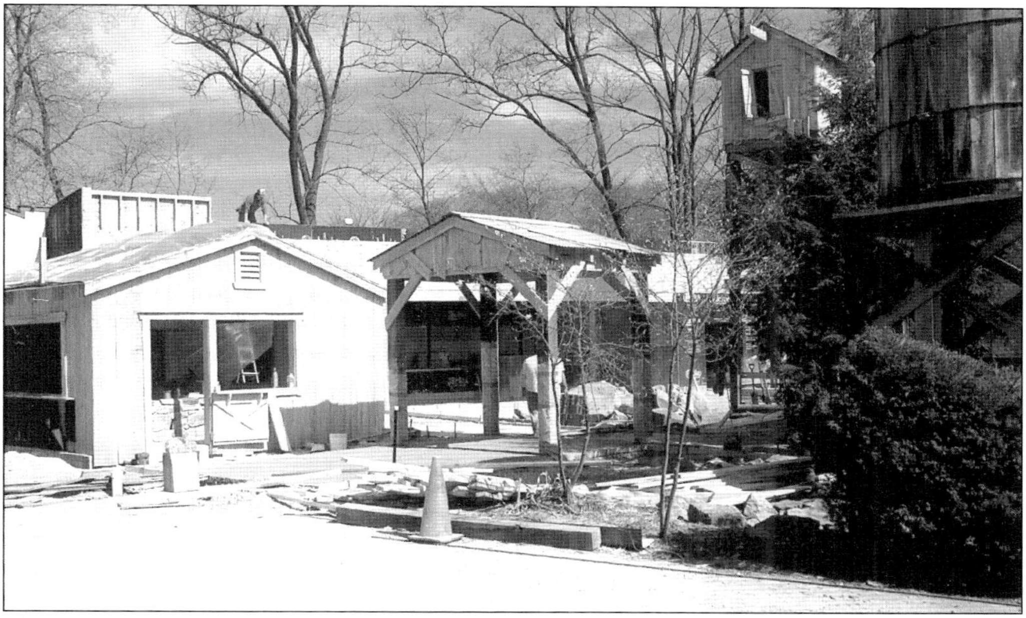

The Mineshaft Kitchen replaced the Wild Horse Saloon. The popular eatery combined many of Idlewild's favorite food choices into a food-court atmosphere. The Barbeque Pit, Potato Patch, a bakery, and a drink stand were the initial occupants, but the building has also housed Big Zack's Hoagies and Loco Roberto's Tacos. The first image shows some of the construction of the food court, and the second image shows the completed western side.

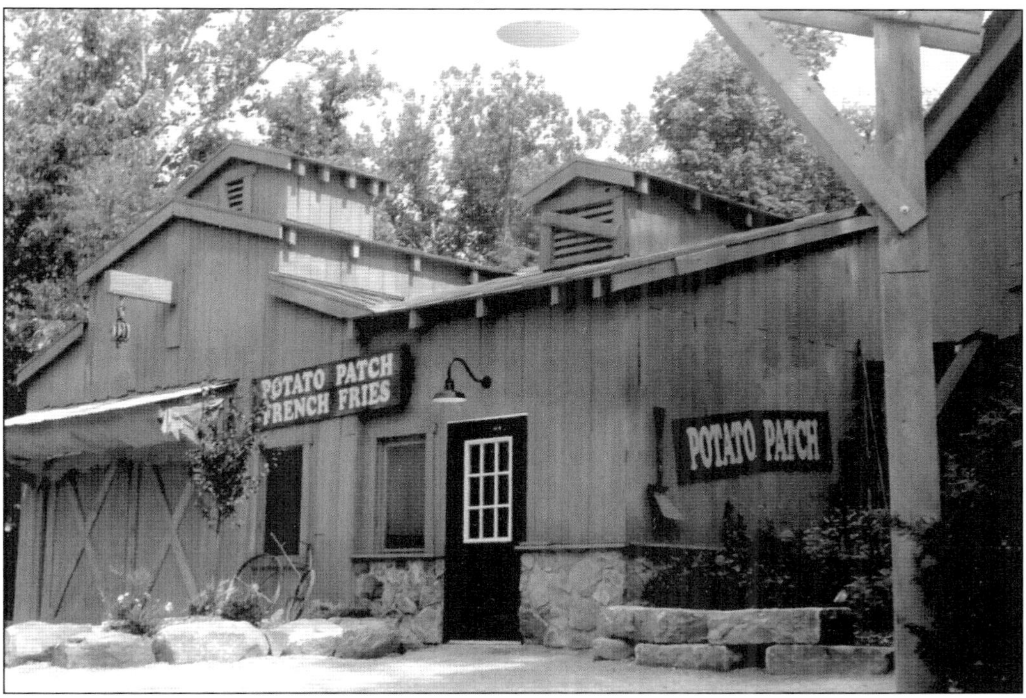

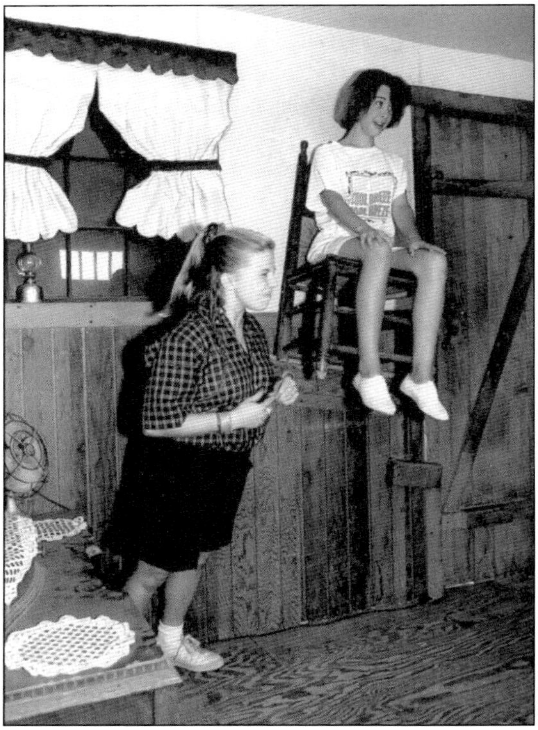

Visitors to Hootin' Holler can stop by Confusion Hill for an eyeful of illusions. Water runs uphill and chairs magically balance on two legs. The walk-through attraction has been a fixture of Hootin' Holler since the theme town's inception in 1984. Tracy Peltz-Palko is pictured here, leading a tour through the crooked hotel while a lucky guest gets to try out Half-Pint Pete's unusual chair.

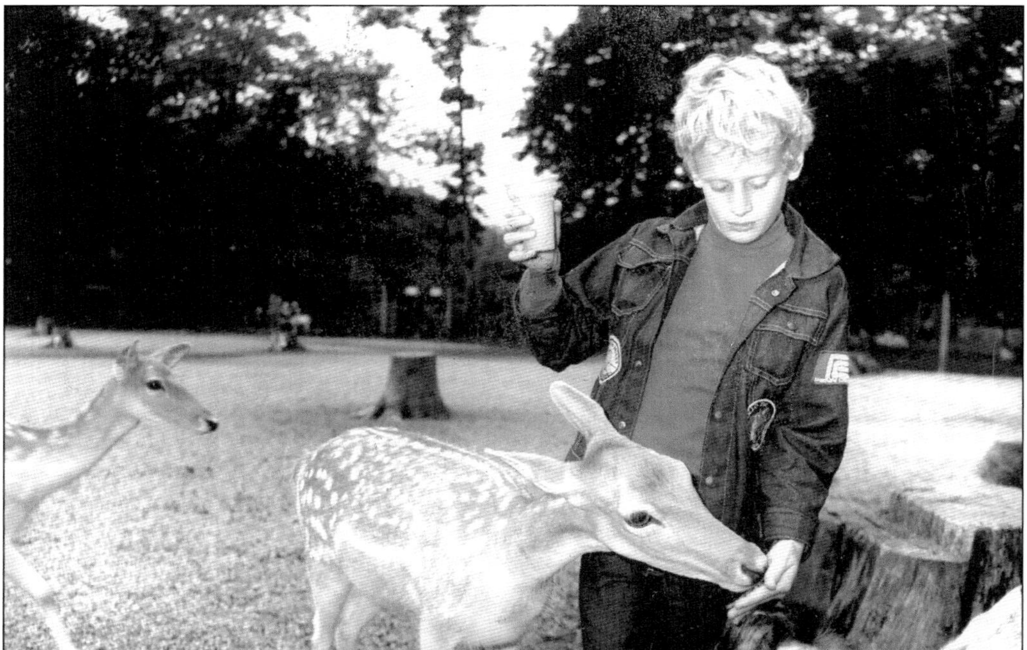

Charles Macdonald feeds the deer near the Frontier Zoo in this undated photograph. In 1986, the New Zoo Revue replaced the Frontier Zoo. It featured a petting zoo, prairie dog mounds, and a humorous circus sideshow. Raccoon Lagoon took over the entire area in 1990.

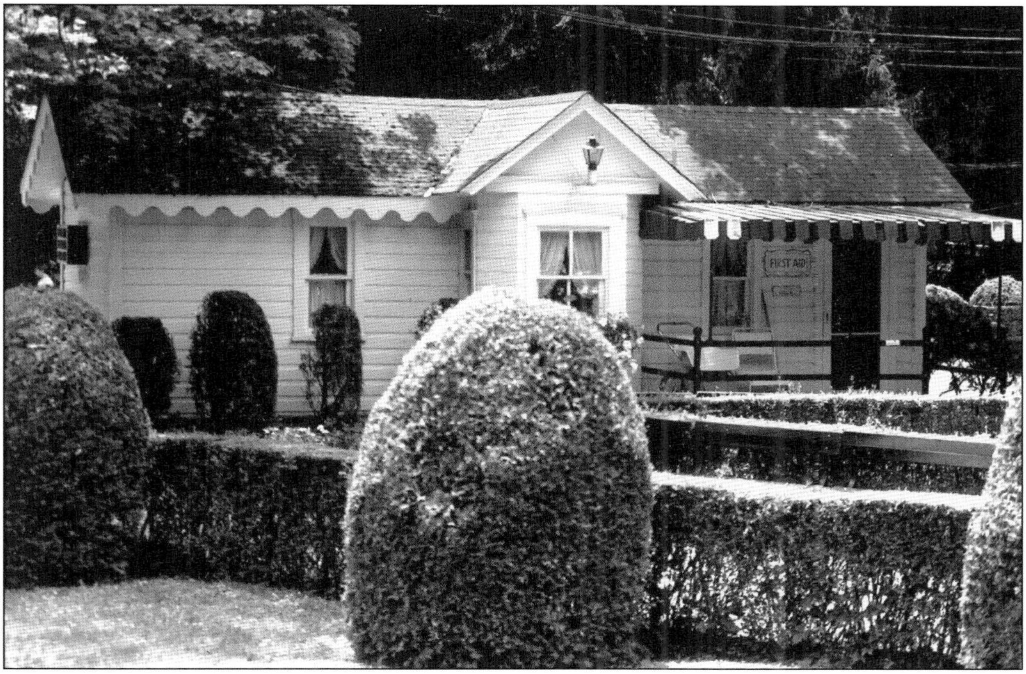

The original Idlewild depot has been well maintained throughout the years. These 1988 photographs show both sides of the building while it served as the park's first aid station. In later years, the building became guest services. In 2002, it was converted into a small museum, displaying photographs and artifacts and honoring the park's 125 seasons.

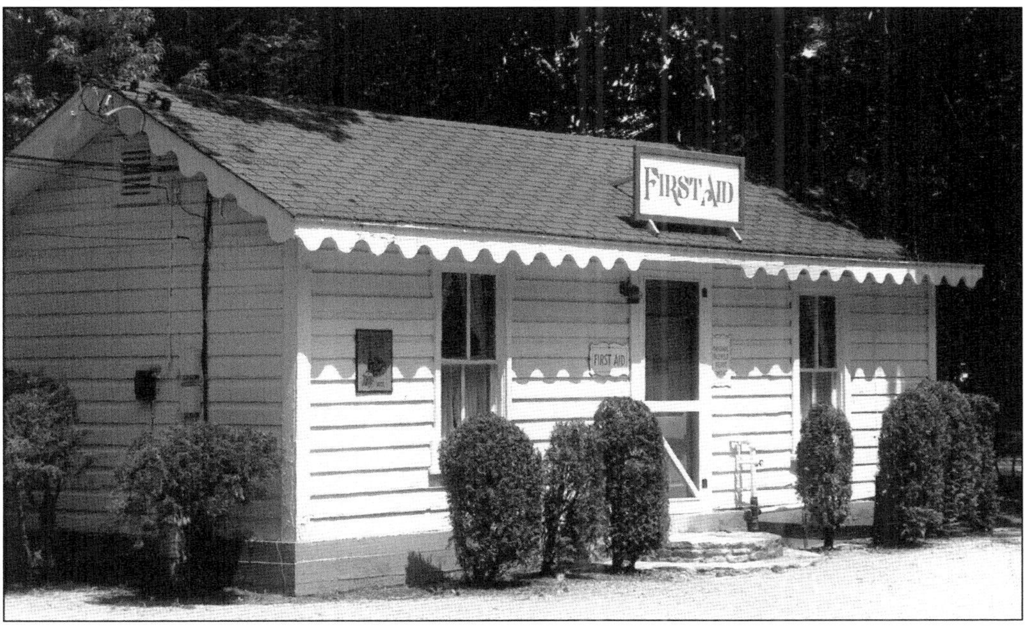

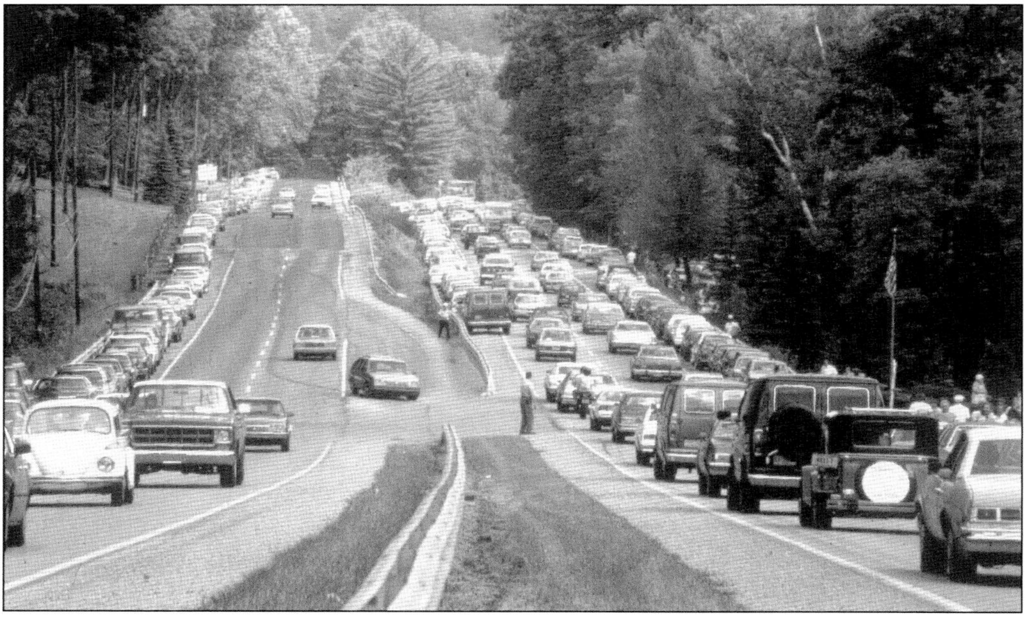

With all the new attractions added to the park in the early- to mid-1980s, attendance began to skyrocket. This photograph was taken on September 1, 1985, when Idlewild was hosting a picnic for the Greensburg Catholic Diocese. All parking lots were filled to capacity and cars were forced to park along Lincoln Highway.

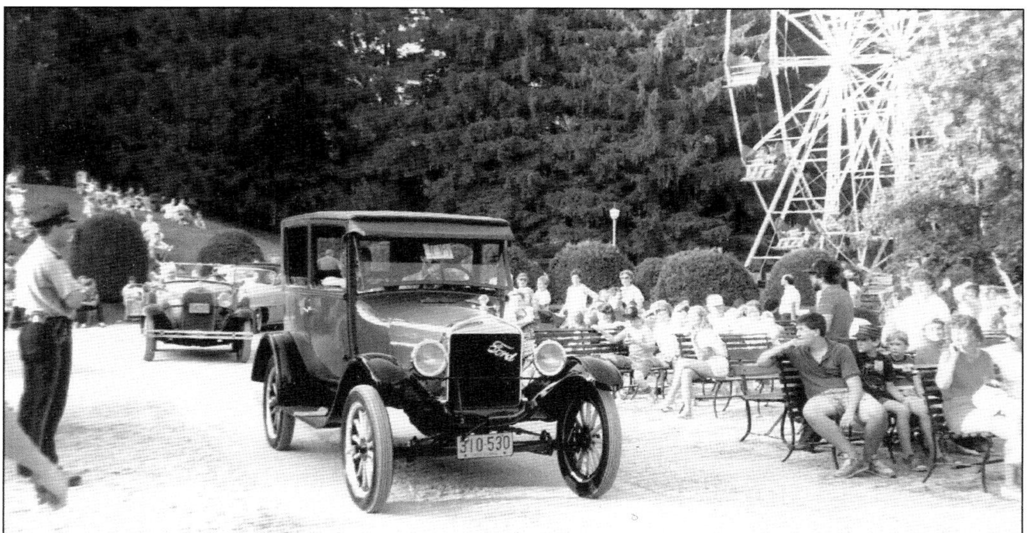

The annual week-long celebration of Old Fashioned Days features artisans, craft booths, street performers, and dancing and musical acts. The highlight of the event is the antique car parade held each evening through the center of the park. It draws classic automobile buffs from all over western Pennsylvania. In recent years, it has proved so popular that the park has, unfortunately, had to limit the number of entrants. Since the parade necessitates the temporary closing of some of the park's midways, a parade too lengthy tends to strand guests in one portion of the park.

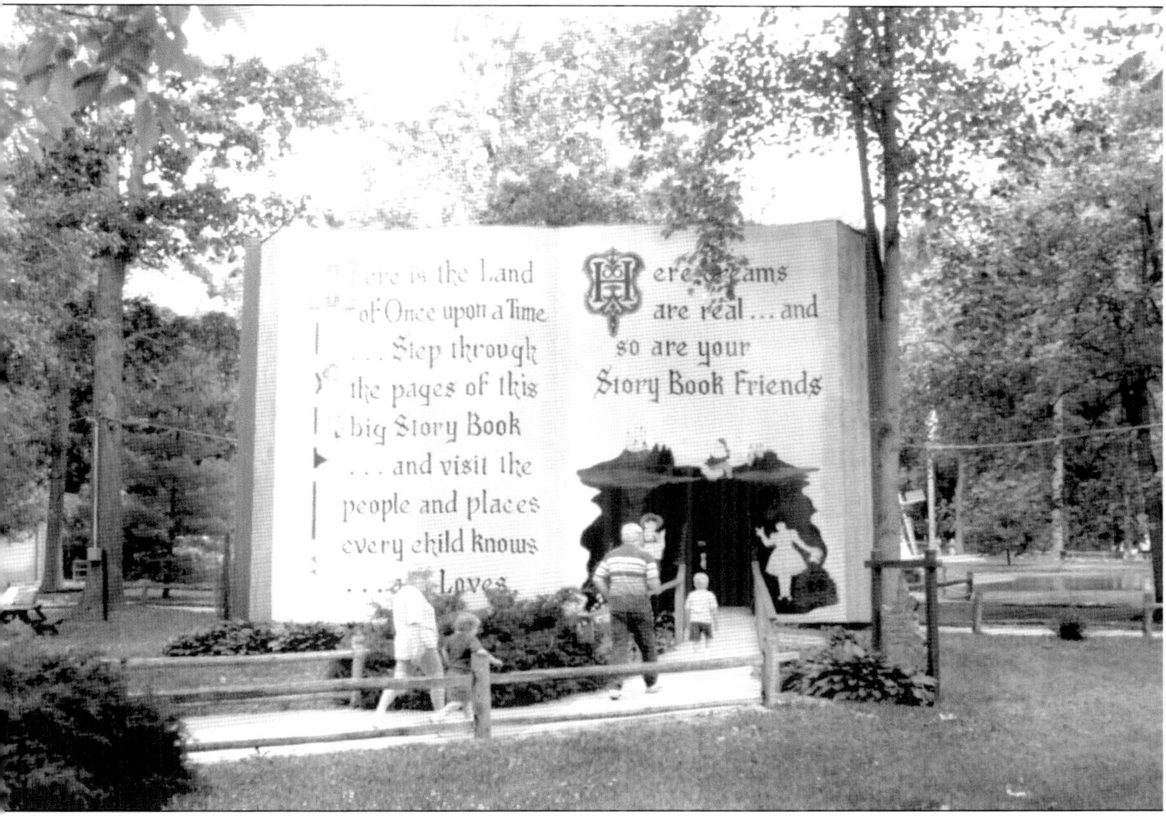

Affectionately known simply as "the Book," the entranceway to Story Book Forest was relocated closer to the Idlewild amusement rides when Kennywood Park Corporation decided to operate them as a single attraction. With a new entry point, passenger traffic through the forest was redirected clockwise from its previous counter-clockwise route. The backward route took several years for faithful visitors to get used to and still garners comments of confusion from some guests who have not visited since childhood.

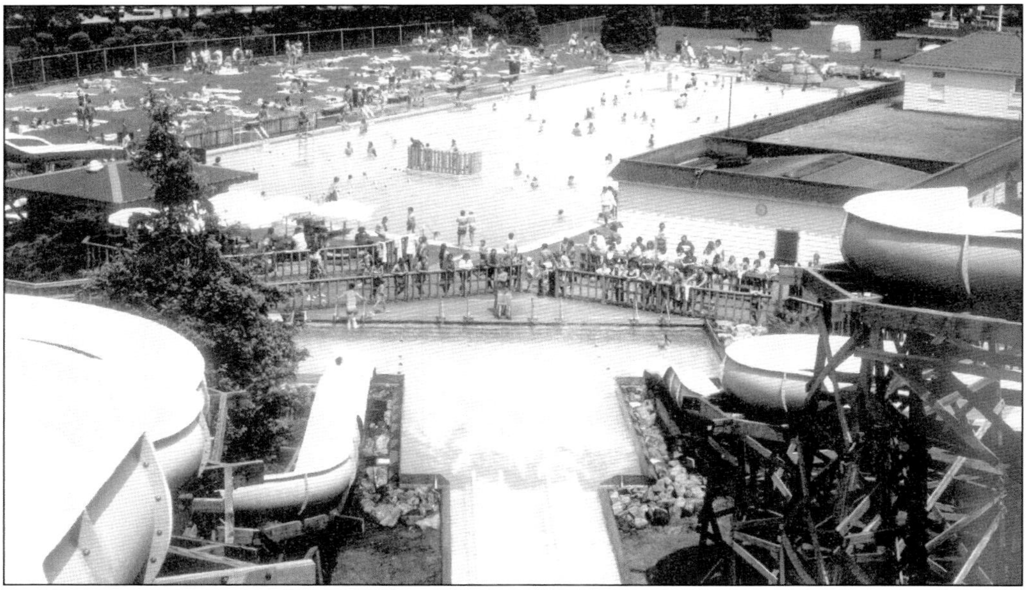

Two winding body slides and two speed slides were added near the swimming pool in 1985. Two shotgun slides, emptying directly into the swimming pool, were added the following year. The entire water complex, known as the H2Ohhhh Zone, allowed Idlewild to compete in the water park boom that was erupting around the country. The top of the water slide tower provides an excellent view of the pool and beach.

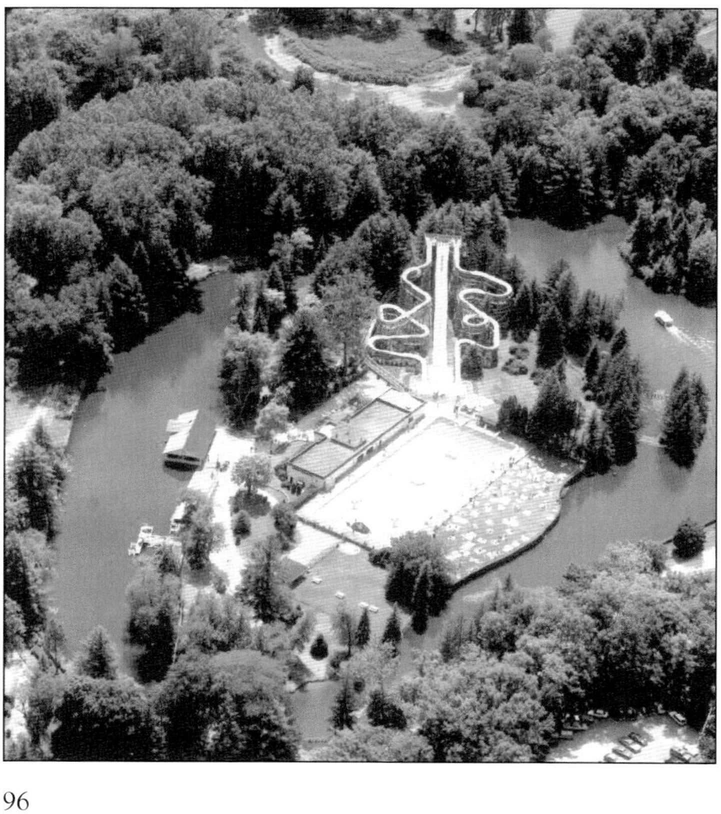

Once known as Flower Island, the home of hundreds of trees, shrubs, and flowers, the island looks remarkably different in this aerial view from 1985.

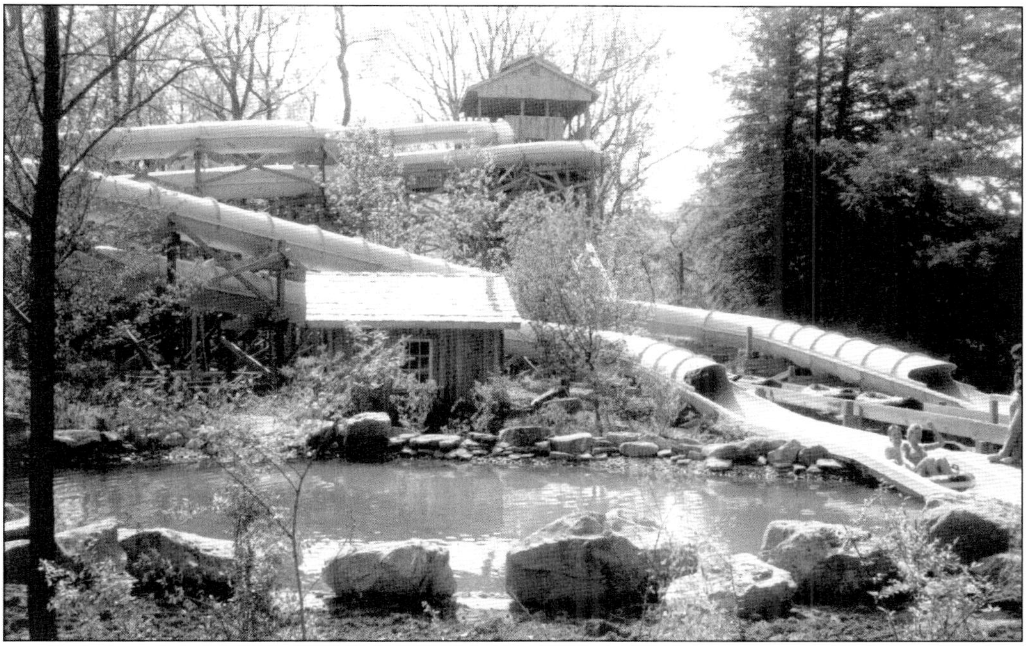

Rafter's Run was constructed adjacent to the H2Ohhhh Zone in 1986. At this popular attraction, two-person rafts run down one of two winding tubes, ending in a splash pool.

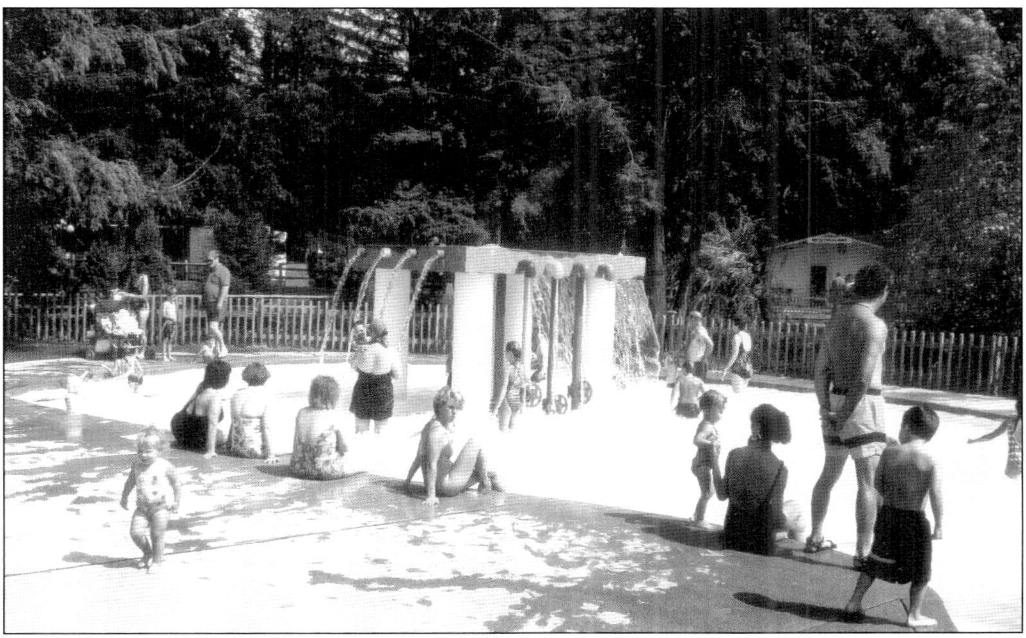

Built as an addition to the H2Ohhhh Zone in 1992, Little Squirts is a children's pool with fountains and sprayers. For families with younger children, the new feature provided an area away from the large crowds cooling off in the park's main pool.

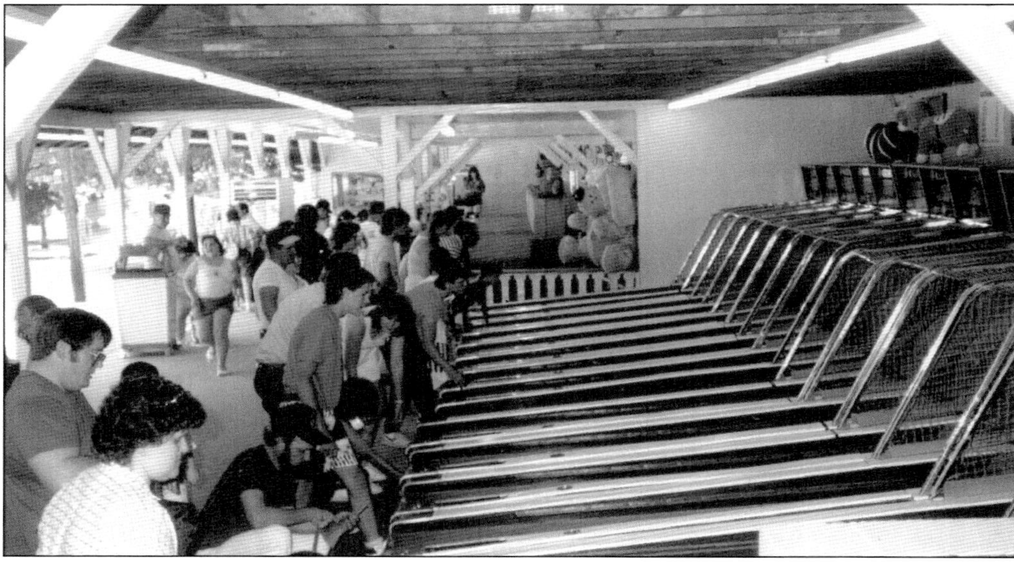

The Skee-Ball alleys were a popular place on this day in the mid-1980s. Since the early Macdonald years, Skee-Ball has offered guests the chance to redeem tickets won from the game for various prizes—from toys to household appliances. In 2000, the prizes were changed to stuffed animals only. In 2003, after 75 years, Skee-Ball was officially retired, giving way to the new water-gun race game, Rising Waters.

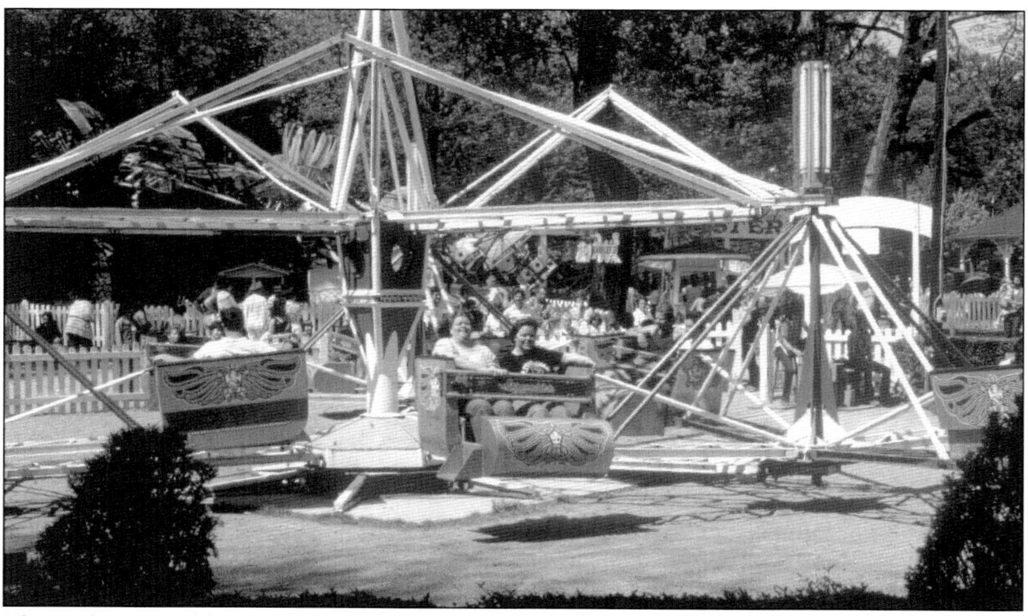

The park's Scrambler, manufactured by the Eli Bridge Company, first appeared in 1977. It sat on the western side of the carousel for many years before moving to its current location on the eastern side of the carousel.

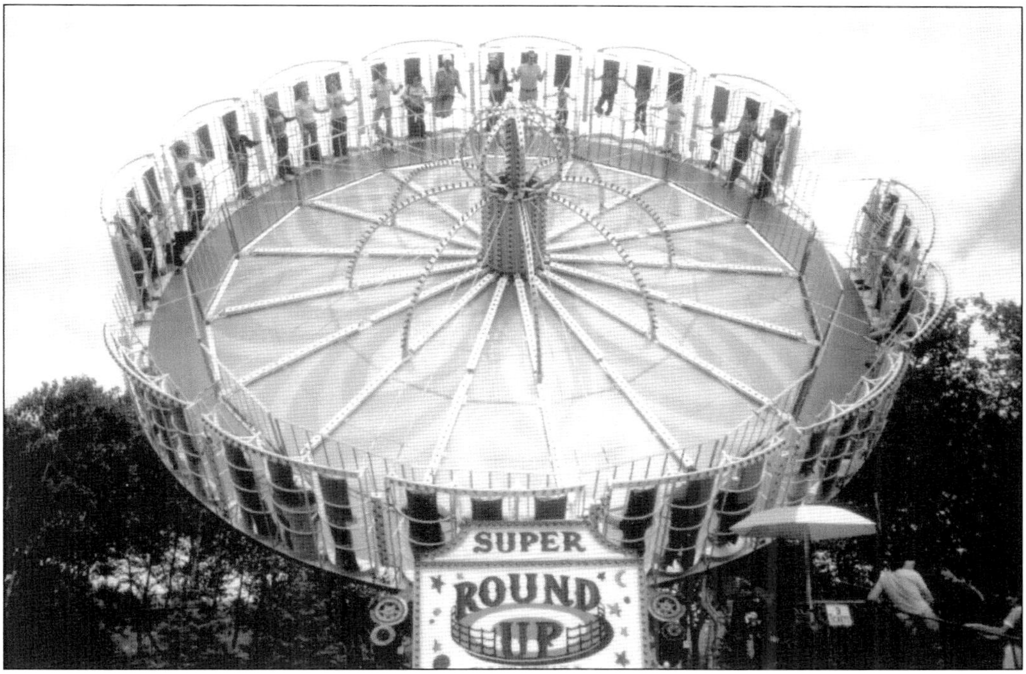

The Super Round-Up, a larger version of the ride that was retired in 1983, was added in 1986. Manufactured by Frank Hrubetz and Company, the 42-person ride is located along the Loyalhanna Creek at the former site of the circle swing.

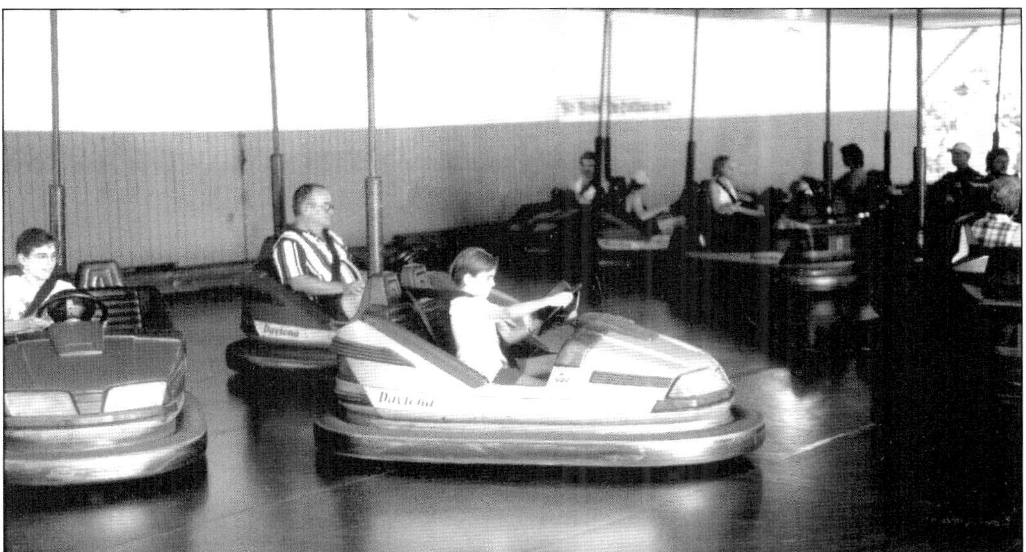

The first electrically operated amusement ride at Idlewild, the septuagenarian skooter ride, has not lost any of its popularity. When this photograph was taken, the ride was on its third set of cars.

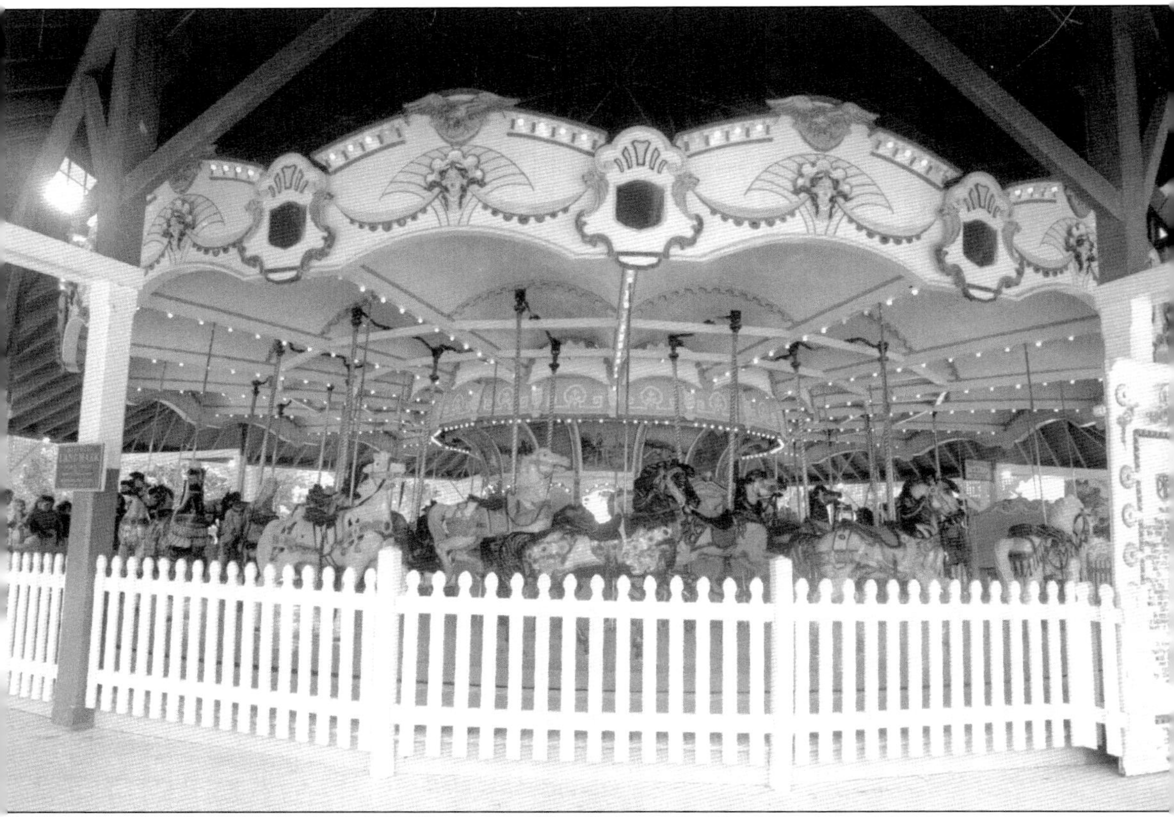

Park artists lovingly restored the beautiful 1930 Philadelphia Toboggan Company No. 83—Idlewild's carousel—over a two-year period. In 1984, Ed Ostroski, Rosemary Overly, and Dale Johnson stripped and repainted all 48 horses and two beautiful chariots. The following year they worked on the carousel facade, decking, and organs. Idlewild's carousel was one of the last built of the solid-wood horse variety; newer models are made from metal or plastic.

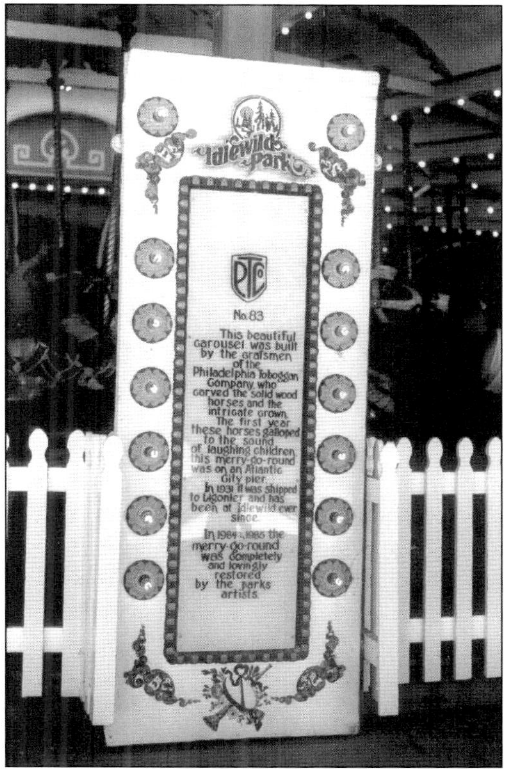

The attractive placard above is featured as an informative history of a classic ride. On July 21, 1987, Edward F. Nowlin, president of the Westmoreland County Historical Society, designated the Idlewild Carousel a historic landmark.

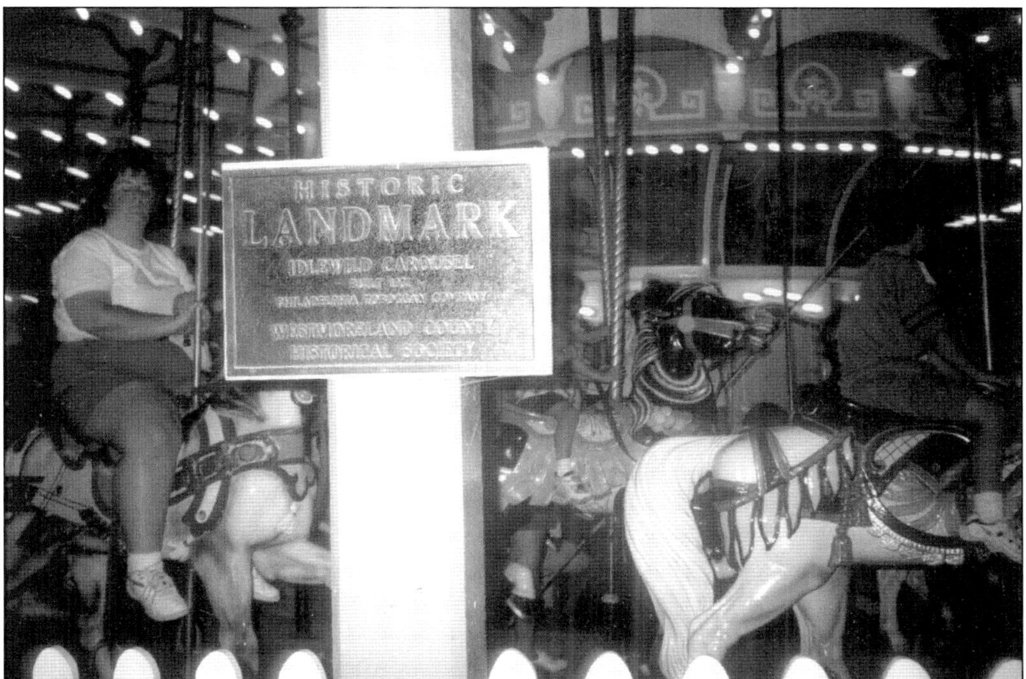

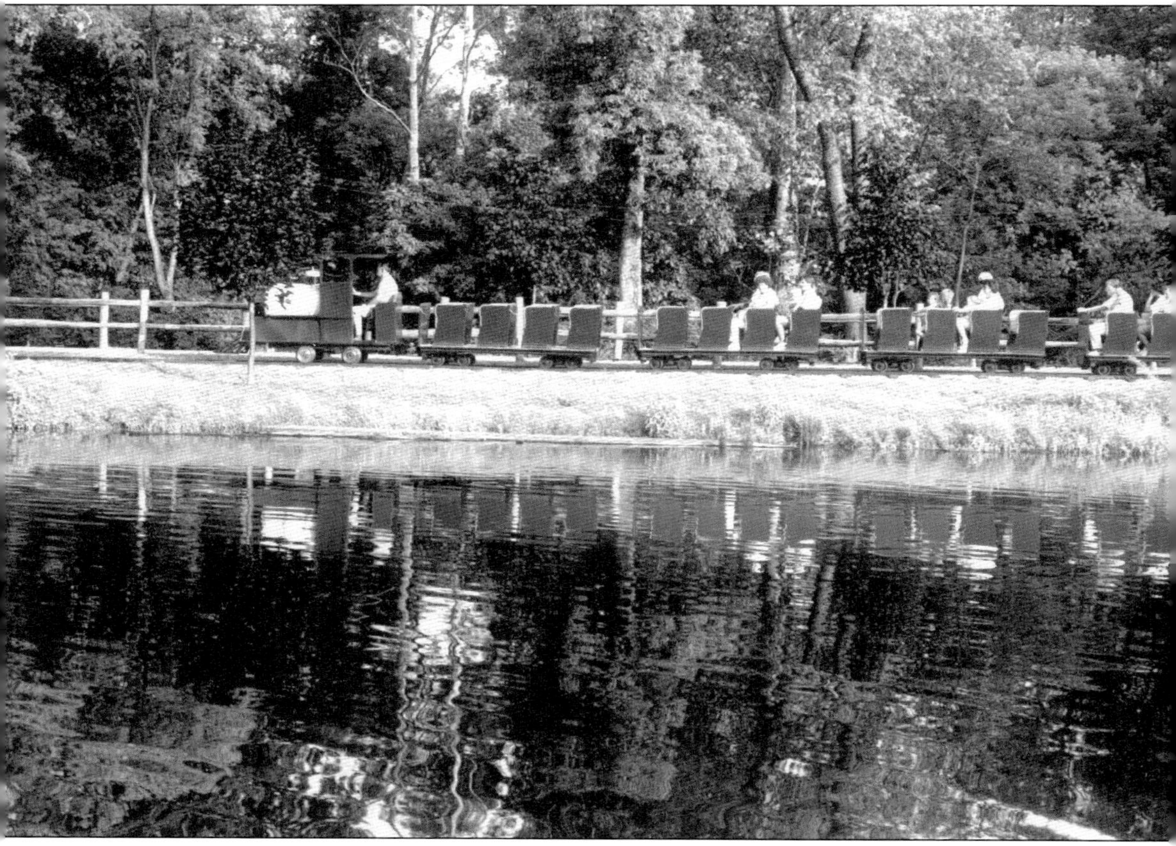

With the closing of the Ligonier Valley Rail Road in 1952, only the Idlewild Express continued to run along the banks of Lake Bouquet. Due to the expense and difficulty in finding parts for the aging ride, it was removed in 1997.

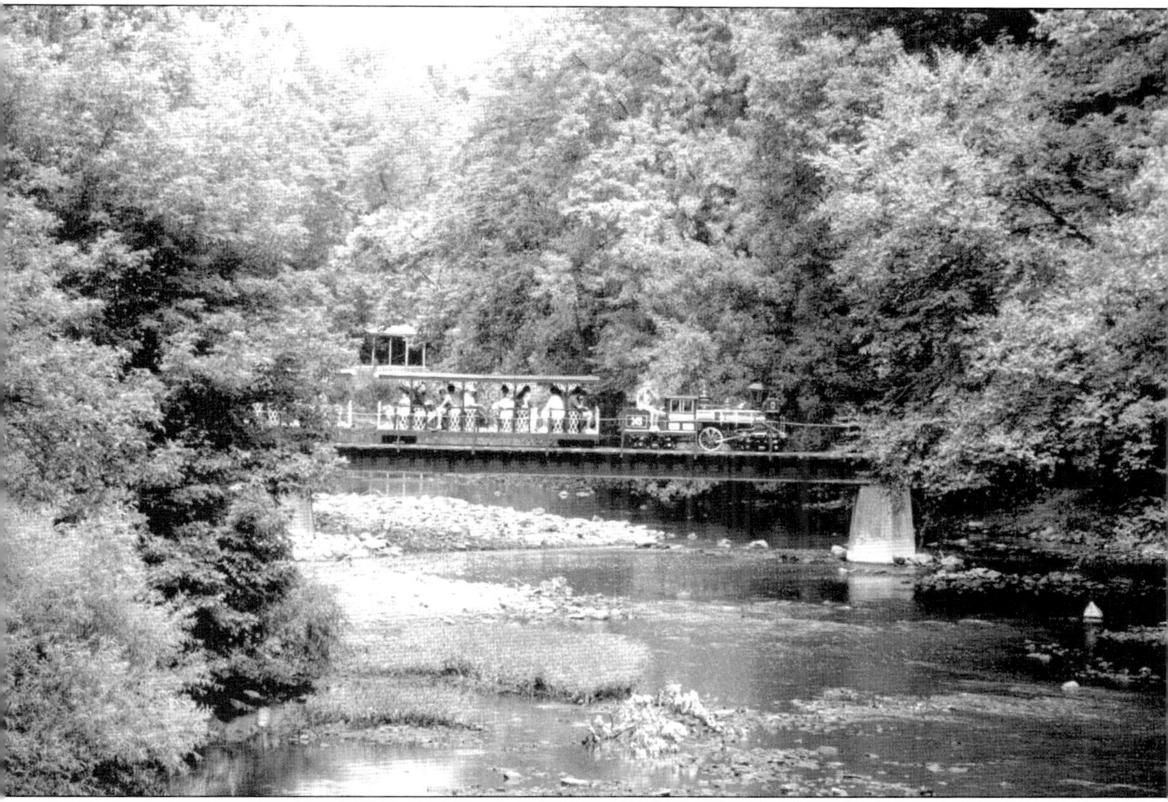

The Loyalhanna Creek flows through the center of Idlewild. Four bridges have been constructed over the years to cross its waters. The Loyalhanna Limited's C. P. Huntingdon trains use two spans, whereas two others are for pedestrian traffic.

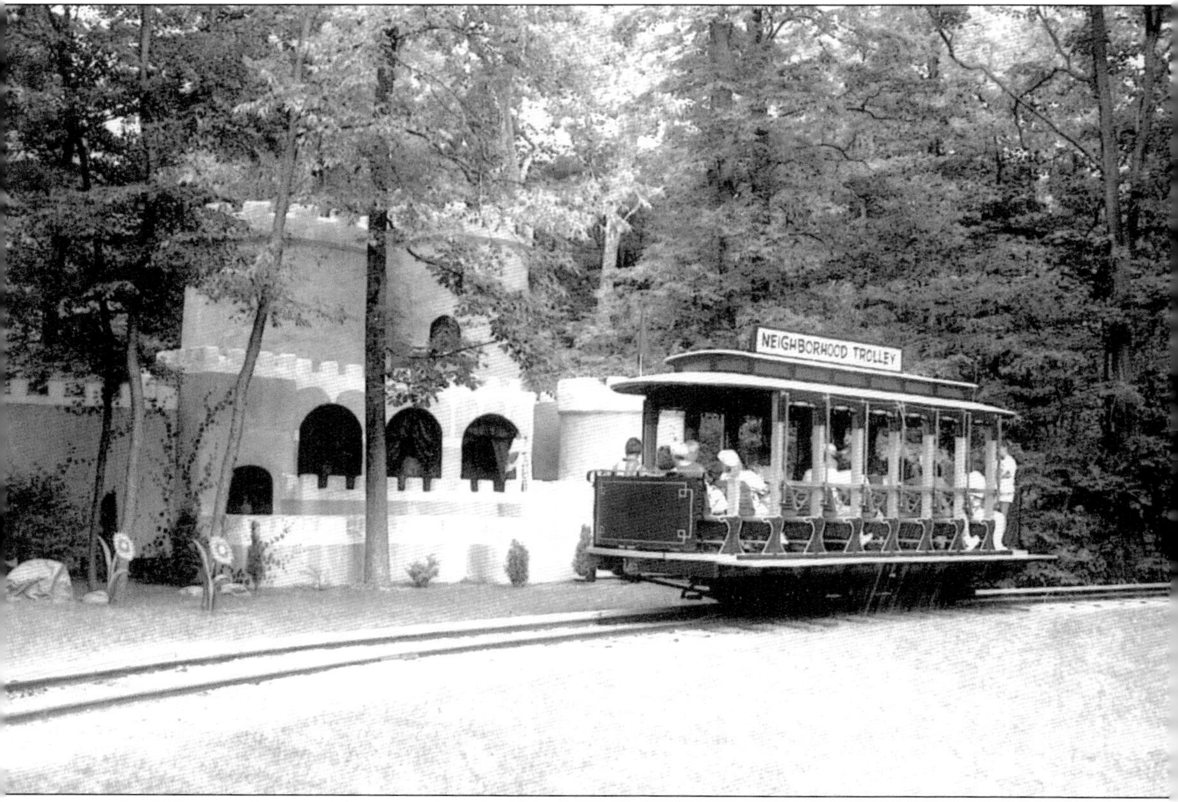

Fred Rogers, host of the popular children's series *Mister Rogers' Neighborhood*, was born March 20, 1928, in Latrobe. As a child, he attended the park for family and school picnics. He enjoyed its family atmosphere so much that he approached the Kennywood Entertainment Company about designing an attraction specially for Idlewild. Mister Rogers designed a life size trolley ride through the neighborhood of Make-Believe, where passengers, young and old, interact with animated characters from the series. He wrote the script and provided all the voices for the characters. The attraction, located across the creek near the old zoo area, opened in 1989 to tremendous response. Idlewild's most expensive expansion project, up until that time, had proved to be its most successful.

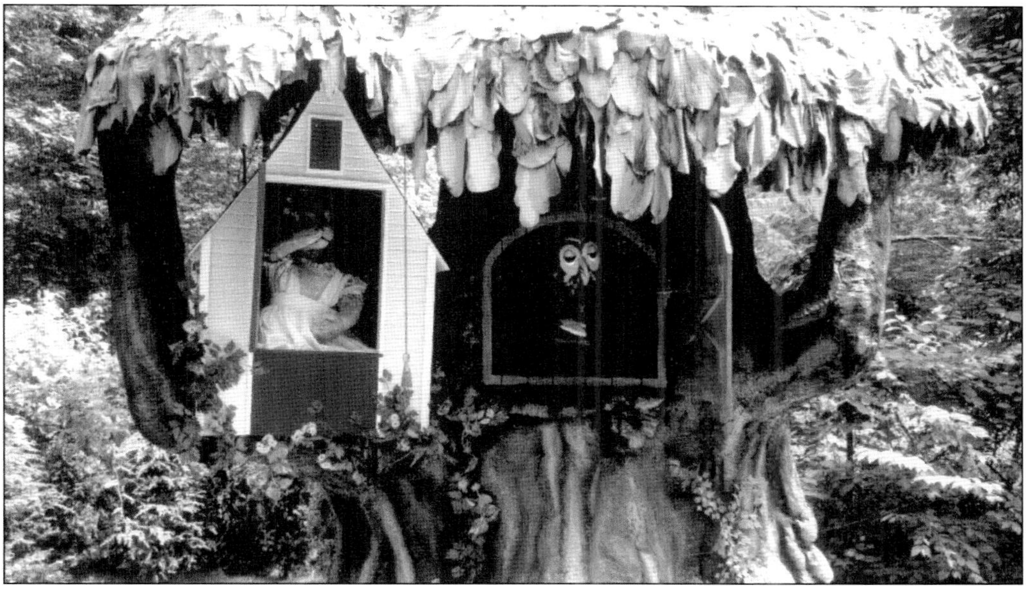

The trolley makes a stop at each character's house, including the tree where Henrietta Pussycat and X the Owl reside. The animated characters and the trolley riders interact with each other along the route. Two trolleys run concurrently on the circular track. It is imperative for the trolley drivers to time their travels precisely so that neither trolley is in sight of the other.

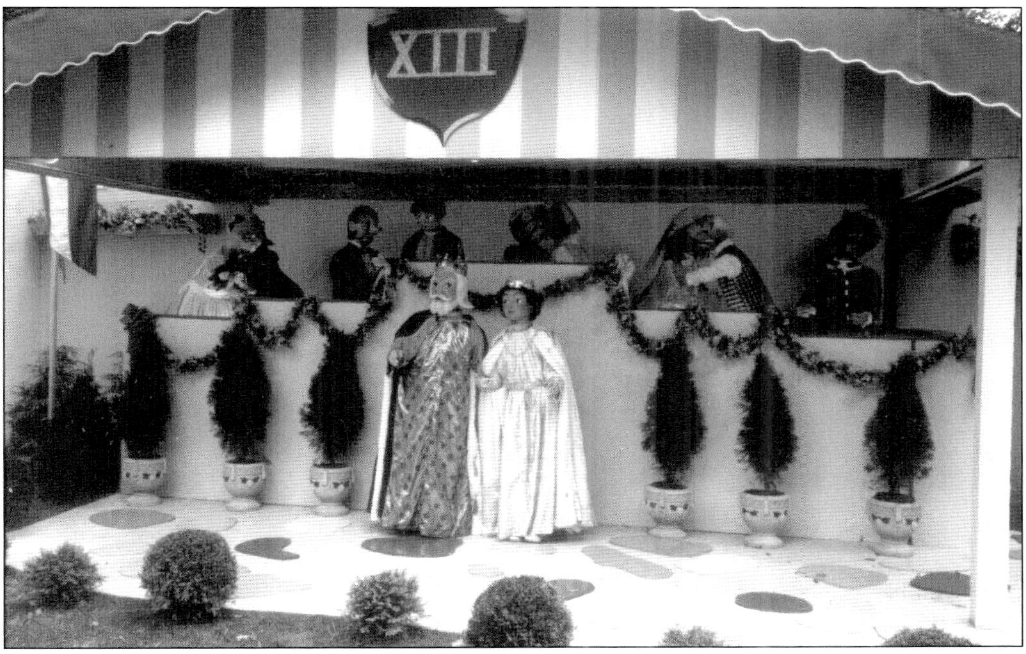

The culmination of the trolley ride is a "hug-and-song party" at the castle courtyard, where all the characters join together. No other amusement ride ends with hugging and the singing of a song. The ride is unique to the world; the management and staff of the park are very proud to have this attraction as one of their own.

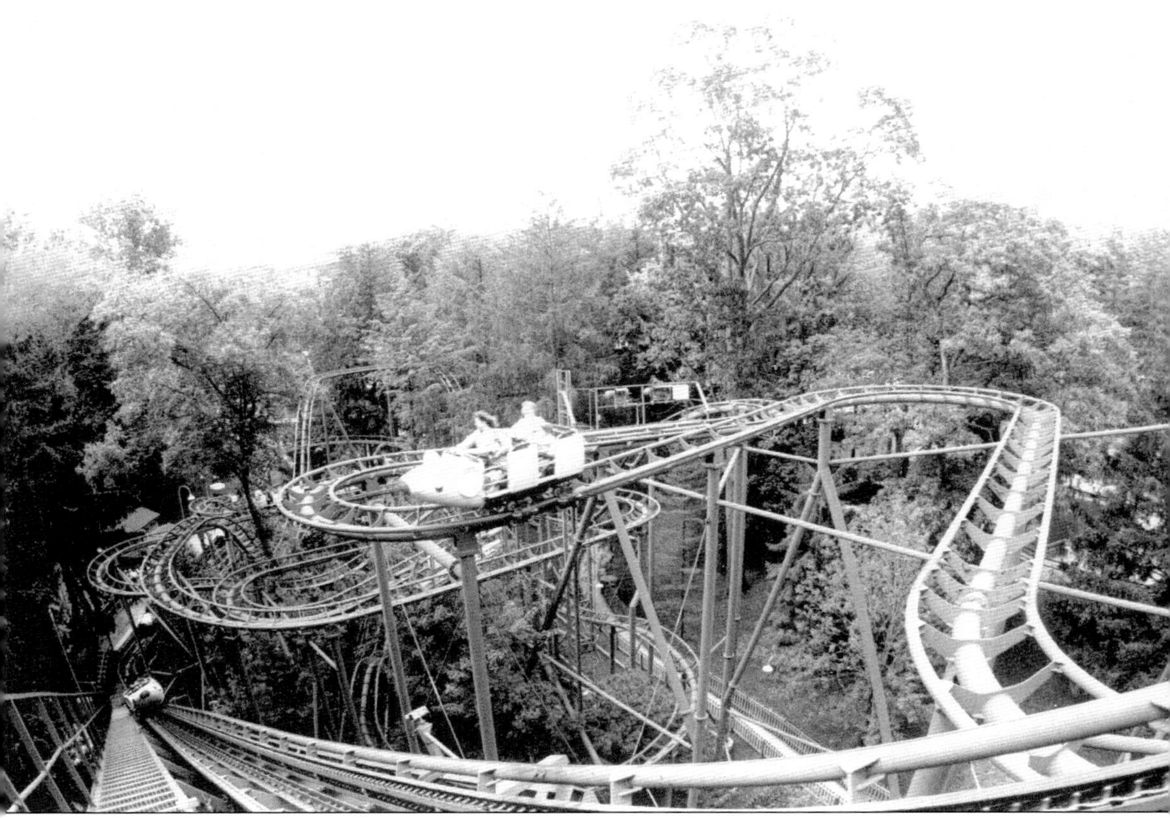

From the top of the lift, one can see how the Wild Mouse steel coaster's sharp curves and dips were intricately nestled among the natural surroundings. The site of the Wild Mouse (which debuted in 1993) was the former Kiddieland on the north bank of the Loyalhanna Creek. Before arriving at Idlewild, the ride stood at Alton Towers, England.

The construction of the Wild Mouse took place in the winter of 1992 and 1993. This is a photograph of one member of the construction crew, perched high among the trees.

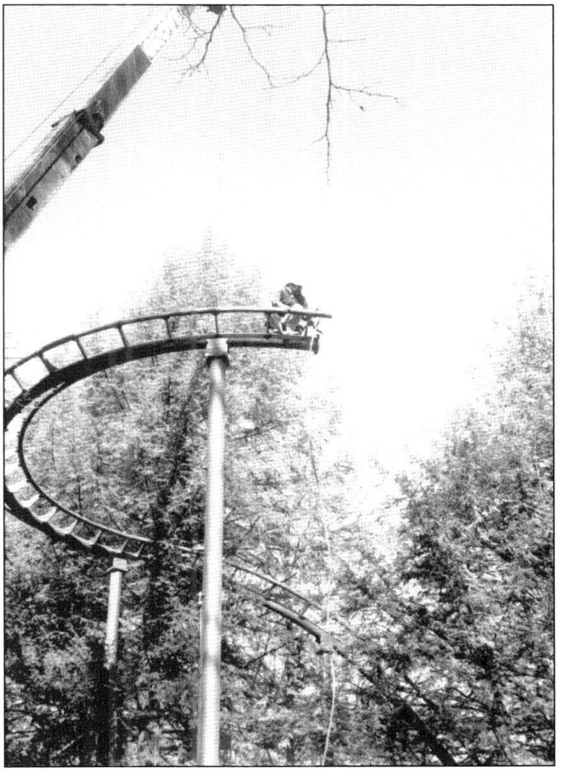

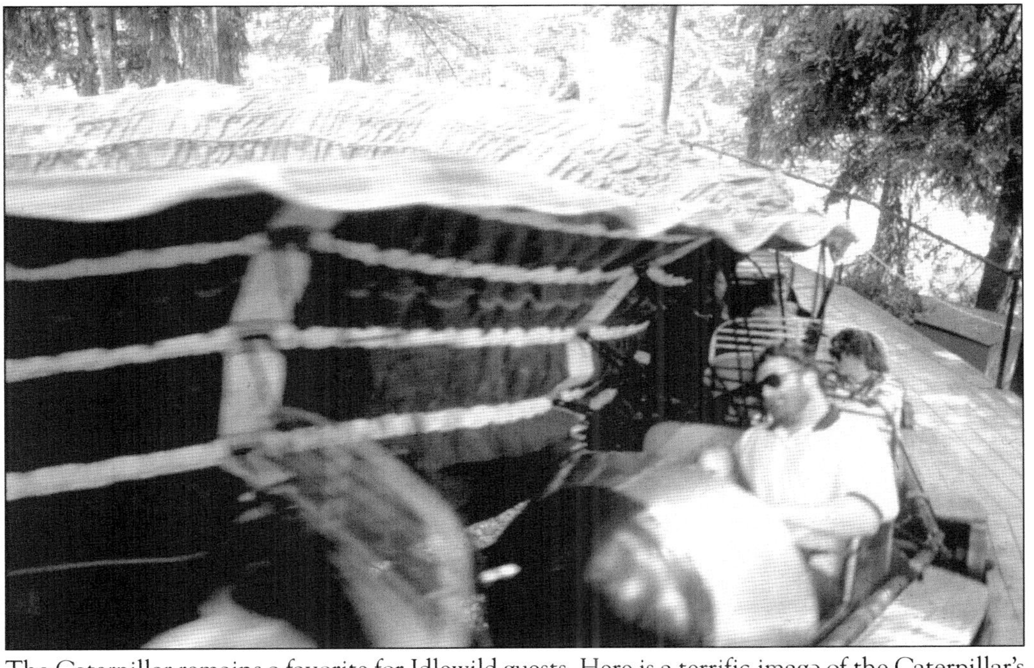

The Caterpillar remains a favorite for Idlewild guests. Here is a terrific image of the Caterpillar's tarp in motion, about to cover its riders.

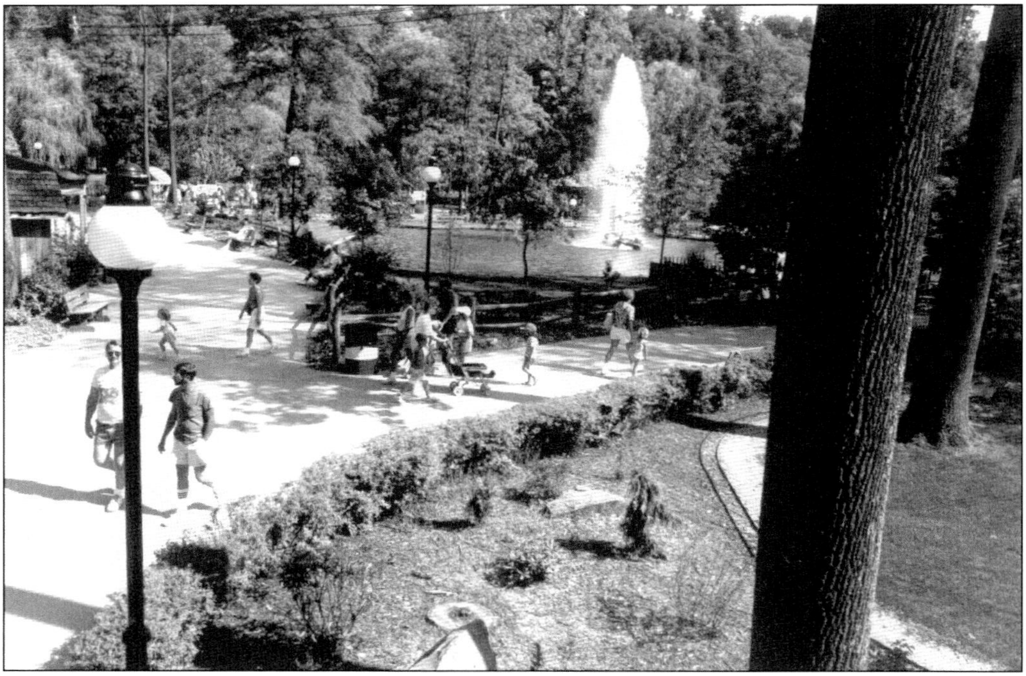

To further enhance its popularity as a family park, Idlewild developed Raccoon Lagoon in 1990. All the children's rides were relocated to this spacious area formerly occupied by the zoo. The area also includes a food stand, gift shop, duck pond, and rest rooms.

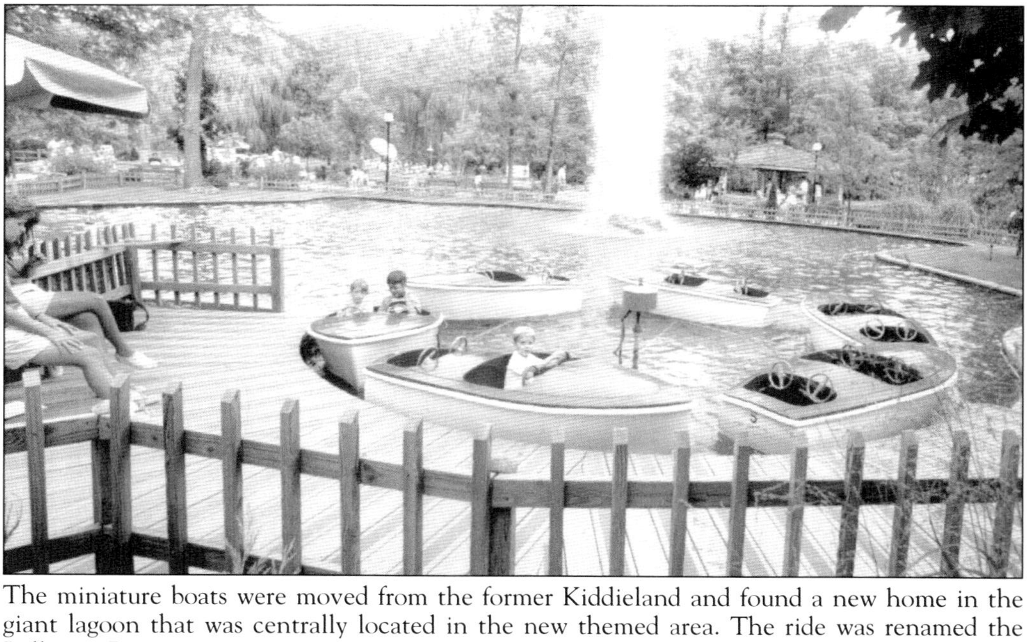

The miniature boats were moved from the former Kiddieland and found a new home in the giant lagoon that was centrally located in the new themed area. The ride was renamed the Pollywog Regatta.

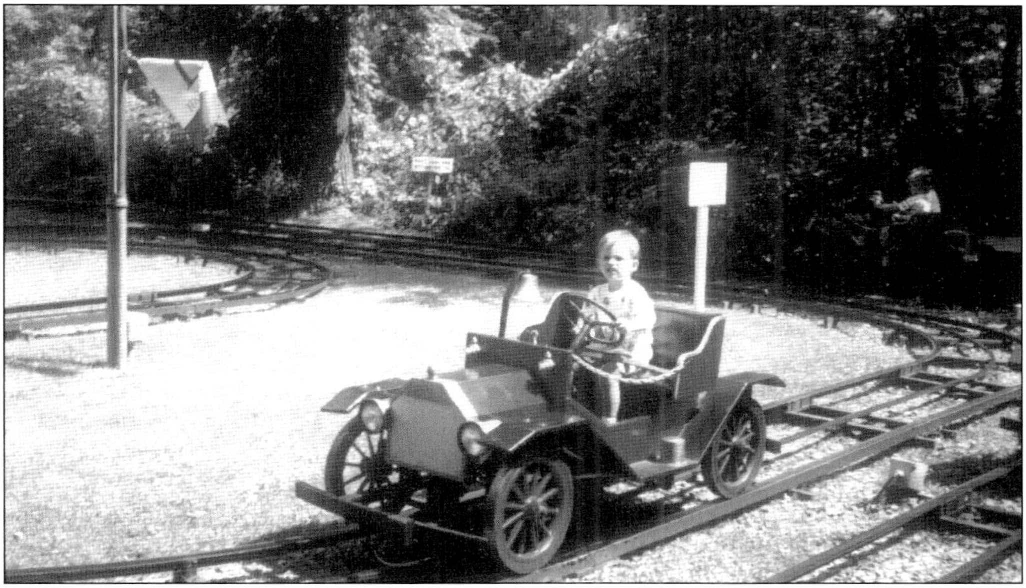

The Flivvers also moved from the old Kiddieland. This ride was themed to commemorate the Lincoln Highway, which played an important role in the growth of Idlewild, especially once the railroad ceased operating. A Lincoln Highway banner hangs from the lamppost to the left of this photograph. (Courtesy Carol Croushore.)

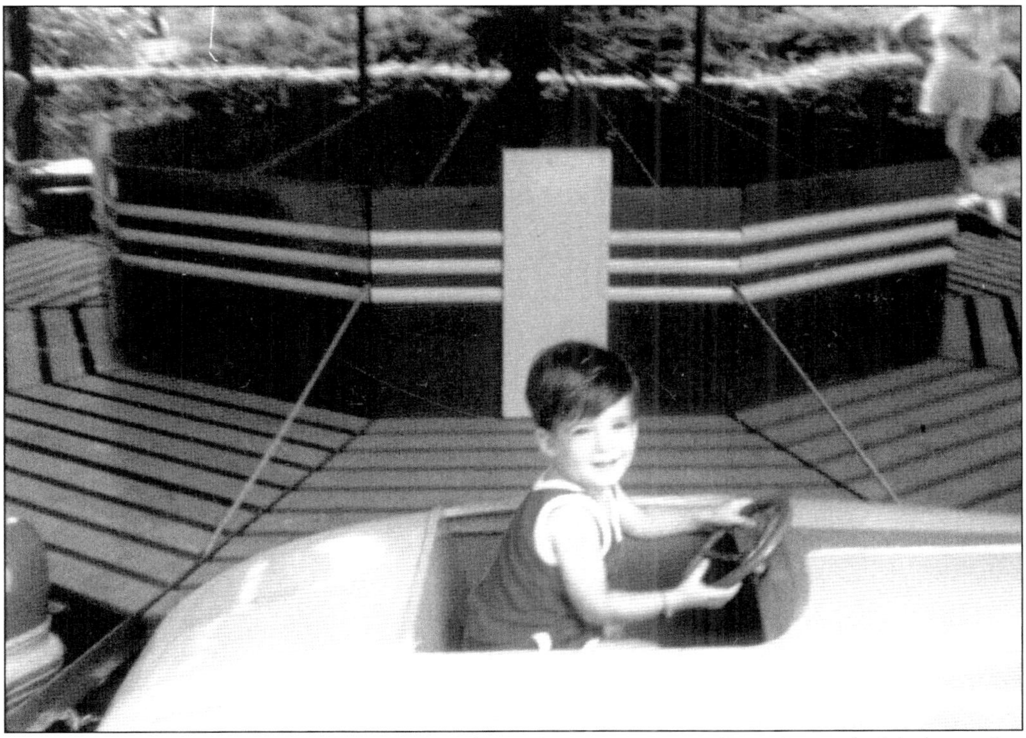

The Scampers have been at Idlewild since the 1950s. Here, young Dan Goswick delights in his turn around the track. (Courtesy Christy Goswick.)

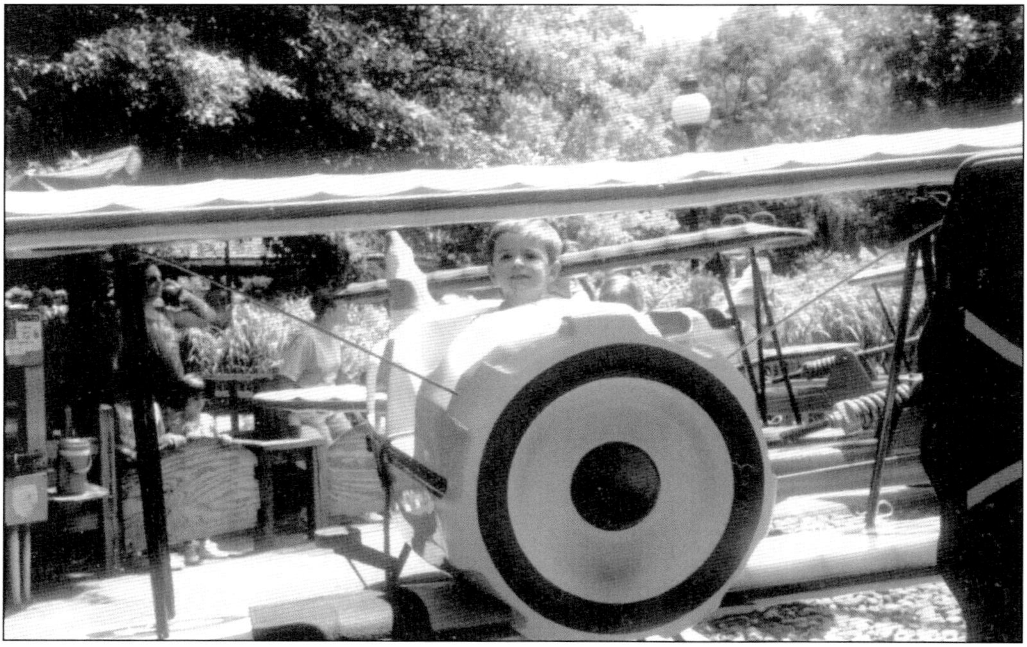

The Red Baron ride gives children a chance to "fly" their own plane. Controls within the cockpit raise and lower the aircraft. In this photograph from July 1999, Christopher Wood prepares to soar. (Courtesy Christy Goswick.)

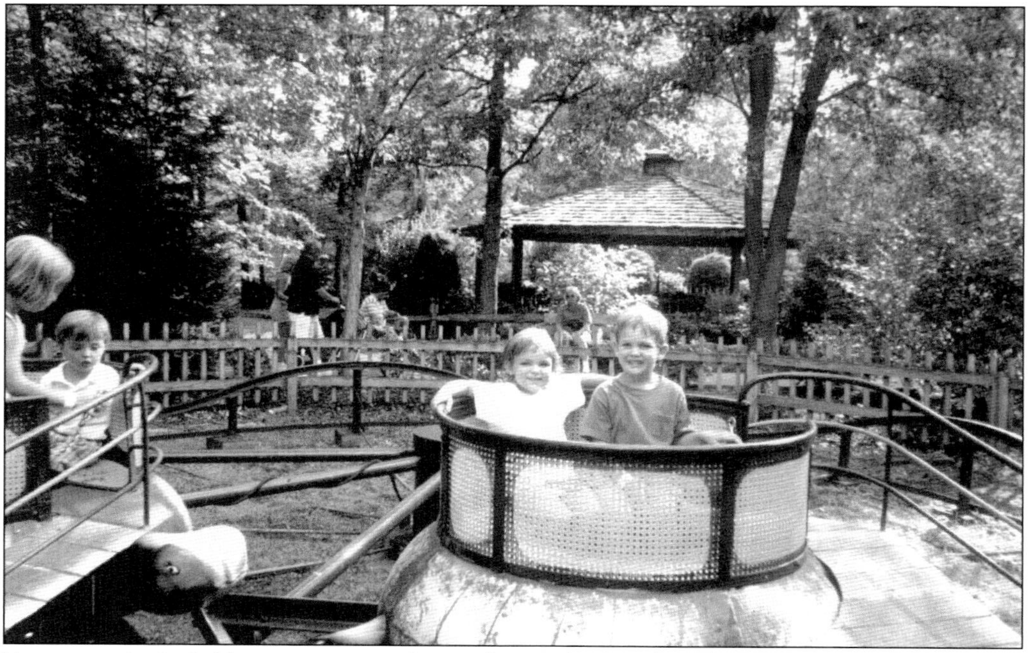

Young, excited children anticipate their ride on the Turtle. The ride, present since 1956, features turtle-shaped cars traveling on an undulating track. Offering more legroom than most children's rides, the Turtle is one of only two in Raccoon Lagoon where a parent can ride along with his or her child. (Courtesy Carol Croushore.)

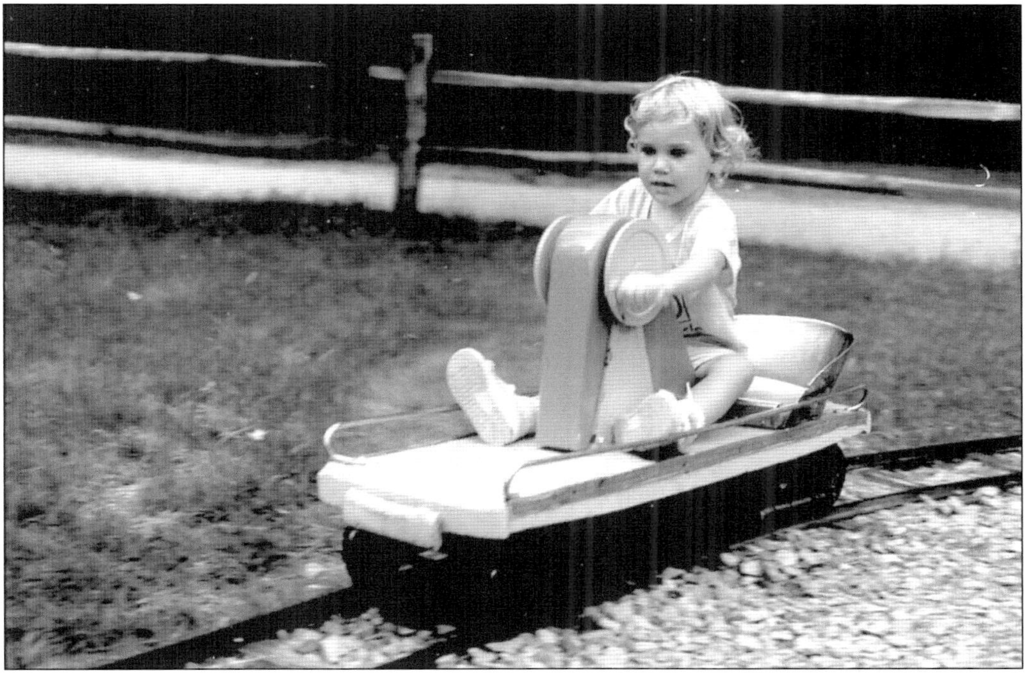

The handcars are truly a classic ride. Idlewild offers two versions: the kiddie and the adult. The kiddie handcars (above) let the child crank the cars around the track. The adult handcars let the parent do all the hard work while the child sits there like royalty. Below, Jacob Croushore waves to the camera as his mother, Kerri, takes him for a spin. (Below, courtesy Carol Croushore.)

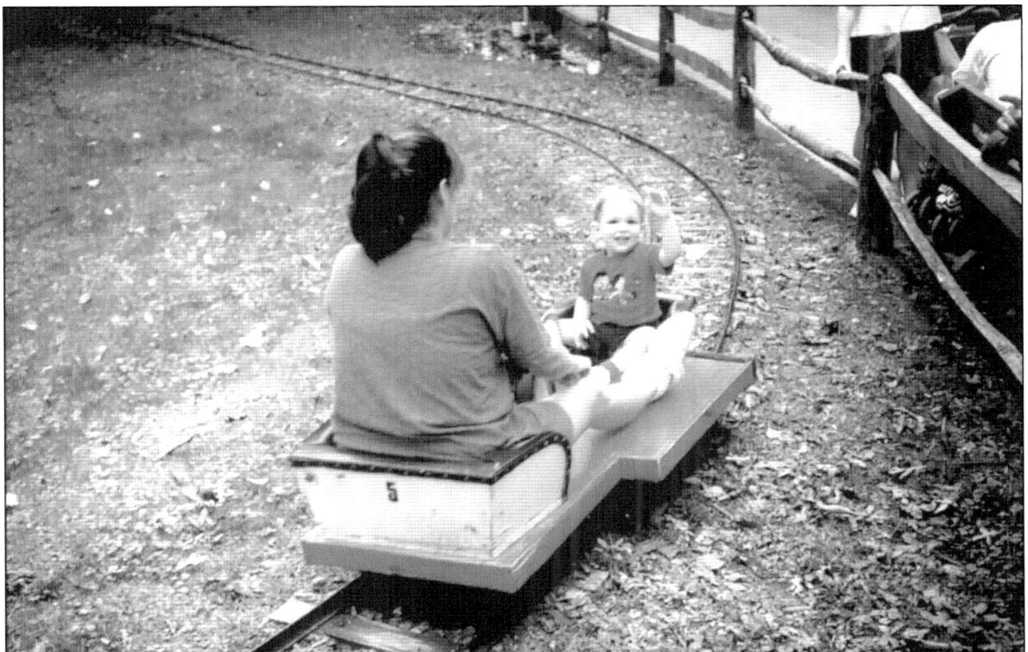

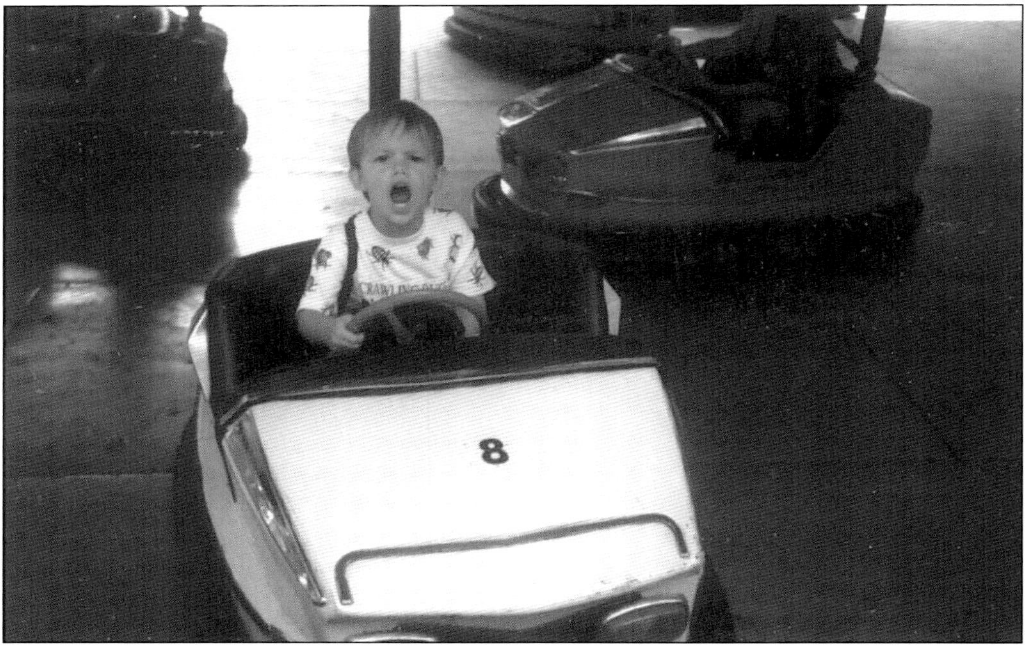

Raccoon Lagoon has its own miniature version of the Skooters called the Cattail Derby. In this image, Zachary Croushore struggles while attempting to drive his car around the derby floor. (Courtesy Carol Croushore.)

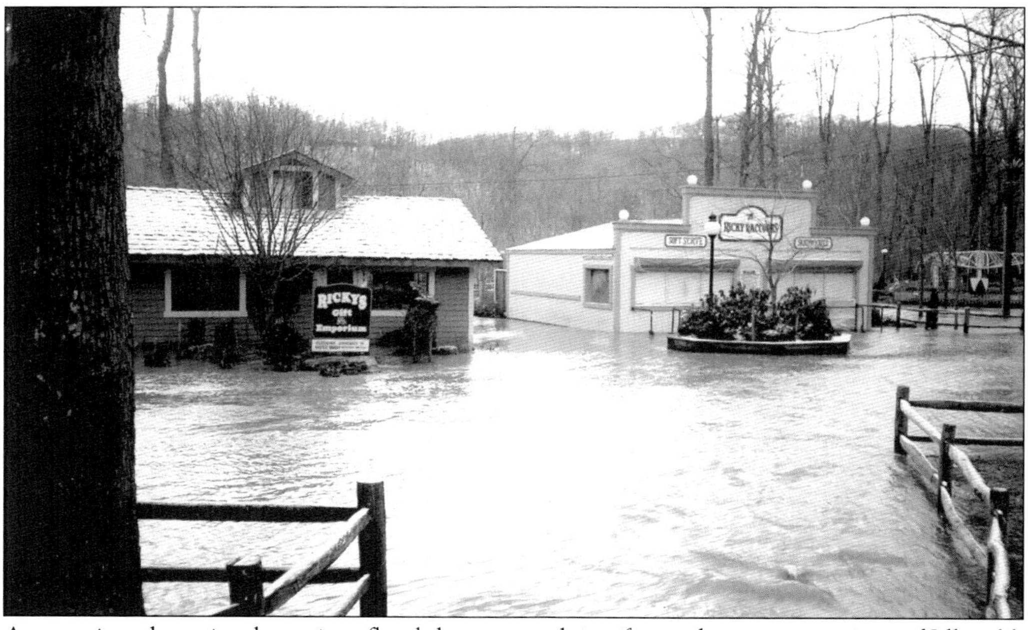

As mentioned previously, various floods have caused significant damage to portions of Idlewild. The usually tranquil Loyalhanna Creek occasionally swells into raging rapids. In January 1996, a warm-weather spell, within days of a heavy snowfall, caused rapid melting of snow. The heavy runoff proved too much for the banks of the Loyalhanna. The walkways of Raccoon Lagoon were left completely submerged.

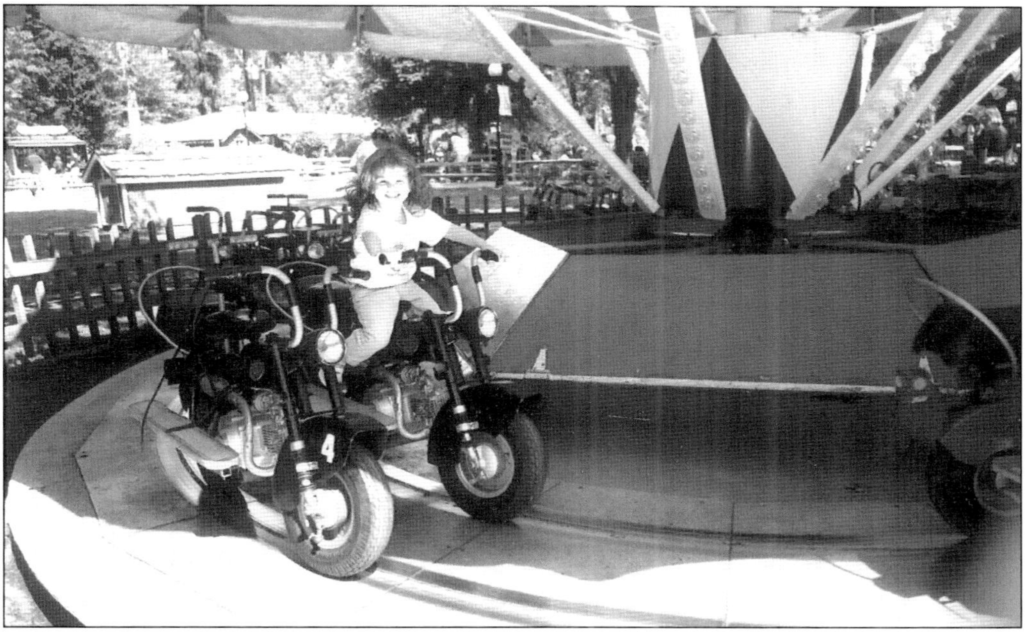

The Little Rascals' Motorcycles are popular among little boys and girls. Here, Rachel Croushore revs the motor as she rides her cycle around the track. (Courtesy Carol Croushore.)

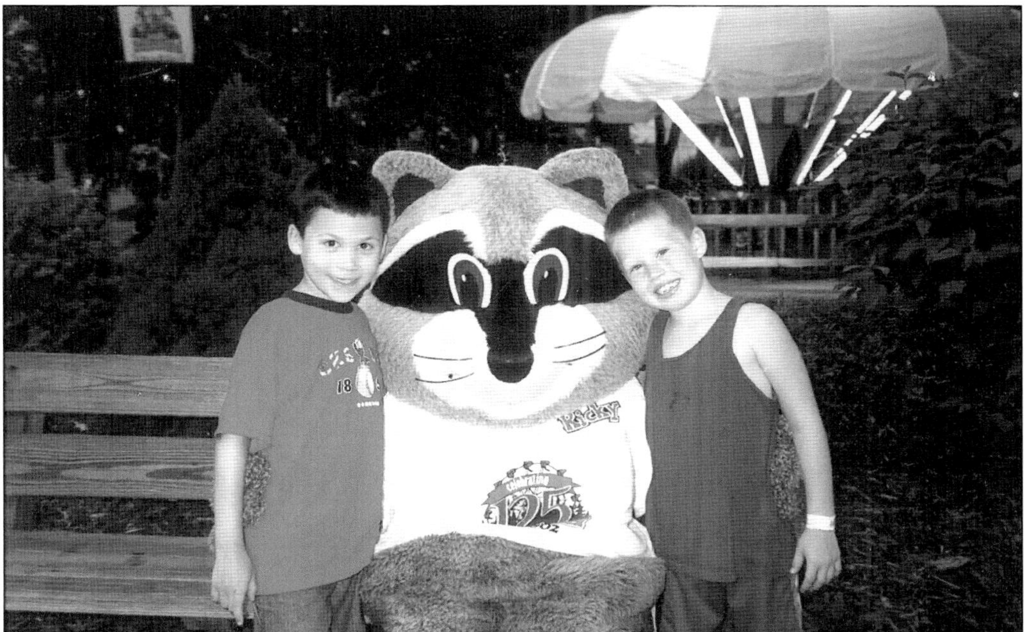

Raccoon Lagoon is the home of Ricky Raccoon. During the summer months, he tours the park hugging, shaking hands, and taking pictures with thousands of children. Two young lads from the Church of St. Therese picnic enjoy a visit with the lovable character in July 2002. (Courtesy Lori Ellis.)

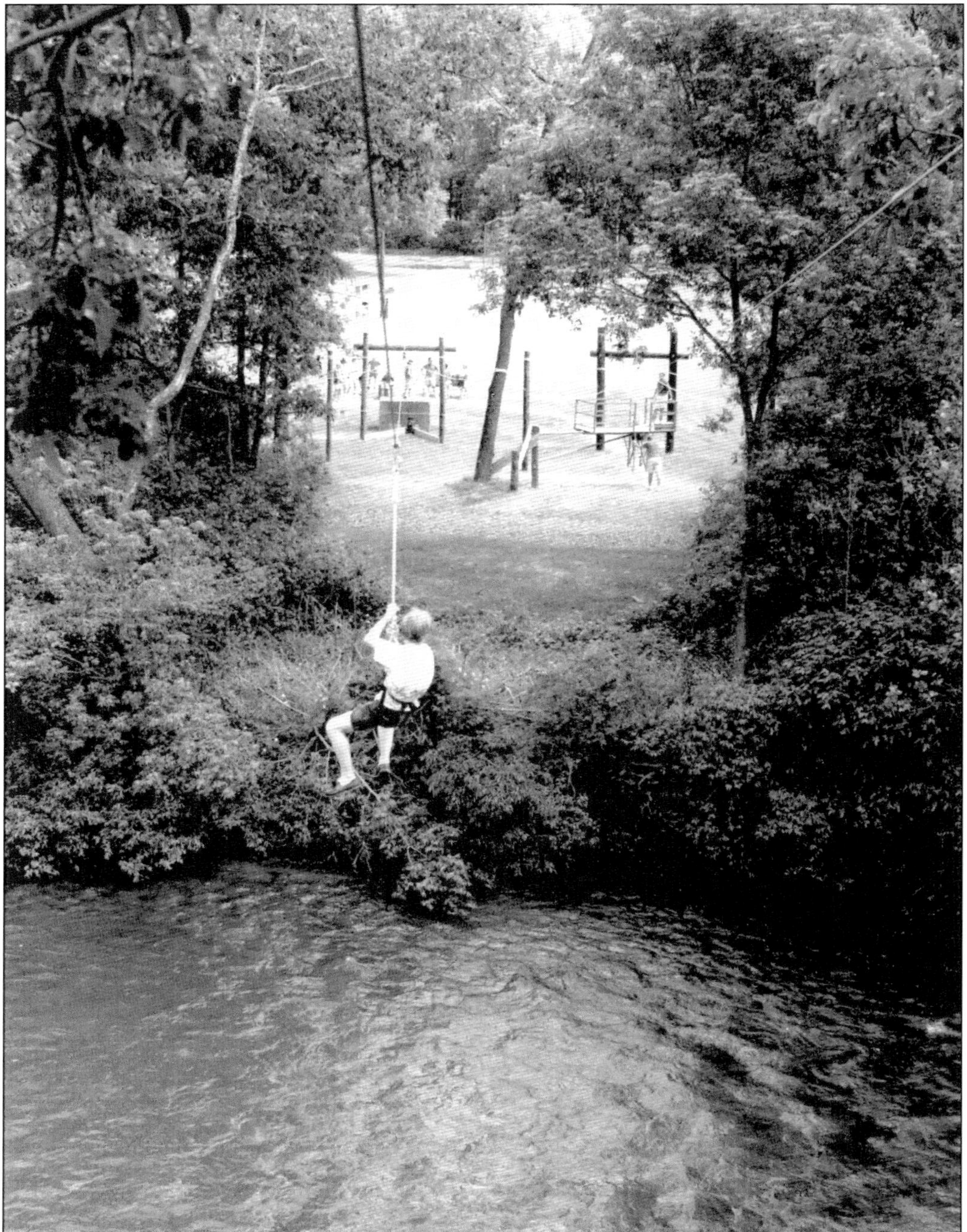

In the 1990s, Idlewild operated a special area called the Far Side. Open only for school picnics, the highlight of the Far Side was the zip line. Park patrons climbed a net to the top of a tall tower located near the entrance to Rafter's Run. There, a specially trained Idlewild team member hooked them onto the line using special harnesses. The patron then stepped (although most preferred to jump) off the edge of the platform where they rode the line across the Loyalhanna Creek. They landed at the ball field.

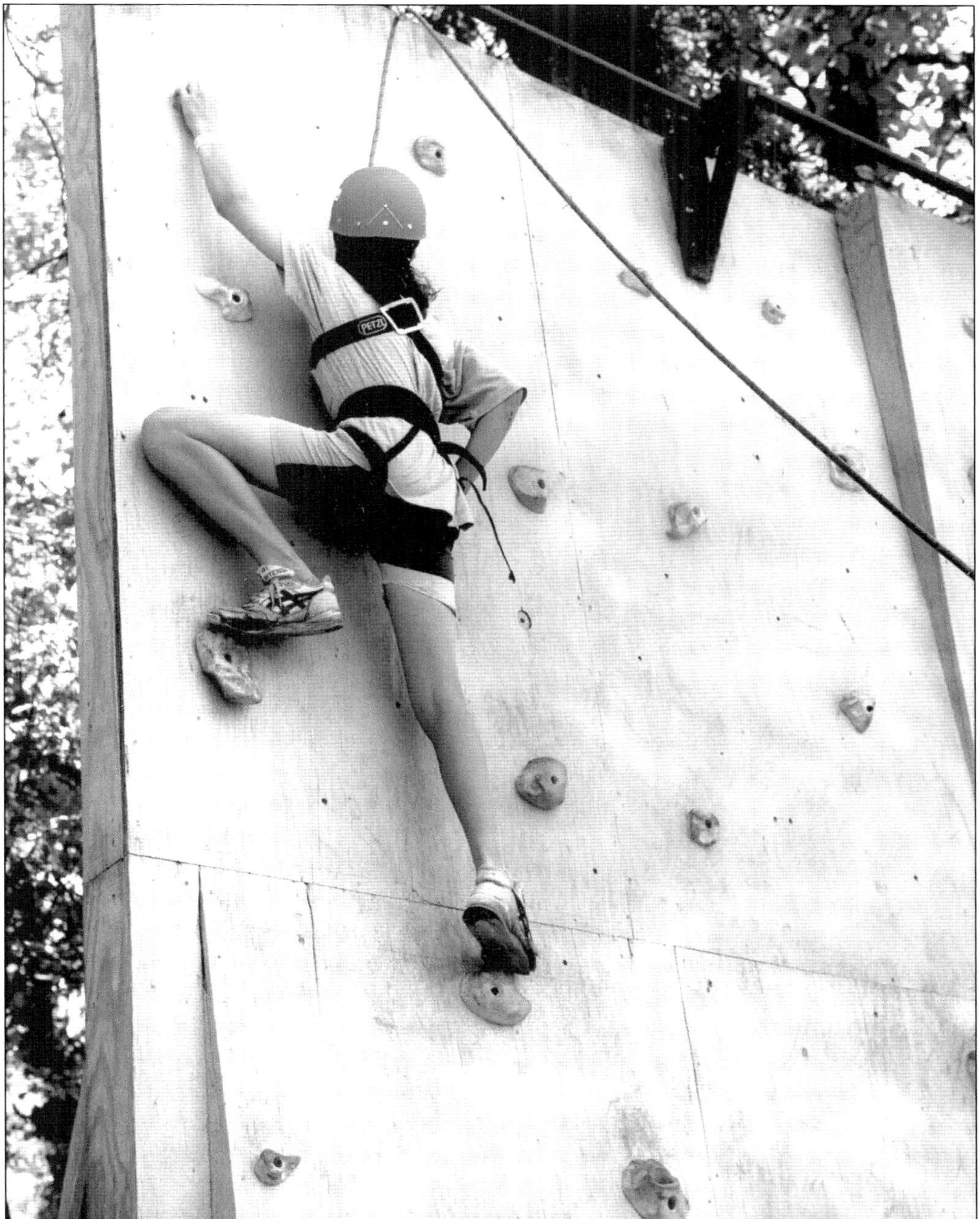

Once the patron rode the zip line to the ball field, they were free to enjoy the other attractions of the Far Side. These included a video game center, batting cages, volleyball courts, a trampoline, and a rock-climbing wall. The climbing wall once again necessitated the guest be harnessed. If the guest ever lost their footing on any of the rocks, they would simply fall away from the wall and just hang in the air. A spotter would slowly lower them back down to the ground by releasing a guide rope. The Far Side was renamed Extreme Elements but was only a fixture at the park for about five years.

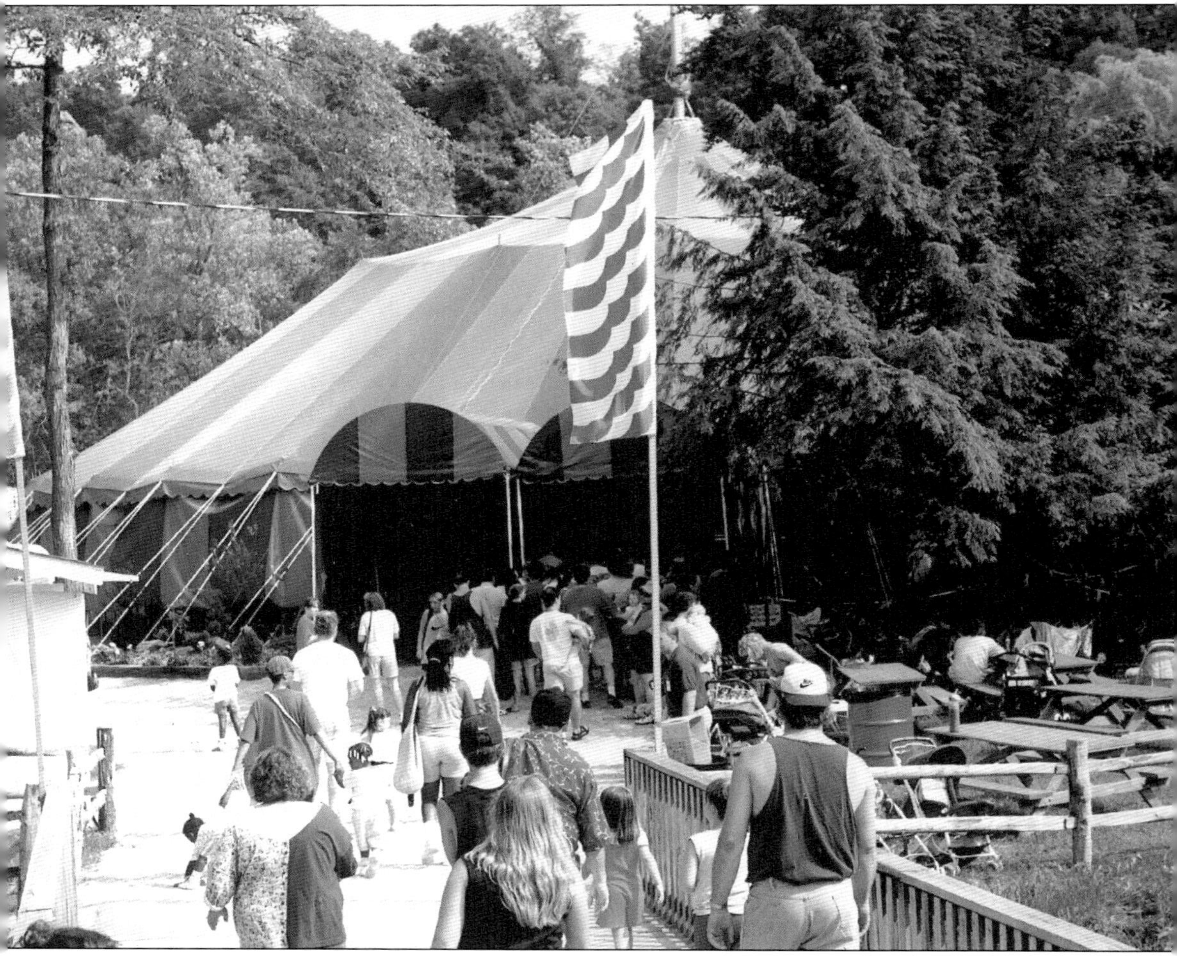

The Royal Hanneford Circus first performed at Idlewild during the 1986 season. In 1996, it returned, and proved so popular that the park booked it again for the 1997 season. The big top was set up behind Raccoon Lagoon at the site of the former Frontier Zoo.

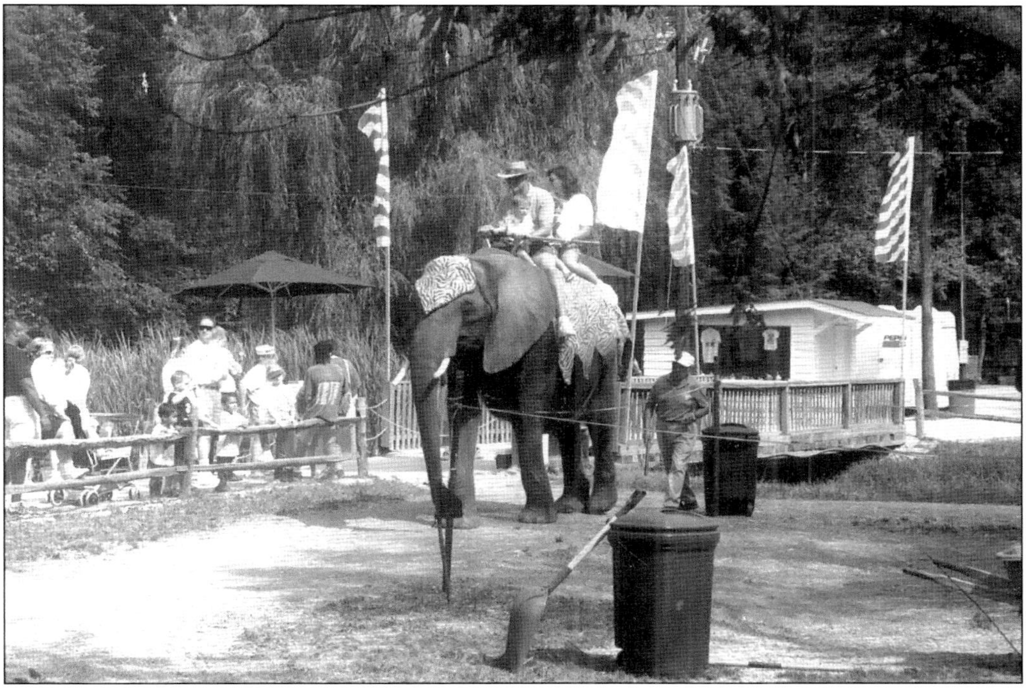

When the Royal Hanneford Circus appeared in 1997, elephant rides were provided just outside the circus tent. Elephants had first appeared at Idlewild in 1936, when the Dutton Circus performed. Below, an equestrian act delights the circus crowd. (Above, courtesy Carol Croushore.)

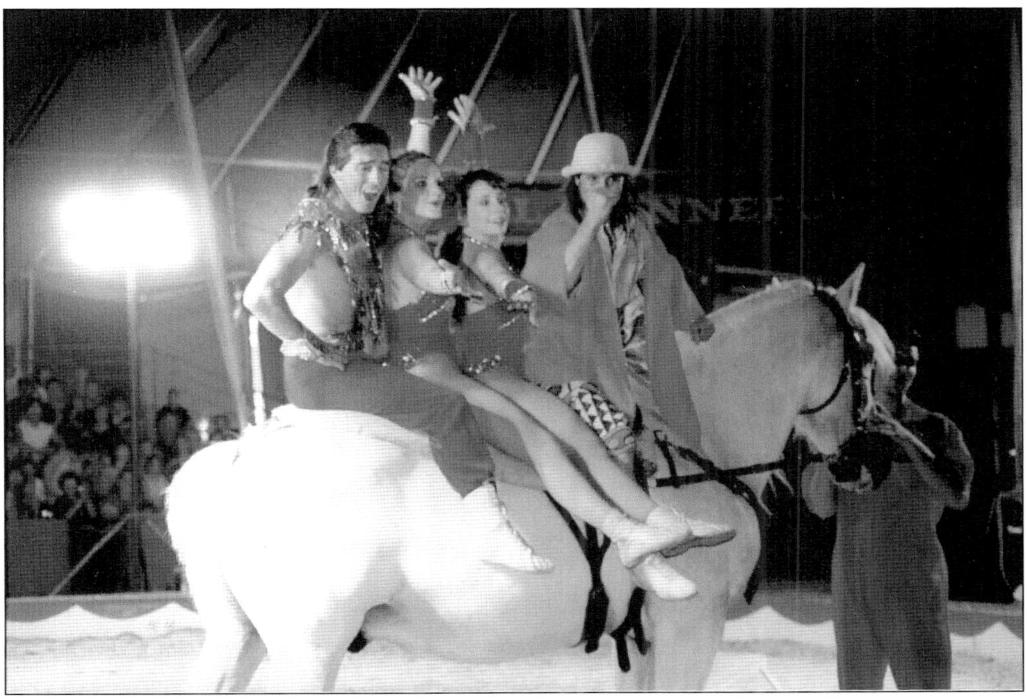

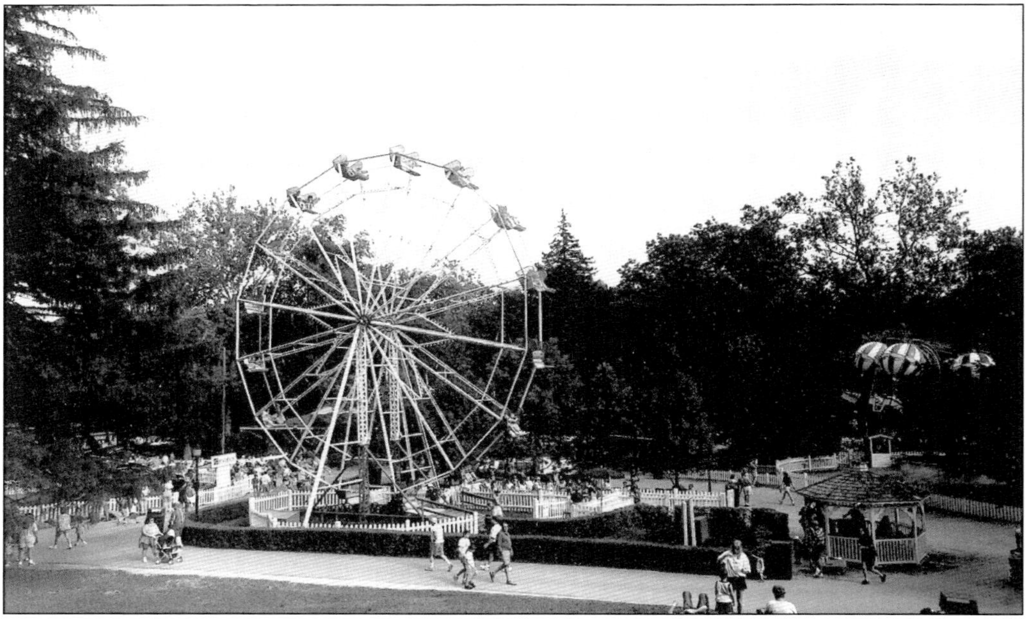

This 1984 Eli Bridge Company aristocrat ground-mount wheel is the second Ferris wheel to call Idlewild home. Located at the base of the hillside, the wheel offers great views of the park's midways. To the right of the Ferris wheel is the Balloon Race, manufactured by Zamperla. A close up of the Balloon Race, which premiered in 1995, is featured below.

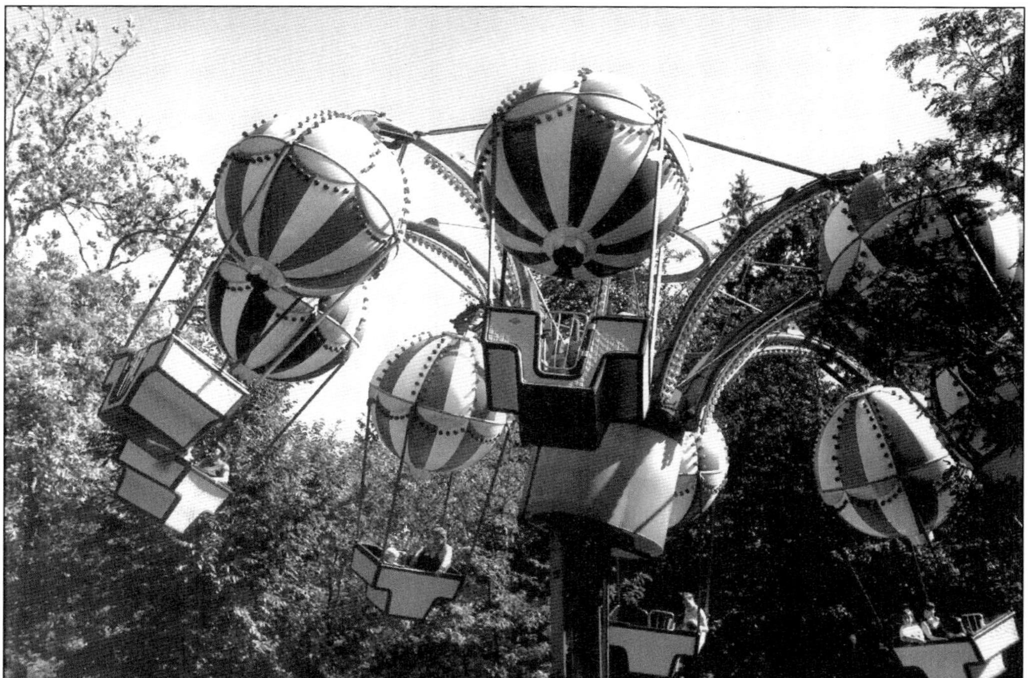

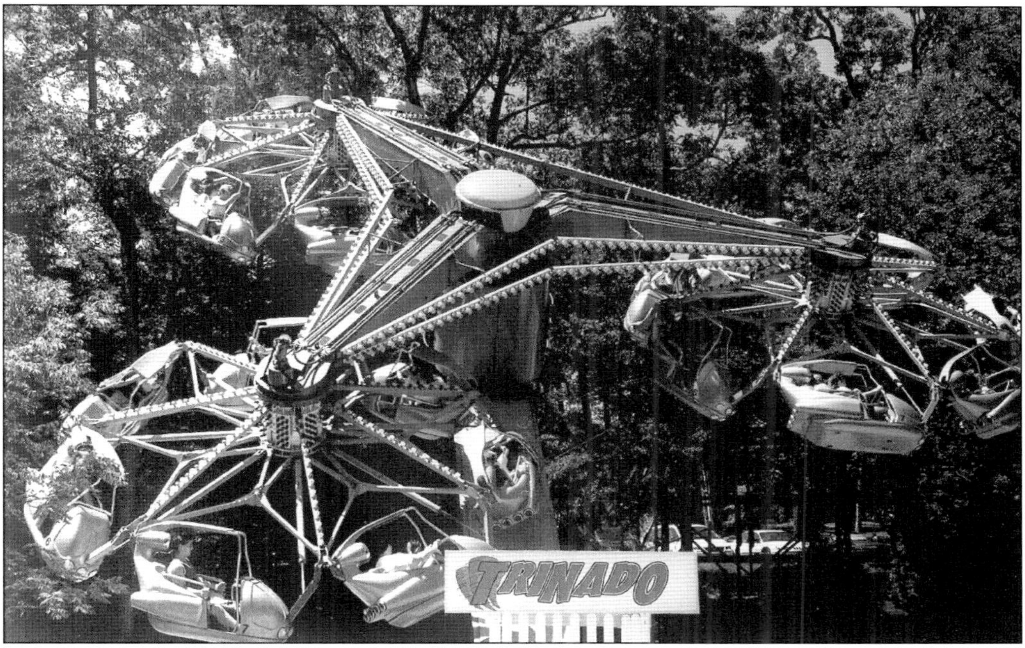

Twenty-one gondolas spin up to 42 passengers on the three-armed Trinado. The Huss Manufacturing ride spent one season at Kennywood before being transferred to Idlewild to launch the 1998 season. The ride, which is manufactured under the name Tristar, was featured in a "name the ride" contest with local schoolchildren participating. For the beginning of its first season, it actually operated under the name "What Izzat?" until the winning moniker, Trinado, was selected. The installation of the Trinado called for the relocation of another longtime favorite, the Paratrooper, from the area near the Rollo Coaster to the front of the Skooter building.

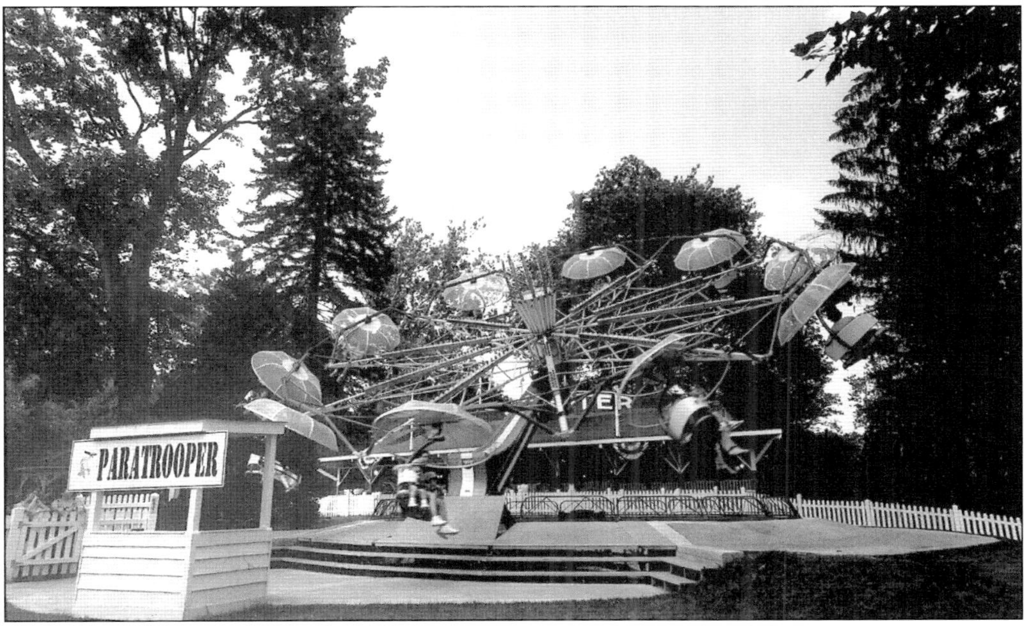

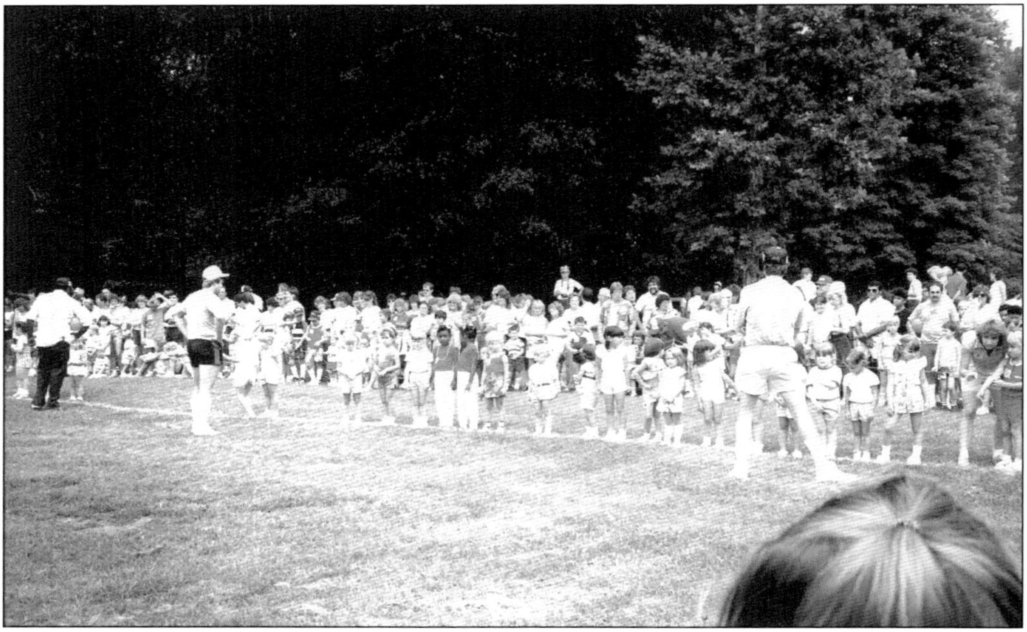

The highlight of many company and community picnics are games and races for all ages, which are often held at the spacious ball field. In 1999, additional game fields became available for use in the new picnic grove designed specifically for corporate outings.

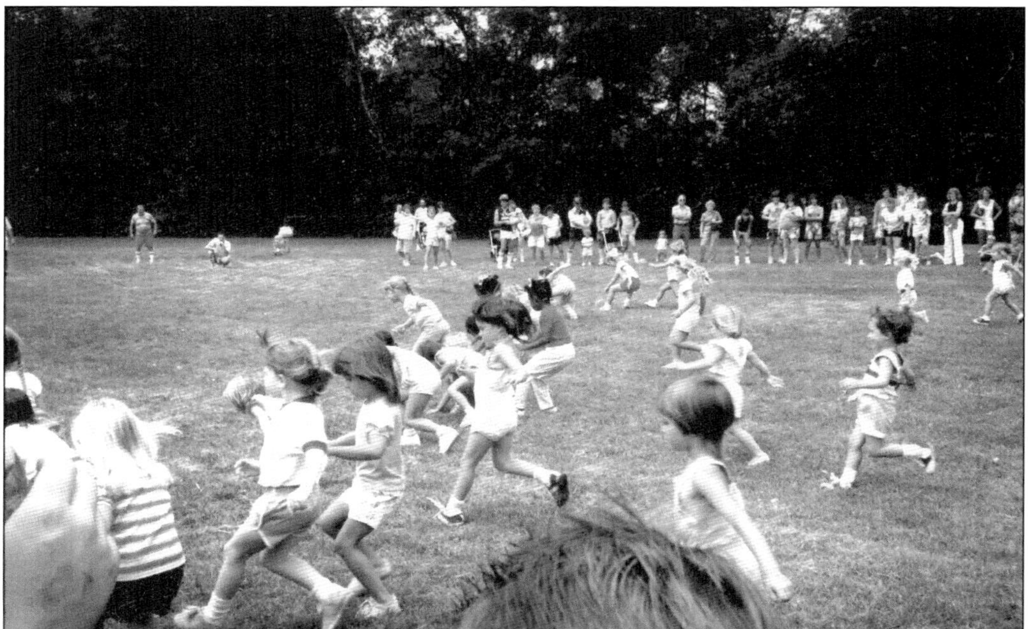

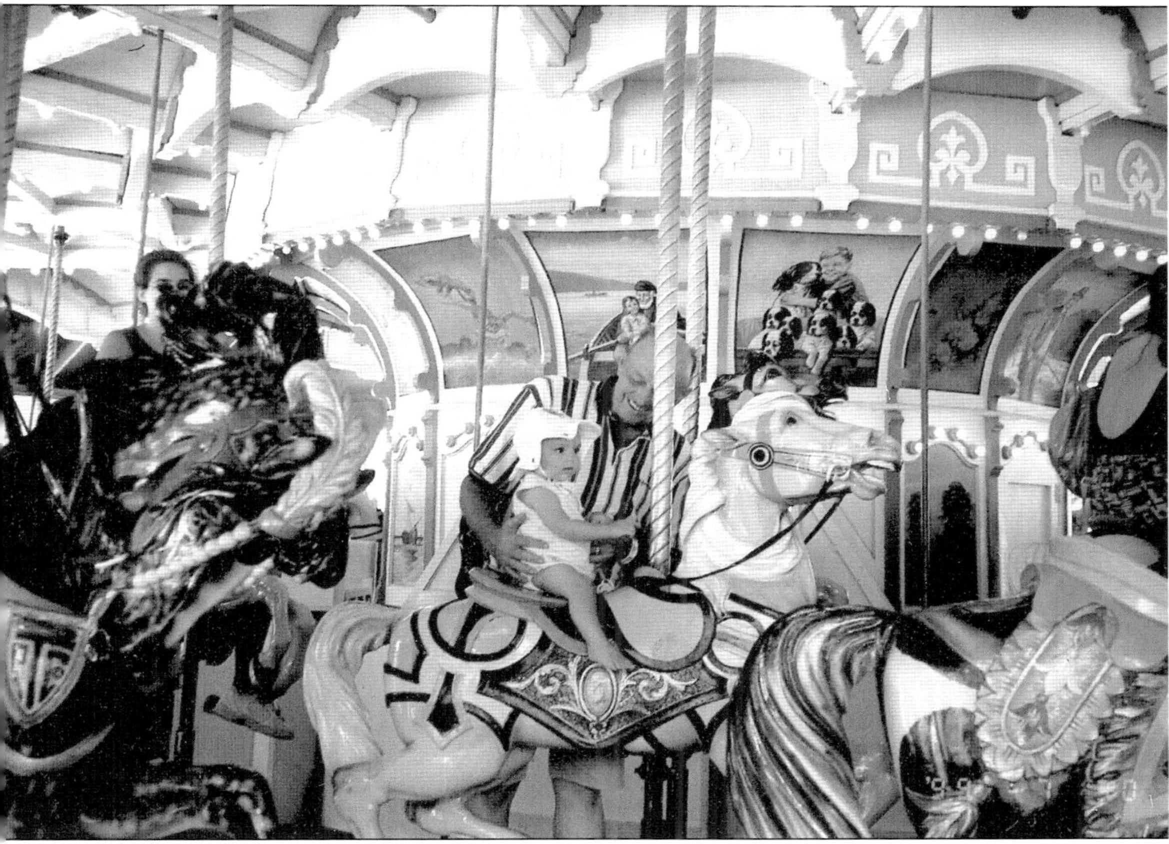

A child's first ride on the Idlewild carousel is always a special event. Shown here riding atop one of the hand-carved wooden horses for the first time is Kaci Croushore, who enjoyed the moment with her grandfather Tom Drew, on a family visit in 1999. (Courtesy Carol Croushore.)

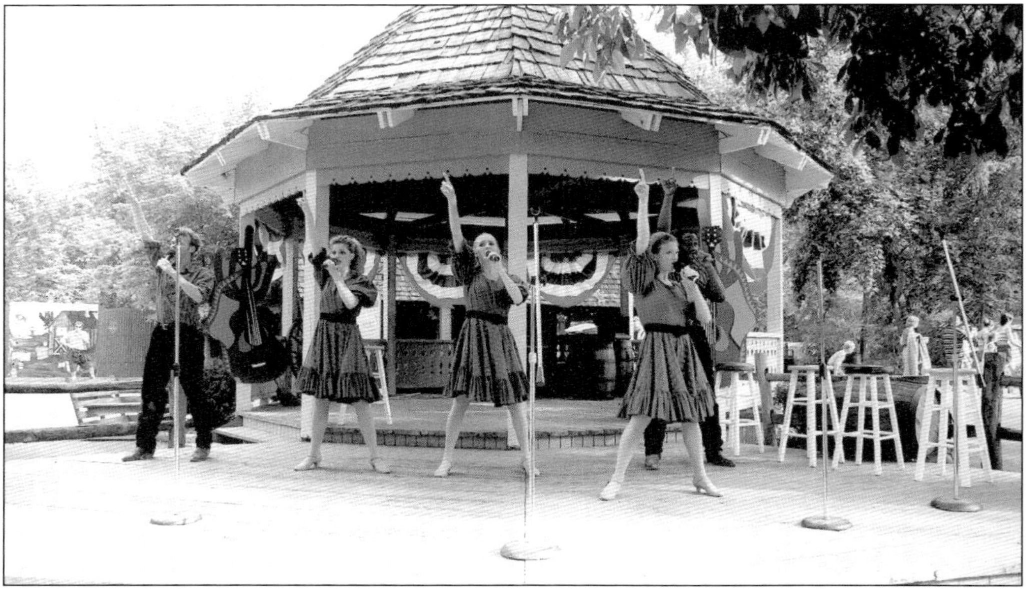

From large stage to small, the free acts continue at Idlewild. Three of the park's stages are used for musical performances while a fourth serves as a puppet theater. In the above image, a 1998 cast sings country western music on Hootin' Holler's gazebo stage. In the image below, they perform a salute to America at the Hillside Theater.

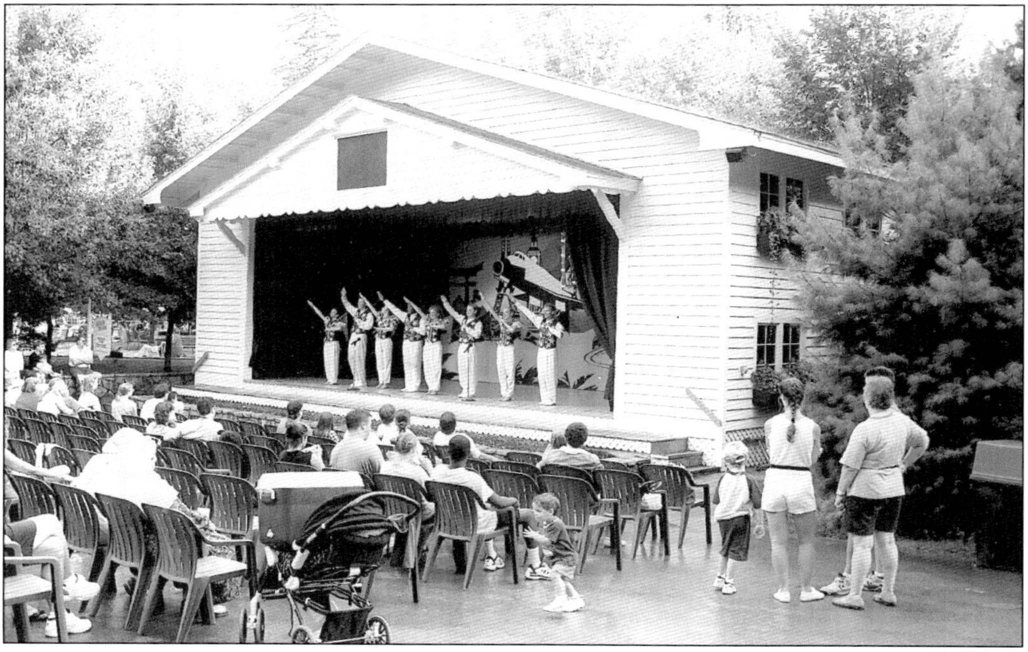

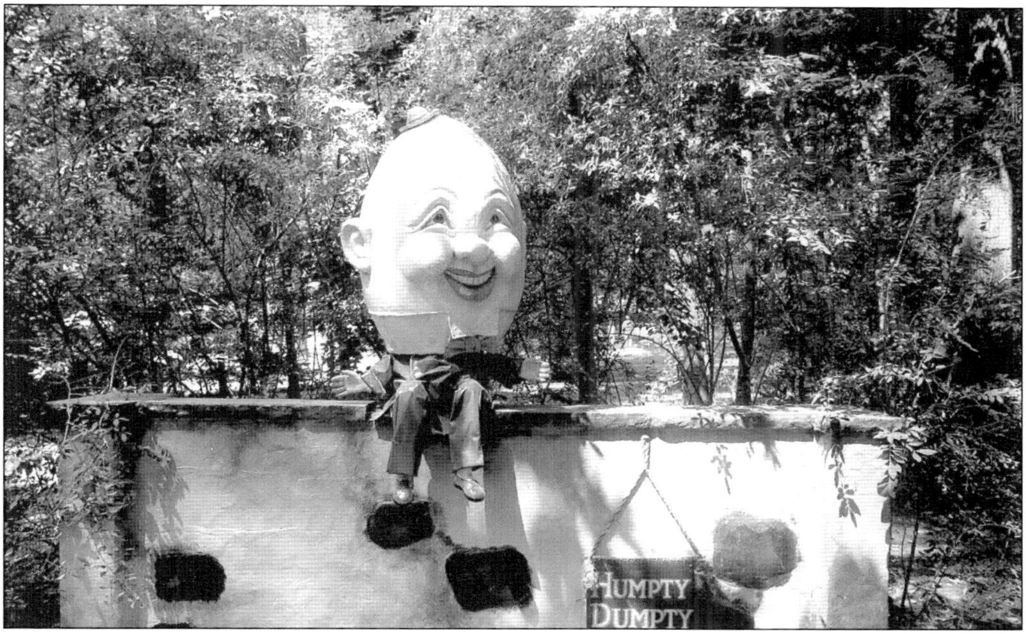

Approaching 50 years old, Story Book Forest has not lost any of its charm. Thousands of people still walk its shaded paths and visit the characters they grew up with. They can see Humpty Dumpty before the fall (shown above) or Goldilocks and the Three Bears outside of their cottage (shown below). While some vignettes have disappeared—Hansel and Gretel, Alice in Wonderland, Bambi the Deer—new ones have taken their place—Raggedy Ann and Andy, the Little Train That Could, and Aladdin's Carpet. All in all, the forest has not lost any of its allure but has only enhanced it.

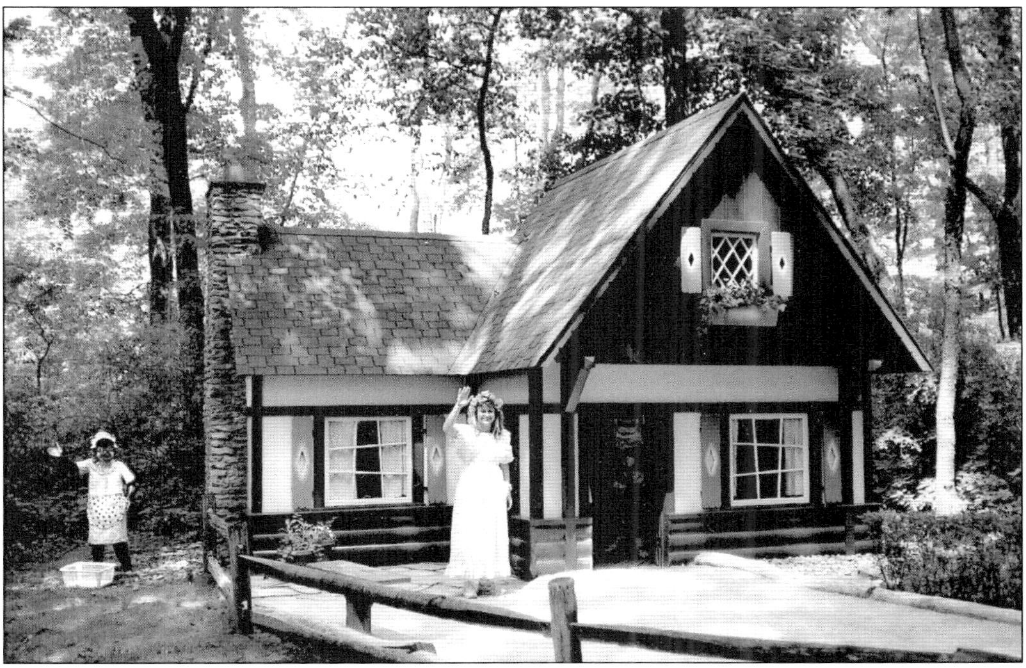

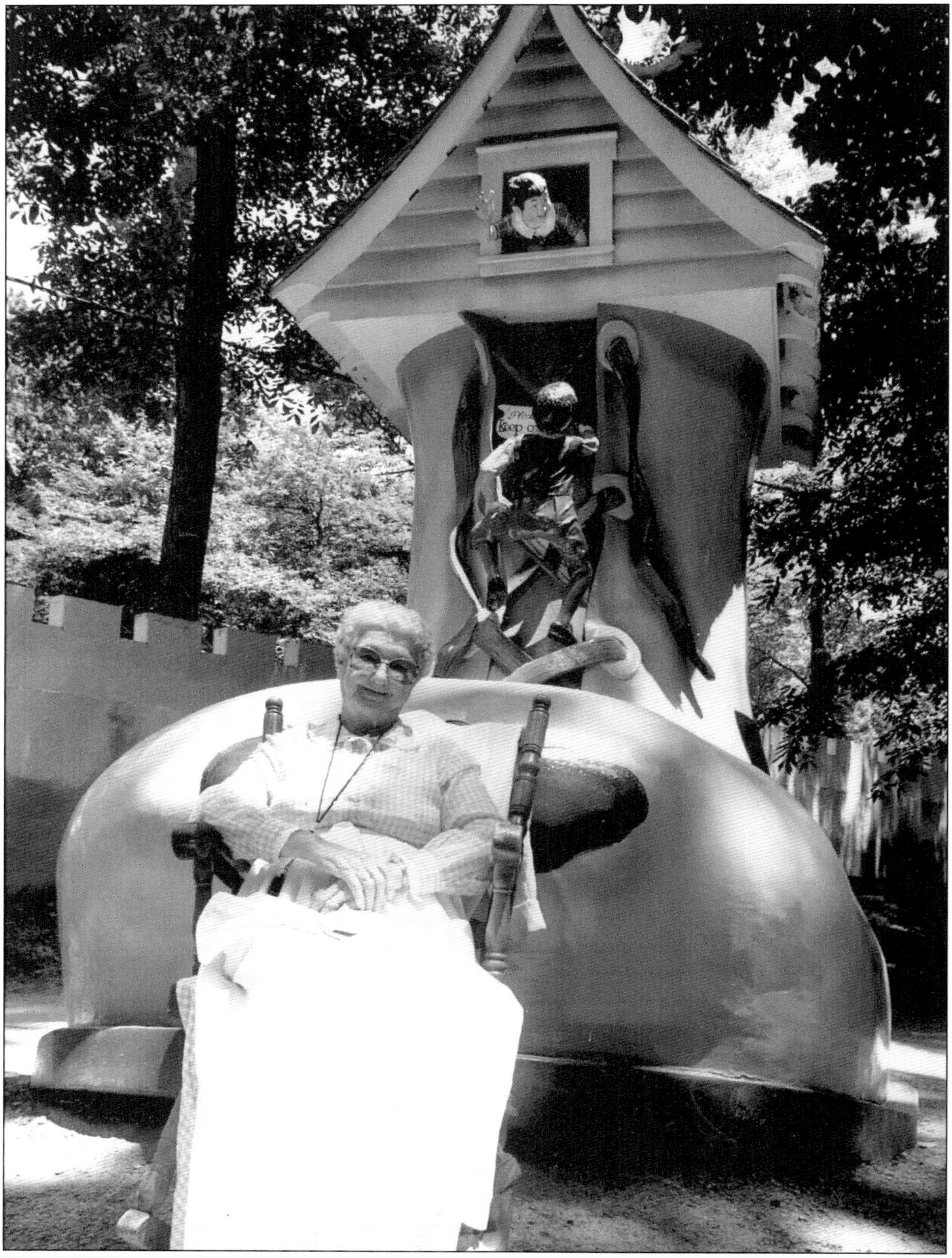

The Old Woman Who Lived in A Shoe has only been portrayed by a handful of people over the years. Nellie Gindlesperger, who retired in 1997 after 25 years, inherited the role from her mother who had played the character for the previous 12 years. Throughout the years, Nellie Gindlesperger became so identified in the role that she received fan mail from all across the country.

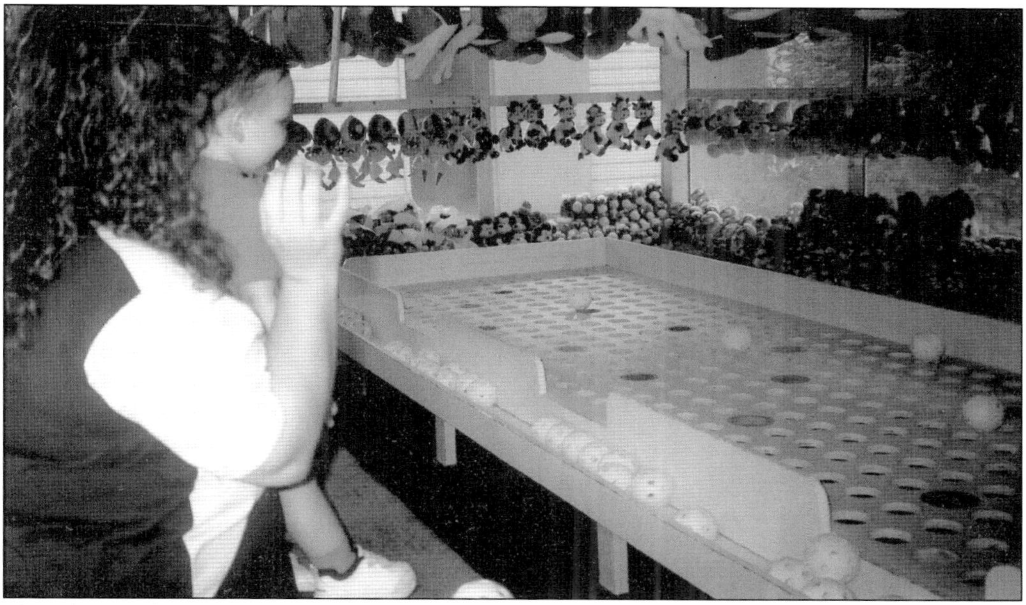

The object of Animal House is to toss a plastic ball into one of the colored holes. It is just one of the many games that line Idlewild's midways. Over the years, mechanical games such as Bowler Roller, Pig Race, and Rising Waters have joined such classics as Milk Bottle, Crossbow, Hole-in-One, Duck Pond, Basketball Toss, and the Fishing Pond.

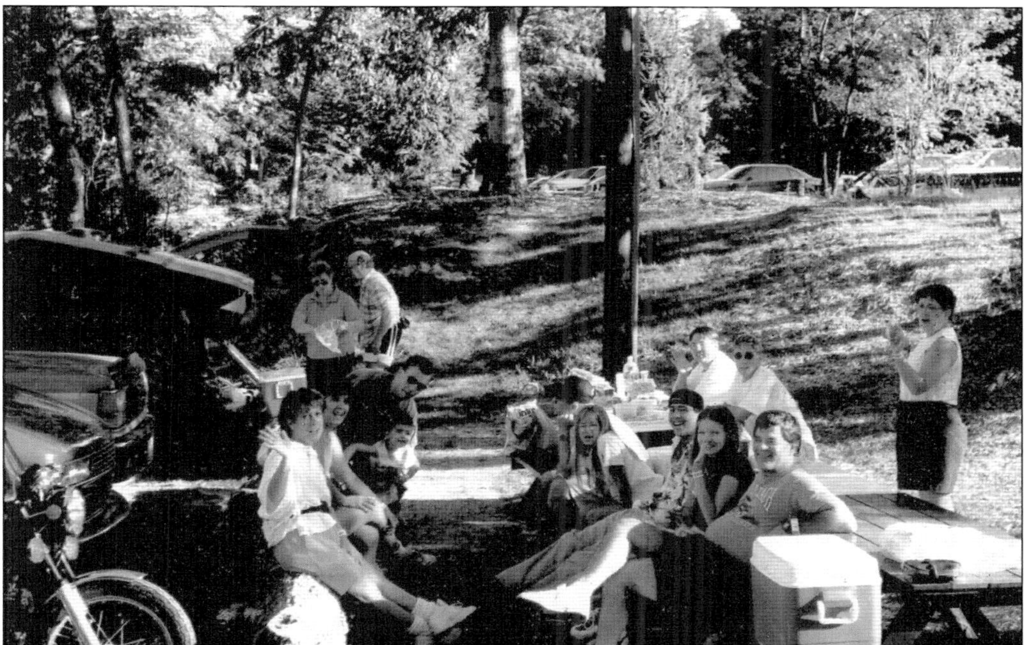

Family reunions, both large and small, are currently a very important part of Idlewild's success, as they were over a century ago. This photograph features the Leezer family enjoying the park's shady picnic groves while on a visit in 1999. (Courtesy Christy Goswick.)

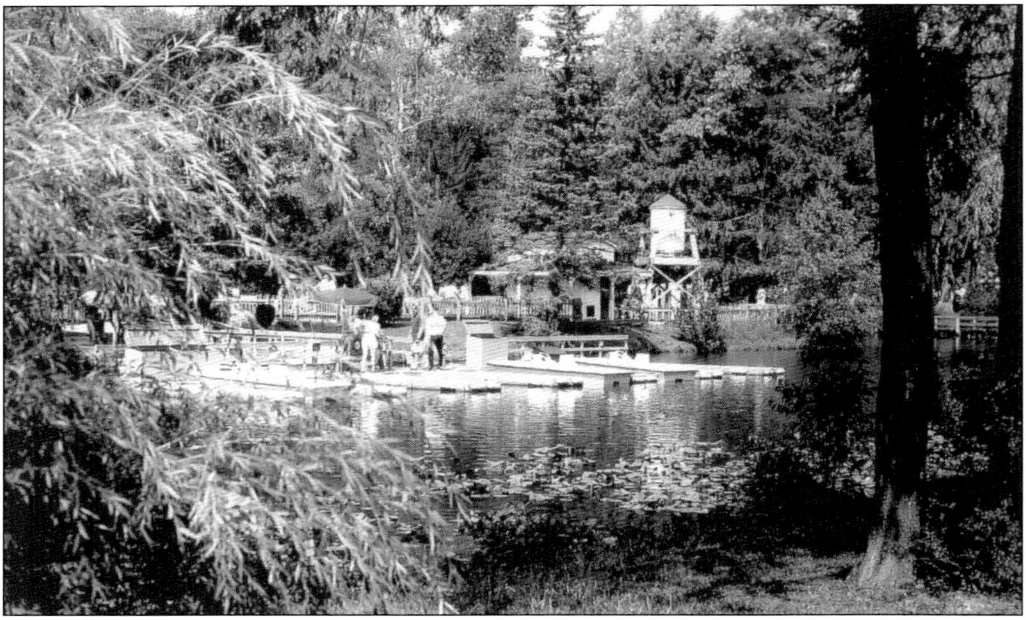

Lake Bouquet has come a long way since it was first dug in 1896. One thing that has remained constant is its usefulness for boating. The rowboats and vapor launches of the early years gave way to motorboats and the Idlewild showboat. Currently, paddleboats cruise the waters of Lake Bouquet. Their dock is seen here with Little Squirts in the background.

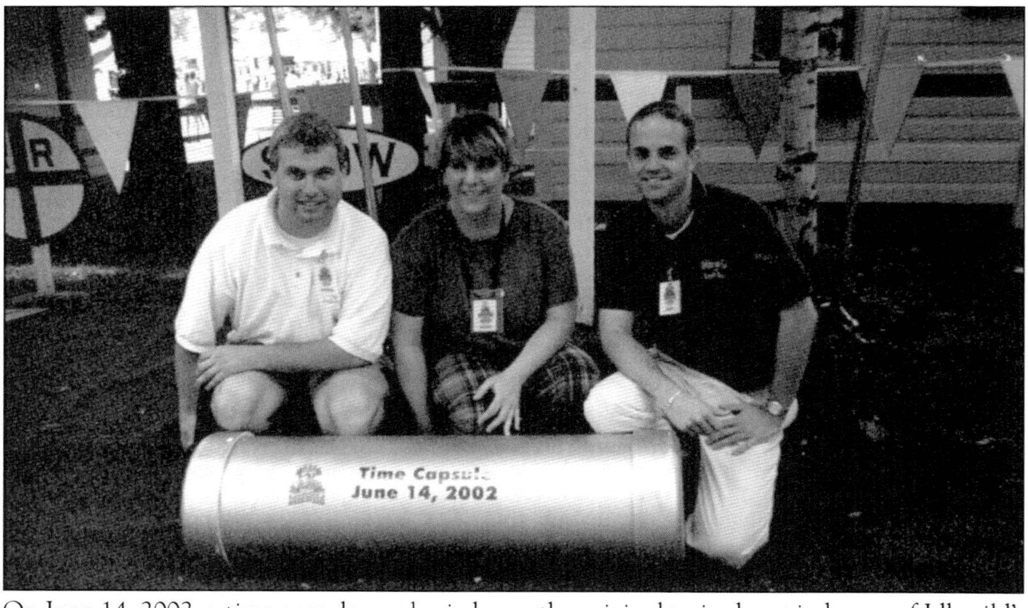

On June 14, 2002, a time capsule was buried near the original train depot in honor of Idlewild's 125th anniversary. Included within the capsule was artwork by area schoolchildren depicting how they believed the park will look in the year 2050. Newspapers, park brochures, t-shirts, and other paraphernalia of the day were also sealed within. The three members of the group sales staff pictured with the time capsule are, from left to right, Dennis Kozar, Kathy Sichula, and Jeff Croushore.

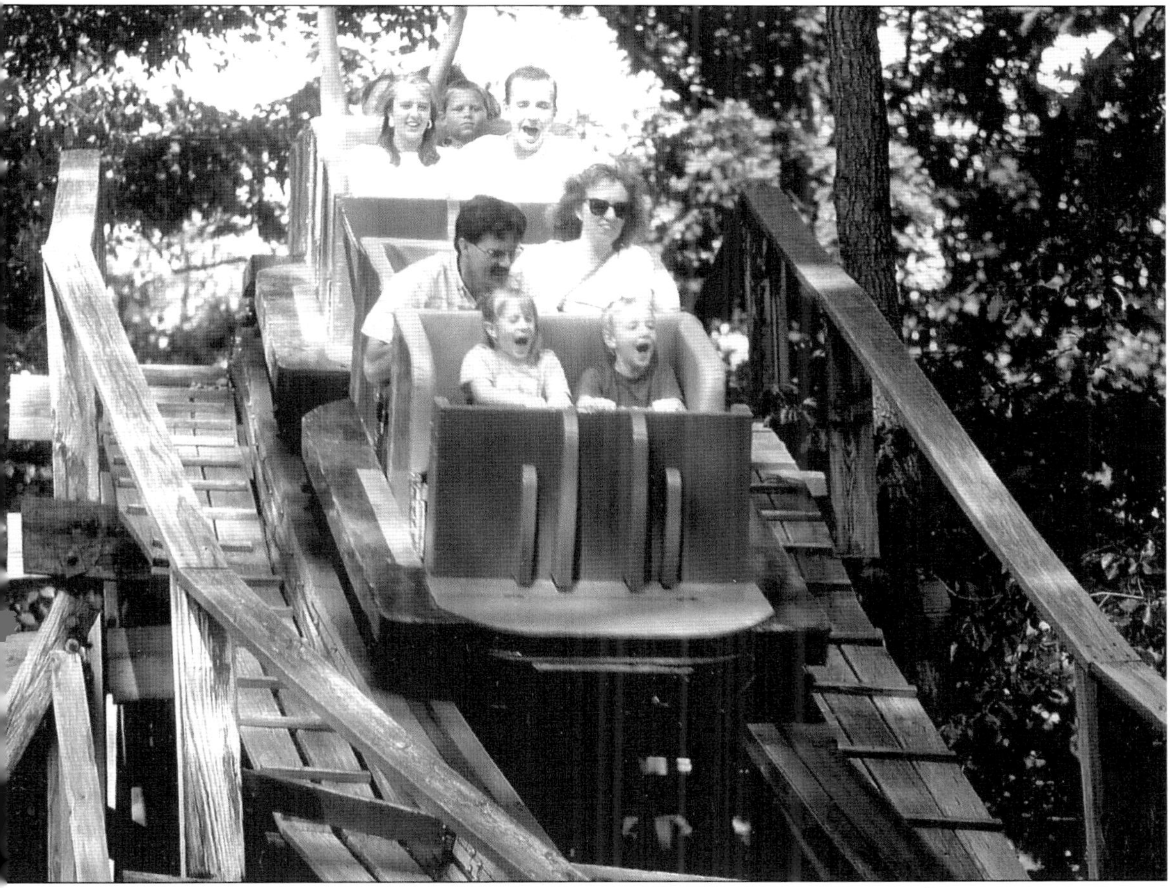

In 2003, the Rollo Coaster celebrated its 65th anniversary. To commemorate the event, a special ceremony was held with prizes for those who rode on the 65th run of the day. Special admission and food prices were also offered as part of the celebration. Albeit a very simple out-and-back wooden coaster, the Rollo remains a favorite for many coaster enthusiasts because of its design, use of landscape, and classic trains.

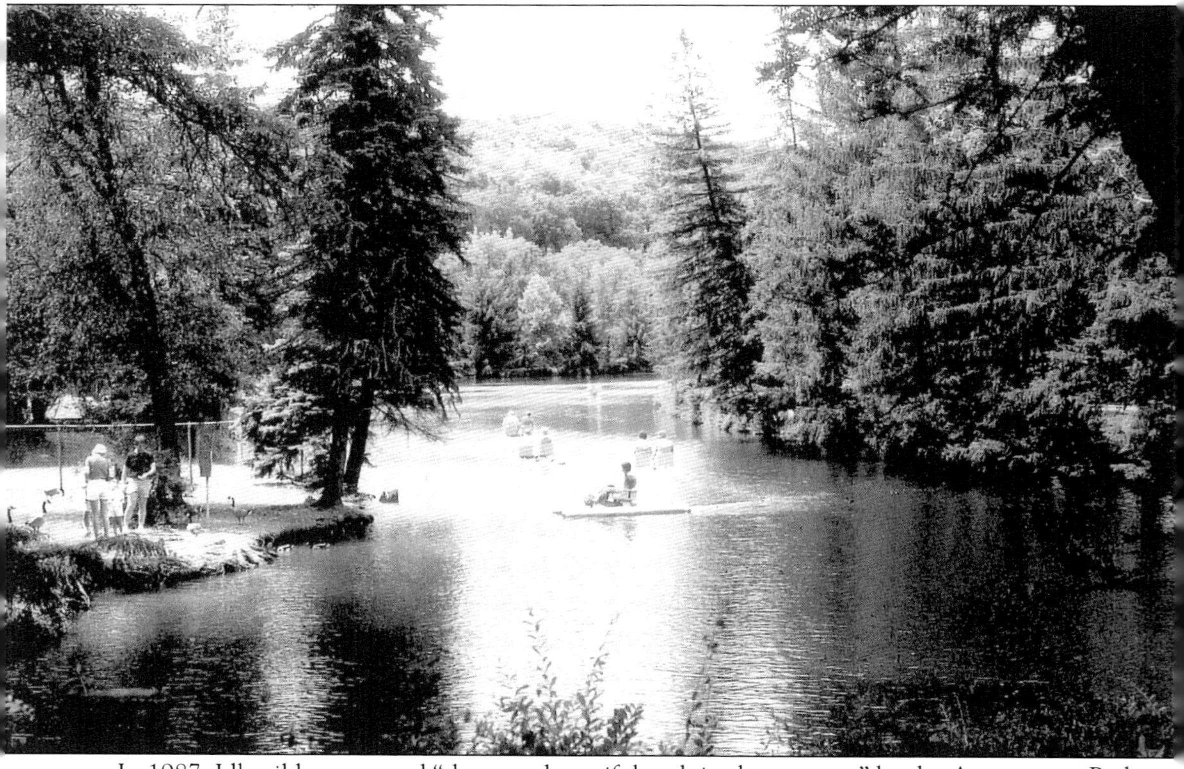

In 1987, Idlewild was named "the most beautiful park in the country," by the Amusement Park Guidebook. The lakes, trees, and rolling hills provide a picnic-perfect setting, packed with so many fun things to do. Idlewild ranks as the oldest amusement park in Pennsylvania, the 3rd oldest in the United States, and the 11th oldest in the world. It continues to offer a family friendly environment within a beautiful natural setting, just as it did more than 125 years ago. The park is ever changing, yet remains familiar to those who come back year after year. The future continues to be bright for this jewel in the mountains.

Tis Hard, indeed, to say thee nay– / Forego the joys of one short day, /
So glad with thee to be exil'd / In the leafy shades of Idlewild

—Rev. J. Q. Waters, from "An Idyl on Idlewild," August 6, 1891